Blue Moose Publishing

Copyright 2011 C.J. Cutayne

1st Edition

Canadian Cataloguing in Publication Data

Because of the Moon

ISBN 978-14752806-9-2

ISBN 10 1475280696

Dedicated to the First Nations People
of the Pacific Northwest.

Chapter 1

A beefy hand squeezed the back of Jay's neck. Jay struggled but the grip tightened thrusting him closer to the building. The assailant reached with his other hand and pulled wide a door, heavy as a bank vault. The door resisted, and then picked up speed like an 1800's locomotive, slamming into the frame with a spine-jolting crash. All activity inside the garage stopped. Jay turned his head to get a look around but only caught a glimpse of glossy red lacquer paint and chrome. Oil and paint fumes mingled in the air.

"What do you think you're doing bringing a kid in here?" yelled the painter.

"I caught him out in the alley, spying," said Beefy-hands. He pushed Jay into the middle of the oil stained concrete floor littered with car parts. Jay rubbed his neck where the feeling of clenched fingers continued to sting.

A hissing sound came from the corner. A guy with a blow torch decapitated a BMW. He pushed back his welder's mask, wiped sweat from his eyes and squinted at Jay.

"Is that right, kid? You spying on us?" said the welder, holding the lit torch close to Jay's face.

Jay retreated from the flame. "No, I wasn't spying. I just wondered what was going on. You guys are into cars, right? You modify cars and then sell them like those motorcycle guys on TV. Nice place. OK, I guess I'll see you around then."

Jay took a few steps back.

"You're stupid, kid, if you think we're stupid enough to think you're that stupid," said another guy from behind a desk. His head was shaved to a shine; only a handle-bar mustache gave away his former hair color. He rolled back his chair, and was on his feet in a split second.

1

"Kinda far from the reservation, aren't you?" said Handle-bar. He swaggered across the garage past a rack of wrenches.

"I'm not an Indian," said Jay.

"Yeah, right. What are you doing out this late, anyway? Shouldn't you be in bed, kid?" said Handle-bar, closing in on Jay.

"You're right, I should get going. I have school tomorrow," stammered Jay as he turned toward the door.

Jay was stopped in his tracks by the man with the beefy hands. His bulging arms crossed over his barrel chest. He stood between Jay and the door like a night club bouncer.

"Don't worry about school. You won't be attending," said Handle-bar.

Jay's heart pounded harder. Adrenalin rushed through his veins as his eyes darted toward the open door.

"Shut the door," yelled Handle-bar to Welder.

Jay's attempt to pass failed as Beefy-hands grabbed a mitt full of Jay's hood and didn't let go. Jay took a step back to avoid strangulation by his own clothing.

The two hot dogs he ate for dinner rose in Jay's throat. Welder, lit torch still in hand, moved past Jay to shut the door. Without thinking, Jay pulled the can of spray paint out of his pocket and pressed the nozzle, aiming for the flame. The paint ignited in a whoosh. Everyone ducked and shielded their eyes. Jay dropped the can and ran out the door, down the alley.

Jay had almost reached the safety of the cross street when he hit the ground. The air exited his lungs as Welder tackled Jay from behind, pressing his face into the wet asphalt speckled with gum and cigarette butts.

"Let me go. I won't tell. I promise," pleaded Jay. He breathed through his mouth to save his nostrils from the urine scented alley.

2

"Get up, you little puke," said Welder. He hauled Jay to his feet and back to the garage.

The place smelled like burnt hair.

"You got guts, kid. I'll give you that," said Handle-bar, checking his mustache.

"Are you going to kill me?" asked Jay.

"No, but he might," said Handle-bar, nodding toward Beefy-hands. "Killed his ma a few years back."

Beefy-hands strutted up so close Jay could tell lunch had consisted of either Italian or Greek. "My mother wouldn't get me a beer, so I stuck a knife in her and stuck her to the wall," said Beefy-hands. His lip curled over crooked teeth.

"I, ah, guess you didn't get your beer then," said Jay. The garage went library quiet. He waited for the life to be squeezed from him.

Handle-bar snickered. "I guess you didn't get your beer then," he repeated and roared.

Welder and Painter joined in, laughing and smacking Jay on the back.

"I like this kid," said Handle-bar, catching his breath.

"Are you kidding? He tried to blow us up," said Beefy-hands. He poked Jay in the chest.

"Shows the kid's got balls. What were you doing with spray paint in your pocket?" asked Handle-bar.

"Painting stuff; walls, garbage cans, underpasses, whatever," said Jay, rubbing his chest.

"Just like you used to do, eh," said Handle-bar to Painter. "Maybe we got ourselves a new apprentice."

"That's OK. I'm getting a paper route," said Jay.

"We both know it's too late for that. Unless you want me to talk to your mom or maybe the cops and let them know what you've been up to?" said Handle-bar.

"You'll get in more crap than I will," said Jay. His voice sounded braver than he felt.

"No way, I gotta couple of cousins on the force. We support their charity 'donations for donuts' so they don't mind our little side business. I figure they'll get to us one day but right now we're low on their list," said Handle-bar.

"I was talking about my mom," said Jay.

The room erupted in snorts of laughter like feeding time at the pig trough.

Handle-bar put his arm around Jay. "You could make a lot of money and help us out. How 'bout it, kid? You work for us and we let you reach puberty."

"Do I have a choice?" said Jay.

"You always have a choice," said Handle-bar. All eyes shifted as the door clanged open.

"Freeze! Police!"

Chapter 2

"Call your mother," said the city police officer, pushing the phone across the faux wood desk.

"She's not home," replied Jay.

"Call your dad then," he said, losing patience.

"Don't have his number," said Jay staring at the white and brown linoleum tiled floor.

"If you don't have anyone to call we do - social services," said the police officer. No trace of humor.

"Let me know what you decide. My name is Constable Magee," he said and began filling out some paperwork.

Jay guessed he was mid-forties; brushed-cut red hair with matching mustache and goatee. Freckles crowded his face and hands. The bulletproof vest under his powder blue shirt made him look muscular but stiff.

"All right, I'll try my mom's cell phone," said Jay, his elbow on the desk and his chin in his hand.

He picked up the receiver and tried to figure out which buttons to punch.

"Hit line 3 and then dial 9 and the number or should I do it for you?" said Constable Magee.

Jay ignored him and dialed his mom's cell phone - voice mail. "Hi, this is Tatla Roberts. Leave a message and I'll call you back." Jay knew her upbeat voice was reserved for clients. He did not expect the same courtesy.

Under the watchful eye of the cop, Jay kept the message short. "Hi, Mom, can you pick me up please? I'm at the police station."

He sat on the slat wooden bench under the fluorescent lights and picked at the yellow spray paint on his fingers. *She is going to kill me*, thought Jay. The back of his left hand was swollen red and stung from igniting the paint can. Jay smiled at the memory.

"Why's this kid here?" asked another police officer, swinging open the half door that barricaded the public from entering the inner sanctum of the police desks.

Jay thought the cop was full of himself. He probably imagined he was Wyatt Earp entering a saloon every time he walked through that swinging half door. His hair was white blond. No facial hair. He stood with his hands on his hips resting the right hand on a hard leather gun holster and the other hand on a black walkie-talkie.

"Constable Jorgenson, this lad is part of the stolen car ring we busted tonight," said Constable Magee.

"How come you're stealing cars? Shouldn't you be hocking cigarettes for the reservation?" joked Constable Jorgenson folding his arms across his chest.

"I don't steal cars and I'm not from any reservation," said Jay.

"No? Hawaiian?" asked Constable Magee. He kept his head down over the paperwork, anxious to complete it before handing the desk duties over to Constable Jorgenson.

"No," said Jay.

"Mexican?" asked Constable Jorgenson.

"No," said Jay, irritated.

"Then what are you?" said Constable Magee.

"Nothing," said Jay.

"You must be Indian," said Constable Magee, looking up from a form to check Jay's features.

Jay had black hair, deep brown eyes, and his skin was tobacco brown. He knew he had First Nations blood but Tatla had left the reservation before he was born. She never talked about it so Jay did not consider himself to be First Nations, Aboriginal, Indian or whatever label society came up with.

"Well, I'm not. Can you please just let me go? I was at the wrong place at the wrong time. I'm way too young to drive a car," said Jay.

"You're not too young to handle a paint gun. You're covered in it," said Constable Magee.

"That's spray paint," said Jay. He realized what he'd said but it was too late to take it back.

"Oh, so you're a tagger. Either way, you're busted," said Constable Magee. He smiled at Jay.

"Kid's got more balls than brains," said Constable Jorgenson. "Is someone coming to pick you up?"

"My mom should be here any minute," said Jay. Who knew cops were so chatty. Jay wished they'd get back to work and leave him alone.

"Why doesn't your dad come and get you?" said Constable Magee.

"'Cause he's having dinner with your wife," said Jay. Jay's dad had left when Tatla was six months pregnant. He'd never seen Jay or talked to him. Tatla sent pictures and letters back east but they were all returned unopened.

"How old are you?" asked Constable Jorgenson.

"Thirteen, so you can't do anything to me. I'm a minor," said Jay.

"Yeah, a minor nuisance but wait five years when you're not a minor and still stealing cars or worse. You'll think juvenile detention was like day-care when you walk through the doors of a maximum security prison," said Constable Magee.

Jay wasn't worried. He knew they couldn't touch him. His smugness didn't last long.

Jay's stomach flipped over as he saw his mom enter the building. Tatla marched directly to him, keeping her eyes locked on his. Her waist length, black hair swung behind her.

Jay stood.

"Are you OK?" asked Tatla.

"I'm fine," said Jay, shifting his gaze to the ground.

"What am I doing here at 1 o'clock in the morning on a school night?" she asked, standing eye to eye with him. He had grown taller than her in the past months but tonight she had on her three inch heels she always wore with her fitted navy 'power suit'.

"I don't know," mumbled Jay.

"You don't know? Maybe he knows," said Tatla turning to the police officer behind the counter.

"We caught your son working at a chop shop," said Constable Jorgenson.

"A chop shop? With stolen cars? There must be some mistake," said Tatla, her chin level with the well worn oak counter.

"He was there when we raided the place. Look at his hands," said Constable Magee.

Jay tried to hide them but Tatla grabbed his left hand and forced open his fingers.

"What is this? Your hands are covered in paint and grease and burn marks," said Tatla.

"The burn marks are from hot metal. They had him cutting up the cars with a welder's torch, too," offered Constable Magee.

"The burns are from lighting a can of spray paint when I tried to get away," said Jay.

"Sure son. Take him home and bring him back first thing in the morning to see the senior police officer on duty," said Constable Jorgenson.

"He has school," said Tatla.

"I actually have tomorrow off," said Jay. He was pretty sure his scheme to shut down the school for a day had worked. Not that he wanted to spend it here, but maybe his mom would cool down a little if she knew he wasn't missing class.

"You do? I don't remember a professional development day being scheduled," said Tatla.

"It's not a Pro D day. It's a rat day," said Jay.

"A rat day?" asked Tatla.

"Yeah, like a snow day. They have to fumigate for rats so we're getting the day off. The school sent out an email," said Jay.

Tatla checked her BlackBerry. A message had been sent from the school stating that the school had a rat infestation. Students were asked to stay home while the problem was eradicated.

"Will you be here tomorrow or not?" asked Constable Jorgenson.

"I have a meeting," said Tatla.

"Yeah, she has a meeting. Can we do this some other time?" said Jay. His arm bent as he slouched on the counter.

Tatla shot him a look.

"Would it be more convenient if we kept him here for you?" asked Constable Jorgenson.

"No, of course not, we'll be here in the morning," said Tatla.

"Enjoy your bed kid. It's going to be the last time you sleep in it for a long time," said Constable Magee.

Tatla thanked the officers and click-clacked to the glass exit doors at a near run.

"Were you stealing cars and chopping them up?" Tatla asked, stumbling over words she never thought she'd say.

"No, I thought it was a garage where they fix up cars. I tried to leave but they wouldn't let me. Then the cops showed up," said Jay. He didn't tell her he was spray painting the skate park.

"Don't lie to me, Jay." Tatla knew Jay was avoiding something when he picked the skin around his nails. His thumb was almost bleeding as he peeled back a hang nail with his teeth.

"Who are these guys?" asked Tatla. She pulled his hand away from his mouth.

Jay glared at her.

"I don't know," said Jay and went back to picking at his hang nail.

"You better tell me. This is serious, Jay. You can't protect them," said Tatla.

"I'm not protecting them. Honest. I don't even know their names. I'll take a lie detector test if you want," said Jay.

"What am I going to do with you?" asked Tatla as she led Jay to their car, a dark green four door sedan bought used, seven years ago. "You tormented the babysitters until I finally gave in and let you stay alone. Now you get caught up in something like this. I guess your pranks at school were just the beginning. What's next, Jay?"

Tatla unlocked the door and Jay let himself in, kicking aside the stainless steel travel mug on the floor.

10

"My business is finally doing well and now I have to worry about what you are up to twenty-four hours a day. I'm supposed to go to Seattle for a tradeshow that could make or break us this year," said Tatla.

Tatla operated an events coordination business. In the past she had left Jay with babysitters while she checked convention centers in other cities. Jay had decided he was too old to be babysat. "They talk on the phone the whole time anyway so why pay them?" Jay had argued. One babysitter didn't even know Jay had left via the fire escape until three hours later when he and Tatla arrived home at the same time. The babysitter swore he was in bed. Tatla agreed the babysitters were useless.

Jay kept silent on the ride home. He knew anything he said could be used against him in the court of Tatla. Instead he thought about his greatest prank to date - rat day.

Chapter 3

Jay hadn't been planning a prank. It just came to him out of the blue; an inspired idea with opportunity too good to waste. As usual, Jay was kept after school as punishment for skipping class. Gym class, that shouldn't count. Jay got plenty of exercise at the skate park or walking around the city at night. Now that was an education. Who cares if he missed a gym class or ten?

To ensure Jay was on school property at 2:45 pm every day, the principal arranged for Jay to do the office photocopying for Mrs. Whittaker or Witty as the kids called her. It was more like clearing paper jams every two minutes from the piece of crap copier. Except today was a special day. The school had received a brand new, high tech copier that was also a printer and a scanner.

"We need 1500 letters printed on school letter-head. Your job is to remove the copies when the tray is full and to add more paper when the red light comes on. When that's done I'll find some other boring menial job for you to do," she said. Witty at least had a sense of humor unlike the principal.

Using the computer in the copier room, she sent the letter to the copier where it started printing immediately.

Jay watched the copier spit out the paper in rapid succession. Much faster than the last machine.

He sat at the computer and looked for games. *Nothing, not even Solitaire, just the stupid letter that half the parents won't read anyway,* thought Jay.

He looked around the room he had come to know so well. Rows and rows of shelves filled with different colored paper, cabinets with toner bottles, pens, staples, paper clips and rubber bands. To combat boredom Jay usually strung the paper clips or the rubber bands together but Witty had since stored them in the locked cabinet. Jay had already memorized the faded cartoons posted on the bulletin boards: "How do you know a man was the last one to use the photocopier?" said a curvy woman standing in front of a copier with symbols of alarm bells sounding. "I don't know," replied her young co-worker. "The lid is up and it's out of paper," answered the curvy woman.

Without thinking, Jay erased most of Witty's letter and typed in his own words:
'Dear parents,

This school sucks. Keep your children at home if you don't want them to grow up and become mindless droids with no original thoughts.'

Witty popped her head in once to ask Jay how he was doing. After blocking the screen with his body, he told her he was practicing his keyboarding.

"Good for you," she said and returned to her desk.

Wow, adults are gullible, thought Jay.

When she had gone he erased the letter and started again:
'Dear Parents,

We regret to advise you that the school will be closed tomorrow due to a rat infestation. Please keep your children home while we eradicate the situation. It could take a day or a week. We will let you know when the health department says it is safe for your children to return to school.'

Perfect.

The letter was worded just like the signs posted by the health department outside almost every restaurant in Jay's neighborhood at one time or another.

Jay hit the printer icon on the screen. The copier beeped. Jay added more paper, placing the letterhead face down.

What a huge copier, thought Jay.

The tan plastic copier took up an entire wall of the copier room. It had that new copier smell. The buttons on the copier were gone, replaced by an LCD panel, where all the commands were done by touch screen.

Jay looked at the options; copier, facsimile, printer, scanner.

I wonder what the scanner does.

He pressed 'scanner' on the panel. The screen flashed and asked for a password.

These people don't trust anyone. What could the password be? Something simple so the stupid teachers don't have to think too hard.

Jay tried 1234 on the numeric key pad and hit 'OK'. "Invalid password."

Ok, something all the teachers will know.

Jay picked up the letterhead and looked at it.

How about the school address? 15469 Shaunessey Street.

Jay punched in 15469.

Bingo.

The screen had boxes with names inside; the names of all the teachers, one called "Staff" and one called "Parents." Jay pressed the button with the principal's name on it. The email address for the principal appeared on the screen.

OMG. I could scan and email my butt to the principal. No, he'd get it right away and know it was me. Too bad, that would have been awesome, thought Jay.

The copier beeped again. Jay moved the stack of warm copies to the out box. The copier fired up again and printed one more sheet.

Jay picked it up and read it. It was his letter. His letter, on school letterhead, signed at the bottom by the principal.

It's like someone up there wants me to do this. I can't not do this. I'll regret it for the rest of my life, thought Jay.

Jay took the letter and put it face up in the copier's feeder. He paused a second, shrugged, and then tapped the screen icon marked "Parents." Before he could stop it, the letter was sucked in through the feeder and spat out again. The screen said, "Scan successful." Jay grabbed the letter and put it in the slot of a blue bin marked "Confidential Shredding."

"All done, Jay?" asked Witty from her chair.

Jay spun around. "Yes, it's a really fast copier," he said.

"And it can scan to everyone's email so you may lose your job soon," she said. "Here, I'll show you."

Jay panicked. The screen still showed the last scan address. "It's OK, you don't have to."

"No, I want to. It's good practice for me," she said. As she entered the copier room Jay reached for the "off" switch.

She swatted his hand away. "Don't touch that. It's very expensive and delicate equipment."

Well that's it for me. I'm dead.

As she turned to face the copier, the screen went black.

Jay didn't realize what had happened until later. Like a computer, the copier had an auto logout. He was safe. It had worked. Thanks to him hundreds of kids would enjoy a day off from school.

Except me, he thought glumly, as the sound of their building's underground parking gate snapped him back to reality.

Tatla grabbed her briefcase from the back seat. They walked to the elevator where Tatla took out her frustrations on the up button. She pressed it repeatedly but the light refused to go on. Jay pointed to a sign from the management company 'Elevator out of service. Sorry for any inconvenience.'

"I can't believe it's broken again," said Tatla.

They'd have to scale five flights of stairs to their apartment. Panting by the third floor, Tatla paused on the landing to remove her high heels. "Why do I put up with this? It isn't worth it."

"Yeah, you should really think about changing to a lower heel," said Jay.

"Very funny, you know I meant the building," said Tatla.

"We should move," said Jay. He took her briefcase.

"Thanks, I was just thinking the same thing," said Tatla.

Jay went straight to bed pulling the comforter with his favorite hockey team on it over his head. He didn't want to face his mother's anger or worse; disappointment. He turned off the matching hockey light but couldn't sleep. His mom was on the phone and he wondered who she was talking to at 2 a.m.

She usually emailed her customers, thought Jay.

Jay pulled back the comforter and opened his bedroom door a crack in time to hear his mother say, "Thanks a lot, Dad. I am sorry to have to do this but I didn't know who else to call. I'll talk to you soon. Goodnight."

Her dad? Why was she talking to her dad? They haven't spoken in years.

Jay gnawed on his index fingernail.

Chapter 4

"Get up, Jay," said Tatla, banging on the door. It was not the usual gentle tap followed by "Time to get up, Sweetie."

Ten minutes later Jay was still in bed.

"I mean it, Jay. Get up and get dressed, now. We have to buy you a dress shirt and dress pants," said Tatla while brushing her hair.

"Why? I think the cops already know I'm not exactly a church-goer," said Jay.

"Jay, I'm not in the mood," snarled Tatla shaking her hair brush at him.

Tatla rarely got angry but when she did, look out. This morning she was choked. The incident last night combined with the lack of sleep put them both on edge.

They rushed to the nearest mall and grabbed the first dress shirt and dress pants they saw. His beat up sneakers, with paint splotches the police officer later pointed out as evidence, would have to do. Tatla, despite Jay's protests, got on her hands and knees to pin up the cuffs. They were back in the car within twenty minutes weaving through the morning rush hour traffic made worse by the rain.

Tatla pulled into the same parking lot of the police station they had left only hours ago. She turned off the wipers and stared out the window.

"Before we go in, I want you to promise not to smart mouth anyone. Just say 'yes, sir' or 'no, sir'. This is serious. It is up to them to decide what happens to you," said Tatla.

17

Jay didn't answer.

"OK?" asked Tatla. She searched his face for a sign he understood the gravity of the situation.

"OK," snapped Jay.

Tatla stepped around the puddles. Jay stepped in the puddles. They climbed the concrete stairs and entered the building. After waiting in line, the desk sergeant told them a senior officer would be with them soon.

Thirty minutes later Jay had picked the skin around one thumbnail until the blood was pooling in the nail bed. He sucked on it to make it stop. Tatla pulled his hand away from his mouth when she saw an officer of Asian descent approaching.

"Are you Jay Roberts?" asked the police officer.

"Yes," said Jay. He and Tatla stood up.

"I'm Tatla Roberts," said Jay's mom, extending her hand.

"Senior Officer Fung. Follow me," he said after shaking hands with Tatla and Jay.

They followed Officer Fung to his office; a cramped windowless room with an L- shaped desk, a computer and three file cabinets. It was stark, impersonal and impeccably clean. In the corner, a flag drooped from a flag pole like a naughty child with its head hung in shame. The current prime minister cast judgment on all from the portrait on the wall. He did not look amused.

"Please sit down," said Officer Fung, motioning to the two black vinyl stackable chairs.

"Jay, were you involved in this stolen car ring?" asked Officer Fung.

"No. I was cutting through the alley and they grabbed me. They said I could either work for them or they'd kill me," said Jay.

"All four of them are saying the same story; you came to them looking for a job and they used you as a gopher," said Officer Fung.

"They're lying!" Jay shouted.

"Do you have any evidence to support your story?" said Officer Fung.

"No, but…" said Jay.

"Then it's your word against theirs," interrupted Officer Fung.

"Why do you believe a bunch of criminals and not my son? He's never been in trouble before," said Tatla.

"If you were in the wrong place at the wrong time as you say, chances are you didn't get there by taking a wrong turn to the library," said Officer Fung.

Wow, thought Jay. *Do they teach this in cop school, 'Trust No One 101' or 'Advanced Skepticism'?*

"I have read your file, Jay. Is there anything you would like to add to your statement?" asked Officer Fung.

"No," said Jay.

"Is this your first offense?" asked the officer.

"You got my file," said Jay. Tatla pinched him under the knee.

"Yes, sir. It's my first," said Jay rubbing his leg. "And I'm so glad it's with you."

"Listen, son, you can quit the tough guy act. No one is impressed," said Officer Fung as a knock came at the door.

The door behind Jay and Tatla opened. Tatla looked up, "What are you doing here?"

Jay stared at the old man as he entered the room. He had shoulder length silver hair, thinning at the front, dark eyebrows and wavy lines across his forehead. He wore a beige corduroy jacket and work jeans. His eyes were the same color and shape as Jay's.

"Can I help you?" asked Officer Fung.

"I'm Mr. Roberts, the boy's grandfather," said the man.

Jay's eyes grew wide and then turned into a scowl.

"Is that true?" Officer Fung asked Jay.

"No, I've never seen him before," said Jay, looking Officer Fung in the eye.

Officer Fung turned to Tatla.

"Let me explain," said Tatla. "My dad and I haven't been on speaking terms since Jay was born. They have never met."

"Until today?" said Officer Fung.

Tatla nodded.

"So why today, Mr. Roberts?" asked Officer Fung. He put his pen down and leaned back in his chair.

Mr. Roberts entered the room and closed the door. He put both hands on the back of Tatla's chair.

"My daughter called me last night to ask for help. After council with the elders of my village I spoke with an aboriginal court-worker named Penny Wilson. She told me to come down here and talk to you." His voice was low, almost monotone and the words slow, smooth and deliberate.

"Yes, I know Penny quite well," said Officer Fung. "Where is your village?"

"It is about three hours north of here," said Mr. Roberts. "If you find Jay is responsible, we hope you'll allow him to live on the reservation with us. The elders and I can oversee his sentence," said Mr. Roberts.

20

Jay looked at his mom. Her cheeks were flushed and her eyes were brimming. Jay couldn't tell if she was furious or about to cry.

"I was going to refer Jay to a community restorative justice program," said Officer Fung.

"He needs guidance and support from his people," said Mr. Roberts.

"Mom, don't let them do this. Please, I'll come home straight from school and I won't go out. I'll do all my homework and I'll stay away from the skate park," pleaded Jay.

"Jay, you've given me this speech before. If Officer Fung agrees, I think this is the best solution. Maybe it's time you got to know your grandfather and our people," said Tatla.

"I think this is best, but there will be conditions, Jay. You will be under your mother's or grandfather's supervision at all times except for school. You will also have to do fifteen hours a week of community service. We'll send up a probation officer, probably Mrs. Thornton, to do random checks on your progress. If she feels you are not getting the rehabilitation you need we will look at other types of extrajudicial measures," said Officer Fung.

Community service, a probation officer, extracurricular something or other? No way is this happening, thought Jay.

"Jay will learn the ways of our people and our traditions of honor and respect," said Mr. Roberts.

Is this guy for real? thought Jay.

"I'm not going," said Jay. "I'll run away. I'd rather live on the street than move to some Indian reservation."

"Go with your grandfather to the reservation for six months. Otherwise, you may end up in juvenile detention where you will eat, sleep, and shower with a hundred other boys. And trust me, they will teach you about tradition and respect," said Officer Fung.

Chapter 5

Jay, Tatla and Mr. Roberts returned to the front counter and signed the documentation sealing Jay's fate. A humorless woman about fifty years old approached the counter.

"I'm Mrs. Thornton," she said and waited for a response. None came. Her eyes bore into Jay.

"Your probation officer," she snapped.

Tatla put her hands on Jay's elbows and led him forward.

"This is my son, Jay. We're pleased to meet you," said Tatla. She put out her hand and smiled her "win over the customer" sales smile.

Mrs. Thornton did not smile back. Her handshake was done with only the finger tips. She did the same to Jay and to Mr. Roberts. Tatla had told Jay many times you could tell a lot from someone's handshake. Jay almost laughed when he saw how little this woman wanted to touch another person.

When Mr. Roberts told her where the village was she rolled her eyes and said they better pay her mileage and a meal allowance. She outlined the terms of the probation and warned that they must be adhered to exactly.

"Just because I am three hours away doesn't mean I don't have spies," she said. She gathered up the paperwork banging the sheets on the desk until a neat pile formed. Satisfied everything was in order she headed back to her office.

Jay thought she would have made a great CIA agent if her bulging feet ever passed the physical. Tatla was on her BlackBerry as usual. She stabbed the "end" button and glared at Jay.

What now? thought Jay.

"That was your principal. He said there is no rat day. The school wasn't infested and nothing was being eradicated, except maybe you. It was a prank. He wanted to know if you had anything to do with it?" said Tatla, shaking her BlackBerry at him.

"How could I send an email to every parent?" asked Jay.

"I don't know but I wish you would use your brains for something more productive," said Tatla.

"Does it matter? I'm not going back to that school anyway," said Jay. His stomach felt like he'd swallowed a bag of marbles and one of them was stuck in his throat.

Tatla walked in front. Jay and Mr. Roberts followed behind.

"How did you know the message was sent by email to every parent?" asked Mr. Roberts in a low voice so that Tatla did not hear.

Jay stopped. He knew he was caught. Keeping silent was usually the best defense.

Mr. Roberts didn't say anything either.

Outside the police station Tatla introduced Jay to his Grampa. Jay noticed that Tatla had not hugged her dad or made sustained eye contact with him since he arrived.

"Do I call you grandfather or warden?" said Jay.

"Call me Grampa or sir," said Grampa, extending an aged hand covered in dark spots like a week-old banana.

Jay reluctantly shook his hand. They zig-zagged through the parking lot to the car. Jay and Grampa both reached for the handle on the passenger door but Jay got there first. The ride home was quiet except for the sound of the wiper blades even though it had stopped raining ten minutes ago.

Grampa waited in the living room while Jay and Tatla packed up three suitcases and several boxes. The movers would bring their furniture later. Grampa had secured the house next door to him, recently vacated by the Martin family who had moved to the city to find work.

Since the elevator was still broken, Jay, Grampa and Tatla struggled down the five flights of stairs with the suitcases and boxes, pausing to let other tenants pass on their way up. Grampa's overnight bag did not allow the trunk to close. He put it in the back seat and closed the door while Jay got in the front seat.

"Get in the back please, Jay," said Tatla.

"What for?" asked Jay.

"Because your grandfather is sitting in the front," said Tatla.

"Great. This is what life is going to be like; delegated to the back seat, back of the squad car, back of this car. It's where I belong, right?" said Jay.

Grampa got in the front seat, reached behind for the seat belt and didn't say a word.

Jay had never sat in the backseat of his own car. He didn't even know what it looked like. Staring at the back of Tatla's and Grampa's heads for three hours was going to be real fun. It was the longest consecutive time Jay had spent with his mom in over a year.

The ride was quiet especially when they reached the mountains out of radio range. Tatla switched the radio off after an hour of static that no one had noticed until it was gone.

This was as far from the city as Jay had been. He stared out the window at the mountains as trees snagged the clouds and were pulled apart like cotton candy. Beneath his feet Jay found a notepad and half a pencil with teeth marks. He sketched the scenery to take his mind off the growing despair he felt. Each road sign marked the distance to the village or rather the closest town to it, in smaller and smaller numbers. The village itself was too remote to warrant its own road sign. Without a gas station or restaurant why would anyone want to stop there?

Grampa and Tatla attempted a few conversations, catching up on the village news but it was strained and never lasted for more than a couple of sentences.

Huge logging trucks careened down the hills towards them turning just in time before a head on collision occurred. Jay wished the brakes would fail and put him out of his misery. The engine struggled through the winding mountain road getting stuck behind a passenger bus. Jay smelled the toxic diesel smoke as the bus trudged up the steep rocky canyon.

"I forgot to ask how your bus ride was," said Tatla. "Did you remember the rule?"

"Sure did," said Grampa.

"What rule?" asked Jay, forgetting about the silence he was waging on his mother. She had refused to let Jay say goodbye to his friends, claiming she didn't want to drive the mountain roads in the dark. Jay thought she was too embarrassed to face their parents.

"The rule is, when you board the bus, if you find two empty seats together, don't sit there. You never know who is getting on at the next stop, could be someone with overactive sweat glands or a non-stop talker with Halitosis," said Grampa.

"Hal-o-what-sis?" Jay asked.

"Halitosis. Bad breath," answered Grampa. He turned his head as much as possible toward Jay but couldn't face him.

"Oooh," said Jay, crinkling his nose.

"Did you sit by someone who met the criteria?" asked Tatla.

"I sat next to a lady about your age. She gave me a dirty look because she knew there were empty seats at the back. When she found out I was from the village she changed seats," said Grampa casually.

Jay's and Tatla's eyes met in the mirror as they suppressed their shock.

"We're getting close now," said Tatla. She took a deep breath.

Barbed wire stapled to wood posts protecting green and yellow fields gave way to sagging, gap toothed picket fences. As they crossed a rusty bridge spanning a swirling river below, Jay sensed he was in a different country. It wasn't like a wooden arm rose and fell to permit entry; it was more the abrupt end of the smooth asphalt onto a bumpy dirt road without sidewalks or street lights. Jay thought he might heave if the car didn't stop bouncing up and down like a carnival ride. When the car bottomed out for the third time Jay looked out the back window to see if the muffler had fallen off.

"There's my old school. Your new school, Jay," said Tatla.

Jay felt like acid was boiling in his stomach. The small, run down school was perched on the edge of a cliff above the river. The adjacent soccer field had a chain-link fence around the perimeter and a sheer drop off on two sides.

"I wouldn't want to be the one to get the ball if it goes over the fence," Jay commented.

"Definitely a three ball minimum otherwise you have to hook up the carabineers and repel down to get the ball before it rolls into the river," his mom joked.

"If you show up at the field with only one ball everyone asks 'Are you new?'" Jay bantered.

"Yes and at the end of the season, the lumber company downstream brings back all the balls. They attach a boom to the

27

tugboats and everyone stands on the riverbank and retrieves their ball. It's an annual event," said Grampa.

It was a brief moment that broke the tension during the long drive. Jay was not looking forward to his new home but couldn't wait to get out of the car and stretch his legs.

Jay swallowed the bile that crept up his throat.

"This is it. It will be nice to have a grandchild around. I think I'm the only man in the village without one," said Grampa.

"Great, you can take me to the park and push me on the swings. Here is something to hang on the fridge," said Jay. Jay passed Grampa his sketch: a passenger bus going off a cliff and bursting into flames while hawks circled overhead with body parts in their claws.

Tatla took her eyes off the road to see what Jay had given her dad. She didn't see the pot hole in time and swerved to avoid it, nearly running into a man walking down the middle of the road. He carried a bag of groceries in one hand and a case of beer in the other. Tatla honked at him to move. He turned and raised his case of beer toward Grampa and smiled. Grampa waved.

"Dad, things have really changed," said Tatla. "Except the trees." Hemlock, spruce and cedar trees towered over the houses on three sides of the village. The village butted up against a mountain. The bottle green trees grew up the side of the mountain, one behind the other so all had a clear view of the village, like rows in a movie theater.

Most of the houses were small bungalows with crooked steps and peeling paint. Some were newer, but unkempt yards gave them a look of being abandoned. Flags and aluminum foil hung in a few windows in place of curtains. Jay wondered if the detention center might have been the better choice.

Yard by yard the village passed by filled with windowless school busses, car doors, tires and gutted vehicles. *This is like one big chop shop except no luxury cars and no one to put them back together,* thought Jay.

He pointed to a house with a full sized inflated pool inside a double garage.

The swollen sides of the pool expanded beyond the concrete floor. It looked ready to burst at any moment.

"Is that the aquatic center?" asked Jay. "I guess they don't have much of dive team."

"Aren't they worried about flooding the house if it gets a leak?" said Tatla.

"Or if someone hits the remote on the garage door opener?" said Jay.

Rusted appliances and decrepit cars littered several yards.

"Maybe if they attached a lawn mower blade to the bottom of one those junk heaps, the grass might actually get cut," Jay said.

"Don't they know that cars go in the garage and pools go in the yard and not the other way around?" asked Jay.

"You can't tell people how to live their lives," said Grampa.

"Unless they're kids," said Jay.

Tatla pulled the car into the gravel driveway.

"Here are the keys," said Grampa. He handed Tatla a plain silver ring with three keys. "It was too bad the Martins had to leave but I'm glad another house won't be boarded up. Are you sure you don't want to stay with me until you get moved in? You don't even have any furniture."

"Gee, can I have my old bedroom, too?" Tatla caught herself. "Sorry, that wasn't very nice. No Dad, I want to stay independent. I only agreed to live next door so you can keep an eye on Jay."

The pale green house was a two story box with matching mildew on the verandah. The front yard had a few shrubs and several dandelions but no lawn to speak of.

"Ah, fresh air. What do you think, Jay? It'll be nice to live in a house instead of an apartment, right?" said Tatla. She climbed the front steps and unlocked the door.

"It's like we won the poverty lottery," said Jay as he followed her inside. "All that's missing is the police tape."

The house smelled dank like wet towels that had sat in the laundry basket too long.

"If it's the same layout as Grampa's house there will be three bedrooms upstairs. Pick the one you want. I'll use the other one for an office," said Tatla.

Jay grabbed the hand rail to climb the stairs and the whole thing came out of the wall, crushing his foot. "Stupid piece of crap," he yelled and kicked the rail. The brass bracket gouged a chunk out of the drywall.

"Take it easy," said Tatla. "And Dad, stop carrying everything in. I can do it."

Grampa dropped the suitcase just inside the door, said good night and went home.

Tatla shook her head and exhaled.

Jay continued up the stairs leaving the rail where it was.

He flicked on the hall light and took in the water stains on the ceiling and the crayon scribbles around each doorway. He picked the room farthest from his mother's. Probably the kid's room judging by the hole punched in the hollow door.

The light didn't work but Jay didn't care. There was just enough daylight to reveal a twin mattress on the floor and a three drawer dresser with one drawer missing. The beige carpet looked like someone used the room to take an engine apart. Brown

30

streaks, green islands and black splotches dotted the shag. The closet did not have a door, just some wire hangers on the floor and the headless body of a doll. The room had a fishy odor like dirty diapers.

"Perfect," said Jay, out loud. Exhausted, he crawled onto the mattress and pushed himself into the corner, sitting with his knees bent up. He crossed his arms and dropped his head onto his forearms.

First chance I get I'm leaving this hell hole, thought Jay, as he drifted off to sleep.

Chapter 6

Jay ducked as a light spiraled from the sky, illuminating the trees at the edge of the soccer field.

What the heck was that?

A brushed, silver disk with a clear glass dome sat steaming in a nest of bushes. Whoosh. The dome retracted into itself revealing a small, pale being with oil black eyes.

"I know you are there," it said in a childlike voice. "I can smell the carbon dioxide from your breath. Come out."

Jay stepped out from behind the garbage can and bolted across the field. He got about three steps and ran straight into the alien. Its skin was cold and sticky like a slice of processed cheese. Jay shuddered. A scream lodged in his throat and he swallowed it.

"Who are you? What are you doing here?" asked Jay.

"We want the Earth. You humans have polluted the atmosphere allowing my species to thrive here. It is refreshing to have so little oxygen to inhale," explained the alien taking in a cleansing breath. With each breath the alien grew taller until it towered over the trees. It reached down with it's three fingered bony hand and scooped Jay up in its palm. Jay's heart raced. *I've got to stop them,* he thought. *But how?*

The keys around Jay's neck jingled as he tried to stand but fell backward. The alien peered at Jay with an eye as lifeless as a mirrored motorcycle helmet. A milky film moved left to right and back again as it blinked. Jay grasped his key ring and found what he was he looking for. He held the button down and shot the alien directly in the eye with his laser pointer, blinding it. The alien fell to its knees and groped to find Jay. He reached into the front pocket of his hoodie for a can of spray paint but the label said "Pure Oxygen". Jay snapped off the lid and sprayed the space creature. Its eyes bulged as the pasty skin turned bright red. The alien clutched its throat and made a horrible sound…

COUGH, COUGH, COUGH.

Jay kept spraying.

CAW! CAW! CAW!

Jay eyes snapped open.

Stars? No, only holes in the ceiling tiles.

"Stupid crows! Thanks for ruining a great dream. I almost slayed the alien and saved the Earth," Jay mumbled.

CAW! CAW! CAW!

What are those stupid birds talking about? Their plans for the weekend? What they did last night? thought Jay as he covered his ears.

CAW! CAW! CAW!

"That's it!"

Jay threw back the blanket and stomped across the worn carpet.

"Quiet!" he yelled out the window.

Then he stopped and listened; silence.

"Hey, it worked!" Jay said as he climbed back under the blanket and tried to pick up the dream where he left off.

"CAW! CAW! CAW!"

"Get lost," Jay hollered as a knock came at the door.

"Jay? I hope you're not talking to me," Tatla warned through the bedroom door.

"No, I was talking to those stupid crows. They're driving me crazy," answered Jay.

"It's time to get up for school. You don't want to be late for your first day. Are you sure you don't want me to take you?" asked Tatla.

She'd probably try to tuck my shirt in my pants and then lick her thumb and wash my face, thought Jay.

"Oh yeah, that'd go over real big," he replied. "The only thing I want, besides moving back home, is more sleep."

"I swear you teenagers need an hour of sleep for every year you are born," said Tatla.

Jay went back to the window and pretended to throw something. The crows scattered in different directions but soon returned to the fence and continued to chat.

I thought living in the country was supposed to be quiet, thought Jay. He jumped as the alarm clock went off, blasting a whiny country music song. Jay turned the dial up and down but found no other stations.

"I can't wait to get an iPod with the money I've been saving, so I don't have to listen to your squawking," Jay told the crows. *Or that lousy country station. How do these people survive with only one radio station?* He yanked the cord out of the wall of the radio alarm clock he assumed Tatla had plugged in while he was sleeping.

Jay shuffled to the bathroom and back handed the crust off his eyelids. He turned on the shower and jumped as the pipes creaked. The shower head shook and coughed then spat out a blast of water, like an old man clearing his lungs.

"Gross! Mom, Mom," Jay called through the house until he found her in the kitchen unloading cardboard boxes. Crumpled newspaper gathered at her feet.

"What is it?" she said as she climbed onto a chair to reach the top shelf. Jay had passed her five foot nothing height about a year ago. She was tiny and often shopped in the kids section when the clothes in the ladies department didn't fit. Her straight black hair, brown eyes and trendy style made her look more like Jay's sister than his mom.

"The water smells weird," said Jay.

"It's supposed to smell like that. It's well water," replied Tatla.

"More like *unwell* water. It stinks like rotten eggs. I'm not taking a shower. I'll smell worse when I get out. Can't we please just go home?" pleaded Jay.

"And leave all this?" said Tatla as she gestured with her hands to showcase the kitchen, circa 1970's. The orange counter tops, brown plastic cupboards and yellow flowered linoleum struck Jay like a Mac truck the first time he saw it.

"There's nothing wrong with the water. You'll get used to it," she said.

"I don't want to get used to it. It stinks like someone farted," said Jay.

"Watch your mouth," said Tatla.

"Give me a mirror," said Jay.

"Jay, one more smart remark and…" Tatla trailed off.

"And what? You've already taken me away from my friends and my school. What else can you do?" Jay said as he stomped up the stairs.

"Don't blame me," said Tatla.

Jay surfaced fifteen minutes later in his favorite black t-shirt and baggy khaki pants.

"Try to make some friends, Jay. I know it's strange going to a different school but I'm sure the kids will welcome you. They might even think you're cool coming from the big city," said Tatla.

"I don't need any new friends. Once my six months are up we're moving back to the city," said Jay as he grabbed his backpack and pushed the door.

"I hope so. Don't forget to take out the garbage," said Tatla.

"Take out the garbage? Take it where?" asked Jay. He had never lived in a house before. In the city the garbage was put down a chute or taken to the trash compactor in the basement.

"Put it outside somewhere, out of my way," said Tatla.

"And just leave it there? Isn't that littering?" asked Jay.

"No, just do it, please," she said. Her patience was wearing thin.

As Jay reached for the green plastic heaps filled with packing material he saw something in the corner of his eye. He turned to look but it was only a coat hanging on the back of the door. *This place gives me the creeps,* he thought.

Jay scowled at the crows as he trudged past them. Low clouds released a cool drizzle. The kids in the village walked to school, unlike the city where minivans and SUVs picked up and dropped off the students. Jay noticed most kids stuck together in packs of three or four. Only one boy walked alone. Jay thought about catching up but then remembered he didn't need any new friends.

A pack of dogs ran down the street barking and snapping at the kids. The kids stomped their feet and yelled at the dogs. The dogs turned on each other. A fight broke out between a German Shepherd and a mongrel with a black head and white body. Curled lips, wrinkled noses, ivory flashes of canine teeth snapped, tufts of fur flew out, paws and tails entangled. The yelping, like one of

36

them was being murdered, made Jay want to break it up. A yellow Lab beat him to it by bellowing at the two dogs. They stopped fighting, and with strands of saliva swinging from their jowls, carried on down the street like nothing had happened.

Jay looked around to see if anyone noticed the dogs running wild but no one paid any attention.

He continued past houses with missing roof tiles and gutters hanging on by rusty screws. The yards were a source of entertainment, completely furnished from fridge and stove to couches, mattresses and even a pop machine. On a column at the front door overhang, someone had handwritten "The Scott's". The other column, in the same hand writing had the house number.

Jay rounded the corner past bramble bushes taller than him. They encroached on the yard, well on their way to consuming the house. Young girls must live next to the bramble house as pink and purple plastic toy jeeps, shopping carts, and baby carriages were parked out front. Plastic shopping bags from various stores hung on the picket fence. Jay wondered if they were there for people to put things in or to take things out of. He never got close enough to find out. It reminded him too much of the baggies city people carried to the park to pick up after their dogs.

Tarps were a big hit in the village, too. They covered wood piles, cars, and boats which wasn't unusual. However, the orange tarps on the roofs, held down by tires, and the olive green tarp hanging across an entire wall including the window was probably not on the list of uses stated on the tarp company's website.

The last house before the school had really outdone the others in the window covering department. Instead of a flag or broken blinds this person had decorated their windows completely in beer cans. Stacked high enough to keep people from looking in but not quite to the top so light could still shine through, assumed Jay. Or they might not be finished yet he told himself.

Jay's stomach flipped over when he realized there were no more houses to view; only a gravel road between him and the school. He used his sleeve to wipe a water drop from his nose, built up from the mist. The sleeve felt damp.

The school was a one story, crumbling, cinder block structure with a flat, pea stone roof that did not look waterproof, fireproof or earthquake proof. It had the school name "Nelson Junior Secondary School" and a faded emblem of a First Nations symbol painted on the outside. A few kids tossed a basketball into a leaning hoop. The backstop looked homemade and wobbled with each shot. Other kids huddled together to keep the drizzle from soaking their cigarettes. Jay thought they looked as miserable as he felt.

Ignoring the stares as everyone checked out the new kid, Jay found his way to his classes. They whispered something over and over again. Jay was convinced it was a swear word, most likely the "A" word. *They don't even know me and they are calling me names. And what gives them the right to call me names when their names were so weird; Two Feathers, Tailfeathers, Two Gun, Old Hands, Standing Alone. What kind of last names were those?* He had read them off a wall in the office while picking up his class schedule.

No one talked to Jay but he didn't care. School ends in a few weeks then summer vacation for two months.

Maybe the courts will let me go home early for good behavior.

Jay spent his lunch hour in the covered area alone at one of the picnic tables. The rain had picked up, forcing most of the students under cover. No one approached him and that suited Jay fine. To distract himself from the stares and whispers he plotted ways to get rid of the crows.

A BB gun would be awesome, he thought over a peanut butter and jam sandwich. Every day, since grade one, Jay ate PB&J

38

for lunch. At first he ate it because they couldn't afford anything else. Now he just liked it. It was something familiar.

A group of kids gathered at another picnic table watching him, not just out of curiosity but really studying him. A stocky boy elbowed the kid to his left, handed him an apple and pointed at Jay. The boy climbed out from behind the bench seat and made his way to Jay's table.

"Here," he said and tossed the apple to Jay.

"Uh, thanks," said Jay, fumbling to catch the apple.

The boy returned to his seat and the whole table burst into laughter. Jay put the apple down and went back to thinking about the BB gun. He knew his mom would never let him have one. His thoughts were interrupted again when a different kid, from the same table, set an apple down in front of Jay.
"Apple," he said.

"No, thanks, I'm good," said Jay. The kid smirked and returned to his friends. One by one, everyone at the table did the same thing; said "apple" then set an apple down in front of Jay and left.

Bewildered, Jay sat with a dozen or so apples until the bell rang. He got up from the table, put the half eaten sandwich in the garbage and merged into the hallway traffic to his next class. Again he heard the whispers but this time he knew they weren't saying the "A" word. They were saying "apple".

What does that mean? Do they think I'm a fruit or something? wondered Jay.

To put the apple incident out of his mind, Jay doodled. It was either that or pick at his scabby fingers. He drew pictures of crows and aliens, crows with alien heads and aliens with crow heads, and did not complete any schoolwork. Jay lugged home a mountain of books thinking about how much he hated the village.

As Jay neared his house he dropped his backpack in disbelief. Garbage was scattered everywhere and picking through it were the crows.

Chapter 7

Jay charged at the birds, waving his arms. A well-fed crow stood its ground.

"Get out of here," screamed Jay.

The bird casually hopped a few steps on wiry feet and then flew away when Jay got within punting distance.

"Hi Mom," said Jay, slinging his backpack on the back of a chair. Their apartment furniture looked small and out of place in the roomy kitchen. The moving company, one of Tatla's clients, delivered the contents of the apartment in one day. Not that they had many belongings but still it must have been some kind of record.

"Hi Honey, how was your first day at school?" she asked, turning from the sink to dry her hands on a towel.

"Great, they made me class president," said Jay.

"It's only your first day. It'll get better. Did you see what that wild pack of dogs did outside?" asked Tatla.

"I think it was the crows," said Jay.

"Can you pick up the garbage while I start dinner?" asked Tatla.

"Why should I? Like it's going to make a difference. There's tons of junk all over this stupid village," Jay spouted.

"Pardon?" said Tatla and raised her eyebrows.

"I've got a ton of homework to do," replied Jay.

"You want to do homework? That's a switch," said Tatla.

"It's better than picking up garbage in the rain," said Jay.

Tatla responded by handing him a folded green, garbage bag.

"I hope those crows choke," yelled Jay as he snatched the bag from her hand and slammed the front door.

As he picked up dirty containers, slimy egg shells, and banana peels coated with coffee grounds, the girl next door teased him from her overgrown front yard.

"Find anything you like?" she said.

"Yeah, your next birthday present," spat Jay.

"Hmfp!" she said and turned toward her house, a yellow stucco bungalow with plywood covering a bedroom window.

Jay's grandfather watched from the porch. The last bit of sunlight found holes in the clouds and turned everything peach.

The crows squawked from a cherry tree, as if Jay was stealing from them.

"I hope you enjoyed your dinner because it's the last one you'll have at my house," vowed Jay.

Jay headed into the house disregarding his grandfather. *Not much time for homework now. I'm going to be up all night getting it done,* thought Jay.

Jay spread his books on the kitchen table and looked at the assignment, "Today's Coastal Indians". His teacher said the government educators were still calling them Indians even though they preferred First Nations.

The back door creaked and Jay's mouth gaped as he turned to see who had entered.

"Hi," said a petite lady. She had white hair with brown streaks like she had started to rust. Her top teeth were missing, causing her lower jaw to stick out farther than her nose.

She stooped over a cane and shuffled toward Jay. The grey, white and black geometric designed shawl she wore dragged on the ground behind her. Dried leaves had attached to the fringes and scratched the floor as she moved towards Jay.

He stood up, shocked that someone would barge in without knocking first. Only serial killers, home invaders and child abductors did such a thing in the city. Jay imagined her sweeping him under her shawl and taking him home to cook in a big, black pot.

"Is your mother home?" she asked. Her voice cracked like her skin had done over the years.

"Um, I'll go get her," said Jay, happy for any excuse to leave. Jay backed out of the kitchen and found his mom.

"Mom, there is a witch in the kitchen. I swear," whispered Jay.

"What are you talking about?" said Tatla as she brushed passed him.

"Mary! How are you, Grandmother?" said Tatla as she bent over to hug the lady who had helped herself to a chair.

"I'm doing OK," said Mary.

Jay didn't think she looked 'OK'.

"I just stopped by to welcome you home. We missed you when you left. Now you are back and have a handsome man with you," she said, flashing a toothless grin at Jay.

Jay cringed.

"This is Jay, my son. Jay, this is Mary Joe," said Tatla.

"Nice to meet you, Jay," said the elderly lady. Her cane hung on the back of the chair.

"Nice to meet you, too, Mary Joe," said Jay.

"Just Mary. Joe's my last name," she said and pulled a cigarette out of her purse.

"Sorry," said Jay as he waited for his mom to send Mary outside to smoke. Instead, Tatla asked Mary if she wanted an ashtray.

What! I can't believe it. She never lets anyone smoke in the house. Even if it was ten below she made them stand on the balcony of the apartment.

Jay's mom looked at him and knew what he was thinking. "Jay, why don't you go watch TV," said Tatla.

"Which channel should I watch? 3 or 6?" said Jay.

"Very funny. The satellite guys will be here next week to hook us up but we'll have to wait two weeks for the phone," said Tatla. "I'll have to run my business from the internet café. Which I found out is an hour drive. The gas will cost a fortune. You're going to put me in the poor house."

"Too late, we're already here," said Jay.

"Oh," said Mary. She took a long pull on her cigarette and exhaled the smoke through her mouth and nose at the same time.

A half hour later Tatla called to Jay. "It's safe to come out now. She's gone home for dinner."

Jay walked into the kitchen and opened the window to air out the smoke.

"I hope she is not having corn-on-the-cob," said Jay.

"Jay, be nice. Not a lot of people here can afford a dentist. The ones the government provided, back in the day, were told to pull teeth instead of filling them. Cheaper," explained Tatla.

"Who is she, anyway?" asked Jay.

"She is an old friend of your Gramma Alice."

"How come you called her Grandmother?" asked Jay.

"It is a sign of respect to call our elders Grandmother or Grandfather," replied Tatla.

"How come you let her smoke in the house?" accused Jay.

"She is my elder and we have to respect their ways. It would have been rude to ask her to go outside. I know I sound like a hypocrite but things are done differently around here. It's just the way of our people," said Tatla.

"Not my people," said Jay as he let the back door slam behind him. The sun had sunk below the horizon and lit the clouds from beneath underlining them in gold.

Jay went next door and found his grandfather sitting on the porch. His squinty eyes gave him the look of an animal on the hunt. He didn't blink as Jay reached the top step.

"Hi Grampa, are you busy?"

"Very busy."

"You don't look busy."

"Just because my hands are not moving on the outside doesn't mean they are not busy on the inside," said Grampa.

"Huh?" said Jay.

"When a duck swims you don't see its feet moving, same thing," said Grampa.

"OK," said Jay as he turned to go back to his house.

"What did you want?" asked Grampa.

"I want to know what my punishment is. Mom says it's up to you and the old folks to decide what I'm supposed to do. Are you going to leave me in a cave or drop me onto some island for six months or what?"

"Elders – not old folks. Come over tomorrow after school," said Grampa, waving his arms like he was shooing a dog. "It's late, go home now."

45

"Uh, OK, bye," said Jay.

Jay headed home wondering what he did wrong.

"Where did you go? You didn't leave the yard I hope," asked Tatla.

"I went to ask Grampa what my punishment is and he told me to go home," said Jay. "He sure is grumpy. I'm going to call him Grumpa."

"Don't you dare. You have respect!" said Tatla, laughing in spite of herself. "Don't take it personally. I think he had a meeting with the elders and it didn't go too well."

"I'm going back tomorrow after school. He said he'll tell me then," said Jay.

"I'm glad you two are getting to know each other," said Tatla.

"Who else am I going to hang out with?" said Jay. He slumped up the stairs to his room.

Chapter 8

CAW! CAW! CAW!

"Whose car alarm?" grumbled Jay. More and more, morning seemed to come as a shock to Jay.

CAW! CAW! CAW!

"Ohh," groaned Jay, when he realized he wasn't in the city.

"Get off my fence you flying rats," yelled Jay out the window. With each 'caw' the big black crow's body puffed up. The tail flicked down to emphasize the force it put into each call.

Jay tried to get back to sleep but gave up. With eyes half shut he dressed for school.

He was surprised to see his mom in the kitchen putting out a bowl of cereal for him. Usually he woke up to an empty apartment. If she did leave anything for him it was a note saying where she was and what time she'd be home.

"Did you sleep OK?" asked Tatla.

"Yeah, it was nice to sleep in my own bed. Who put it together, the moving guys?" asked Jay.

"No, your grampa did it yesterday. It's so strange to be back. It's like I am living next door to myself," said Tatla. She poured hot coffee into a stainless steel travel mug.

"Hmm," said Jay, shoveling Mini-Wheats into his mouth.

"Sorry to do this to you, but can you help me clean the car? I'm late for a meeting with the mining company I've been trying to land as a client," said Tatla.

"But you just took it through the car wash," said Jay.

47

"I know but I parked under the cherry tree where the birds sit. Please hurry," she said and handed Jay the Windex and a roll of paper towels.

Jay shook his head when he saw what greeted him. The grey liquid had splattered across the paint at unusual angles.

They do more than just 'sit'; maybe mom should have added an 'h in between the 's' and the 'i'. How did they hit the door handle?

He squirted the partially dry mess. It became a disgusting paste. Jay turned away before he gagged.

"I gotta figure out a way to get rid of those crows," Jay said to himself.

Maybe there are some bows and arrows around here. I'll bet Grampa has one.

On his way to school a lady waved at him from her front window. He averted his eyes and pretended not to see her.

When Jay arrived at school he checked his schedule and groaned: Third period – Gym. His skinny build did not make him much of an athlete. C minus showed up on his report card year after year.

Jay followed the signs in the hallway to the gym. He peered through the wire-mesh window at the gym's polished concrete floor. A half wall around the court, with Plexi-glass on top made it look more like a hockey arena than a gym.

The right side of the double doors opened. A thickset man with a whistle around his neck hollered to Jay, "I'm Mr. Dunbar, come on in. Locker room is over there. Let's hustle." He pointed to an opening in the white, cinder block wall.

Jay shuffled across the concrete floor over blue and red painted lines, chipped from years of wear.

"Get your gear on and be at the center line in five minutes," bellowed Mr. Dunbar. After ten years of teaching gym he no longer spoke at a normal decibel.

Jay looked around the locker room while the kids put on shoulder pads, knee pads and helmets from a huge, cardboard box.

"You better get in there before they're all gone," said one kid. It was the first time someone, besides a teacher, spoke to him like a human being.

"What for?" asked Jay.

"We're playing lacrosse, ya dumb apple," said one of the boys. Jay recognized him as the ringleader from lunch yesterday.

Frantic thoughts raced through Jay's mind. *Lacrosse? What's that? Must be rough if we need all these pads. Maybe I should fake a stomach ache? Nah, I'll just stick to the sidelines. Teachers never expect much from new kids.*

Jay grabbed a pair of sour smelling shoulder pads and put them on. Then he pulled on some worn out knee pads and a mismatched set of elbow pads. He dropped his arms to his sides and the elbow pads fell to his wrists.

Jay ran across the gym floor and heard snickering.

"Jay, you've got your shoulder pads on backwards," said Mr. Dunbar.

"Maybe you need your mom to come and dress you?" said the big kid.

Great, I think I liked being ignored better, Jay thought. He felt his face go red as he adjusted the shoulder pads.

"That's enough, Miles. Have you ever played lacrosse before?" asked Mr. Dunbar.

"No," replied Jay. "I think I saw it on TV once, kind of like hockey but with a ball, a sort of butterfly net for a stick and no ice."

"Yeah, no ice, just like my old man takes his whiskey," said Miles. The rest of class laughed.

"Miles, one more comment and it's off to Principal William's office," warned Mr. Dunbar.

The big jerk's name is Miles. Good, send him to Principal William's office, thought Jay.

"Lacrosse is a team sport. Win by putting the ball in the net. You can run with it, pass it, or bounce it. Hitting above the waist is allowed if you have the ball. You'll get the idea once we start playing," barked Mr. Dunbar.

Stay away from the ball and you won't get hit, was all Jay heard.

"Everyone grab a stick and an Indian rubber ball and warm up against the boards."

"First Nations rubber ball," said Miles. Mr. Dunbar ignored him.

Jay watched the kids fight for the best sticks, except Miles who had his own stick. Jay selected one with a slightly bent handle and frayed netting. Boom, boom, boom. The Indian rubber balls pounded against the walls.

Miles stood about five feet behind Jay and shot the ball hard against the wall just missing Jay. Jay moved over, so did Miles. Ignoring him, Jay put the ball in the net of the stick, raised it behind his head and flung the ball towards the wall. Or so he thought. Jay watched and waited for the rebound, but the ball had vanished.

"It's right behind you, city boy," jeered Miles. "You don't know nothing about lacrosse."

Jay was about to correct him and say "I don't know *anything* about lacrosse," *ain't that the truth,* when Mr. Dunbar blew his referee's whistle.

Miles and another kid crouched down on one knee and squared off in the center circle. With their sticks parallel to the ground and the ball in the middle, the heads clashed together to gain possession of the ball. Stick clacked against stick. The ball rolled back toward Jay. He tried to scoop it up with the awkward stick. Miles shouldered him out of the way, expertly placed his stick on the top of the ball, rolled it back and dropped it into the mesh.

Miles ran the length of the court, a stampede of squeaky running shoes at his heels. No one came close to catching him. Criss-crossing in front of the goalie, Miles shot the ball clean into the net.

The whistle blew. "Everyone back to the center circle," hollered Mr. Dunbar.

This time Jay's team got the ball first. The right winger ran towards the goal only to be double teamed. The rest of his teammates were also covered by their opponents. The only one open was Jay.

Oh no, don't do it, please don't pass to me, but even as he thought it, the scuffed ball headed right to him.

The ball bounced and Jay put his stick out assuming it would rebound to the right like any normal ball. Instead, the ball bounced left, then right, then left.

What kind of crazy voodoo devil ball is this? thought Jay.

He chased after it and managed to scoop it up. Impressed with himself, Jay turned away from the wall to pass it off. Miles raised his stick across his chest and rammed Jay into the boards.

Jay felt the air sucked from his lungs. He crumpled to the floor. No one took notice. Everyone was too busy chasing Miles down the court. With a twist of his wrist, Miles spun the stick upside down and back. Up, down, up, down, but the ball never left the pouch. Miles pulled the stick behind him and took a shot. This time it hit the cross bar and rebounded to the side. A pack of players scrambled to the corner to get the ball. Jay did a half-hearted hobble to get back in the game. He was crossing the center line when the class turned and ran towards him, their sticks held high in the air like Zulu warriors. Jay wondered what they were doing. And then he saw the menacing ball skipping through the puddles of light on the gym floor.

"Get the ball! Get the ball!" they yelled.

No getting out of this one, thought Jay. He positioned himself in front of the ball and put his stick down to meet it. Jay's eyes followed the ball as it trickled past his stick, in between his legs and stopped at the end boards.

As Miles ran by, he yelled, "You are so lame, Apple."

Jay couldn't take it anymore. He put his shoulder into Miles and bumped him off his stride.

"TWEEET," blew the whistle.

Everyone stopped and stared at Jay.

"Two minutes for interference. Jay, go sit in the penalty box," said Mr. Dunbar.

"What for? He hit me and nothing happened," Jay contested.

"That's because you had the ball," explained Mr. Dunbar.

Miles smirked at Jay, as he went to the penalty box.

Chapter 9

The sun had burned away the morning cloud and warmed Jay as he walked home from school grateful the lady in the window was not around to wave at him. He took his battered body over to Grampa's house. The door was open but he knocked anyway.

"Come on in. We are going to clean out the garage," said Grampa as he met Jay at the bottom of the stairs.

"What about my punishment?" asked Jay.

"This is part of it. And don't think of it as punishment. Think of it as helping out an old man," said Grampa.

"I get it, you just wanted a slave for six months, right?" said Jay.

"Your probation officer, Mrs. Thornton, said you had to do community service. The elders also promised the courts we'd teach you about the history and the culture of the village. I thought this would be perfect. You help me clean the garage and I tell you the stories of the coastal First Nations. You will know our ways and understand your people."

"Not my people," said Jay.

"No? Who are your people, Jay? The men in the chop shop?" asked Grampa. He laced up a pair of work boots and pulled on his jean jacket.

"Well, at least they were there for me." Jay knew it wasn't true and regretted saying it. Something stopped him from taking it back, however.

Grampa stared Jay in the eyes. Jay shuffled his feet waiting for the silence to end.

"You are under my care now. We are going to make things right starting with cleaning my garage. Idle hands do the devil's work, eh?" said Grampa as he raised his eyebrows.

"Idle hands do the devil's work?" repeated Jay. "That doesn't make any sense. If the hands are idle then really they aren't doing any work, the devils' or anyone else's."

"Good point. The sooner we begin, the sooner your community service will end. OK? Then you won't have to hang out with an old man," said Grampa.

Jay and Grampa headed toward a grey-washed, wooden garage the size of a barn. Weathered but otherwise solid. The roof had cedar shingles turned silver by years of sun and clumps of moss from years of rain.

Grampa grabbed a rust spotted door handle. He stepped back three paces to open one of the enormous double doors. Jay did the same with the other door. The garage filled with light revealing the contents. Dusty boxes towered against the walls, a hand cranked washing machine sat in one corner. Tools and car parts were scattered on the uneven concrete floor. Other things that were either last century farming equipment or medieval torture instruments, dangled lazily from the rafters. Two windows cloaked in dirt and algae blocked the sunlight.

Jay ducked as a swallow swooped down from its nest and flew outside.

"She must have eggs in the nest," said Grampa.

The tiny nest tucked in the corner of the rafters had a stream of hardened bird poop running down the wall and a pile was forming at the floor. Jay thought of the stalagmites and stalactites he'd seen in a geography text book and wondered if the poop at the top would eventually connect to the poop at the bottom.

"Want me to grab the ladder and get rid of the nest?" asked Jay.

"No, why would I want you to do that?" asked Grampa.

"Because there's poop everywhere," said Jay, incredulous.

"Swallows have as much right to be here as we do. I am not touching the nest. Believe me, you'll be happy in the summer when she and her partner eat their weight in mosquitoes and flies," said Grampa.

"Believe me, I'll never be happy here," said Jay. He surveyed the garage and felt overwhelmed by the amount of time and effort needed to clean it up.

"Why don't you just put all this stuff on the front lawn like everyone else? Your garage is almost the same size as our apartment. This will take forever," complained Jay.

The only clear spot measured four feet by five feet. Jay screwed up his face in disbelief at how packed the garage was.

"If you keep making that face it will stay that way," said Grampa with a slight grin.

"Is that what happened to you?" said Jay.

"I can see you are not going to make this easy on either of us," said Grampa.

"I should have done my community service in the city. Can't we do something else?" said Jay.

"No, we need to clean out the garage so I can start my project," said Grampa.

"What project?" asked Jay.

"None of your business," replied Grampa.

"You brought it up," said Jay.

"Talk to me with respect, Jay," said Grampa.

55

"I didn't want to come to this hick town in the first place," said Jay as he pulled at a flap of skin on his thumb.

"You must honor my wishes and not ask about the project again. And this isn't a hick town. It's the village where our ancestors have lived for thousands of years," said Grampa.

"No wonder it looks so run down. It's been here forever," said Jay.

"Well, maybe not forever for long," said Grampa. "It looks like no one has any reason to stay here. You and your mom are the first people to move here in years."

"I can't blame them. There's nothing here. Why do you stay?" said Jay. "It would have been easier for you to come live with us."

"This is where my home is and where my people are. The land belongs to us," said Grampa.

"How long have you lived here?" asked Jay. He climbed over boxes and squeezed in between furniture to see what else the garage was hoarding.

"I was born here," said Grampa.

"You weren't born in a hospital?" asked Jay. He rummaged around in a box of toys, all for little girls.

"No, for thousands of years we took care of ourselves. Hospitals aren't natural; too clean and cold. The people there are only too happy to poke you with something or shove something inside you. Who wants to start their life off in a place like that?" said Grampa.

"They do save a lot of lives," countered Jay.

"They have got the science down but they lack any spirit. The lab rats are treated better," said Grampa.

"I guess I can see that, your home is your home. My home is the city," said Jay.

"Well, let's get started," said Grampa. "Are you afraid of heights?"

Jay had climbed down the fire escape numerous times without a thought. "Nope, not afraid of heights. Why do you ask?" asked Jay.

"Those windows need a good cleaning so we can see what we are doing in here," said Grampa. "The ladder is over there." He pointed to a twelve foot ladder resting against the wall. Jay had to climb over boxes and lean it toward Grampa who half lifted, half dragged it outside.

"The bucket and sponge are somewhere," said Grampa. Ten minutes later Jay found the red square bucket labeled Bonsey's Dog Biscuits. The sponge, car wash soap and Armor All sat inside.

Jay moved in slow motion, filling up the bucket with water from the green hose attached to Grampa's house. The bucket was too heavy to carry up the ladder so he left it on the ground and climbed down several times to clean the sponge. He scrubbed the windows alternating between the sponge and an ice scraper, removing the black gunk. Satisfied the windows were clean, Jay stepped inside the garage to see how much brighter the garage was.

"That's better," said Grampa. "Once we get rid of the other boxes you can clean the inside."

"Can't wait," said Jay.

They dragged an empty oil barrel from the side of the garage to the entrance for garbage.

"We'll burn the garbage once the barrel is full," said Grampa.

Jay reached for the box of toys and proceeded to the barrel.

"Stop! What are you doing?" asked Grampa, grabbing the box until him and Jay both had an end.

"Throwing this out. It's just a bunch of girlie toys," said Jay. "You don't play with dolls, do you?" He pulled on the box. Grampa did not let go.

"Those are your mother's," said Grampa. He yanked the box from Jay's hands.

"She doesn't play with dolls either," said Jay.

"She might want something. I'll leave it to the side. She can go through it and then throw away what she doesn't want," said Grampa.

"Are you going to be able to throw anything away?" asked Jay.

"Yes. It's time," said Grampa. He picked up a stack of newspapers and dropped it in the barrel. Bong! The barrel gulped.

They ploughed through several boxes. The clear patch had now extended to a six by six square.

Jay emerged from the garage for a breath of dust free air. The sun ducked behind the mountains that cradled the village. Clouds striped the horizon and turned from pink to purple. The darkness grew and Jay noticed a bright light in the sky to the south.

"Is that an airplane?" asked Jay.

"No, that is Scout. The first star of the night," said Grampa. "The astronomy books call it Fomalhaut, but I know it as Scout."

"Foam-a-lot? That's a funny name. It's not even dark out. There's no way it's a star, it's too bright. It's got to be an airplane or a UFO," said Jay.

"You are not in the city anymore. The stars like it here. They come out in droves, like herds of caribou," said Grampa.

"I only see one. Where are the rest of them?" asked Jay, skeptical.

"Scout waits until the sun disappears to see if it is safe for the other stars to come out. The sun rules the sky and doesn't like to share the spotlight but it can't be everywhere at once so when it goes around to the other side of the earth the stars come out to play. One by one they appear. They dance and wink at us. Sometimes they dare each other to race across the sky. They remind us that even in darkness there are still bright spots to be found and fun to be had," said Grampa.

Jay and Grampa stared at the sky until their necks ached. Then they stretched out on the ground and waited for Scout to tell the other stars if it was safe to come out. Jay counted each one until they overlapped each other and he lost track.

"I could lie here forever. This is better than TV," said Jay.

"That is the Milky Way," said Grampa indicating the streaky white cloud that split the sky.

"That really exists?" said Jay.

"There is the Big Dipper," said Grampa, pointing to the west.

"I saw the Big Dipper one summer when the city had a brown out," said Jay.

"Those three bright stars in a row are called Orion's Belt," said Grampa.

"If Orion's belt falls down will we see a full moon?" asked Jay.

It took Grampa a second and then he belly laughed so hard he almost choked.

"Very good," said Grampa after catching his breath. "I think you're going to like it here."

"It's going to take more than a few stars to keep me around," said Jay.

59

Chapter 10

Jay walked to school by himself again. The same lady waved to him from her front window when she saw Jay checking out the items in her yard. When Jay didn't respond she ran to the door and called to him. Jay put his head down and walked faster until he was out of shouting range.

Why can't people just leave me alone? thought Jay.

After another lousy day at school where the highlight was eating lunch on a curb in the parking lot to avoid Miles, Jay walked home. He kept to the other side of the street to avoid the lady from the morning. When he reached the garage Grampa was already hard at work.

"Why do you keep this junk?" asked Jay after another afternoon of sorting box after box.

"Saving it for my family," said Grampa.

"You saved all this crap for me?" said Jay.

"Jay!" said Grampa.

"Sorry…all this stuff," corrected Jay.

"We didn't have much growing up. Afraid to throw anything away in case I needed it or your mom wanted it."

"I think we should light it all on fire or leave it on the curb," said Jay.

Jay had brought the box of toys to his mother but it remained at the front hall unopened.

"Look at this," said Jay as he held up an old tire. "It is almost as bald as you."

"Just because you're my grandson doesn't mean you can talk to me like that. In fact, especially because you're my grandson means you can't talk to me like that," said Grampa.

"I was kidding, you know, just trying to have some fun 'cause this is boring. I thought you were going to tell me stories about the Coastal Indian?" said Jay.

"First Nations," corrected Grampa.

"I'll tell you one of our stories but first you have to tell me one," said Grampa.

"I don't know any stories," said Jay, sliding another box over to the milk crate he used as a stool.

"Everyone has stories," said Grampa.

"Why do you want to hear my stories?" asked Jay.

"Stories help us find out about each other. Why don't you tell me about the troubles you had in the city? Why you were suspended from school?" asked Grampa.

"Mom told you about that, too?" said Jay. He flipped through a box of record albums keeping only the ones by Elvis, Johnny Cash or Loretta Lynn, as instructed.

"Yes, but I'd like to hear you tell it," said Grampa.

"It's no big deal. I played a joke on a guy at school but I guess not everyone thought it was funny. It was Mike Jones. He's in a grade ahead of me and I noticed whiskers growing on his chin already. He's only fourteen and has a mustache already. As a joke my friend, Anthony, and I filled his locker with shaving cream. You should have seen the look on his face when he opened his locker. It came out in one big blob and covered him from head to toe. When he went to the office there were white footprints down the hall. I thought Anthony was going to pee himself from laughing so hard. I would have got away with it too if my English teacher, Mrs. Olsen, hadn't noticed I smelled exactly like Mr.

Olsen does when they are going out on a Saturday night. But I got her back. I took her hand lotion from her desk and filled it with self-tanning cream. Her hands were orange for a week. It was hilarious," said Jay.

"So you do have stories to tell," said Grampa. "And an extraordinary amount of free time."

"Aren't you mad?" asked Jay.

"It should be Mike and Mrs. Olsen who are mad," said Grampa.

"I had to apologize and clean up Mike's locker and then they suspended me," said Jay.

"Already I am learning a lot about you. Who is Anthony?" asked Grampa.

"He's my friend from the city. I've known him since kindergarten. We even went to this boring summer camp together last year," said Jay. *And we almost got sent home together after sneaking out one night and toilet papering the camp site,* thought Jay.

"It's weird not seeing him every day. I didn't even say goodbye," said Jay.

"Hey, what are these?" Jay asked as he held up a wooden crate. It said 'Drink Pepsi' but that had long since dried up.

"Good, I've been looking for them. Those are wood carving tools. The middle one is called an adze," said Grampa.

Jay grabbed the knife with the curved blade and started digging at a block of blackened railway tie that smelled like creosote.

"Now I will tell you the story of Raven. Raven was born before the earth ever saw light. Everything was in total darkness. There was no light and no color. That is why the raven is black," began Grampa.

"The raven was born before the sun?" asked Jay.

"No, you weren't listening. I didn't interrupt your story, don't interrupt mine. Do I have to get out the 'talking stick'?"

"No need to resort to weapons," said Jay holding up his hands like a shield.

"A 'talking stick' is not for hitting people. Our elders used it in ancient times. Whoever held the 'talking stick' had the floor. Everyone else kept quiet except the person with the talking stick," explained Grampa.

Jay set the box of tools to the side and waited silently as Grampa passed over another box.

"Raven was mischievous and curious. One day he came upon a man and his beautiful daughter. He noticed the man had lots of boxes and kept them close to him. He wouldn't let anyone near them, not even his daughter. Raven had to know what was in the boxes. He saw the daughter going down to the water. Raven called out to the father, pretending to be the girl. Ravens are able to change their shape. 'Help! Help! Father!' The father didn't want to leave any boxes but he had to save his daughter. He picked up every box except one and stumbled through the dark.

Raven spotted the box. It was the smallest one. Raven hoped it would be bigger. He picked it up. It was light. Raven hoped it would be heavier. Raven shook it. It was quiet. Raven hoped it would be noisy. Raven decided there was nothing in the box and almost threw it away, but his curiosity made him open it. As he lifted the lid his eyes squinted. The sun rose from within the box and everything changed. When the man saw the beauty of the earth and his daughter, he was grateful to Raven and regretted keeping it all to himself. Everything changed after Raven brought the light."

"My grandfather told me that story when I was very young. He said one day I would tell it to my grandchildren. Until two days ago I didn't think I'd get the chance," said Grampa.

"A raven is a crow, right?" said Jay, trying to change the subject, as he rifled through another box to avoid eye contact. He didn't know why but he felt a pang of guilt.

"Yes, but not like city crows. Ravens are much larger and have a hoarser call. They are pranksters and tricksters," said Grampa.

"I wish the man had put the raven in a box," said Jay.

"Why do you say that?" asked Grampa.

"Every morning there's this stupid crow that sits on the fence and squawks for no reason at all. He does sound different too, kinda phlegmmy," said Jay.

"The raven is very important to our people. He is so happy to see the sun return every day that he must tell everyone," said Grampa.

"I wish he'd be happy somewhere else so I can get some sleep. After I get my iPod I won't have to listen to him anymore or the kids at school," said Jay.

"What's happening at school?" asked Grampa.

"Nothing. The kids are a bunch of losers. I don't talk to them and they don't talk to me. Do you have any other stories? I don't want to talk about the kids or crows or ravens anymore," said Jay.

"I'm sure not all the kids are losers, Jay. If you accept the school then the school will accept you. It's your turn. Tell me about the police bringing you home," said Grampa.

"I'd rather not but since you probably know anyway, I'll tell you." Jay looked at the ground and began. "Mom was out of town. I decided to paint something at the skate park. So I put a couple of cans of spray-paint in my pocket and went out. You have to do it at night 'cause everyone is there in the day and the paint has to dry. I get to my spot and start tagging. My design is going exactly as I planned, when this cop car comes around the corner. I ran away and hid in the alley. That's when those goons caught me. They probably thought I brought the cops with me and that's why they ratted me out," said Jay.

"Why did you paint the park?" asked Grampa.

"I don't know. So people would know I was there. Anthony and the other guys think my designs are awesome. They said it's like art and tons of people will enjoy it," said Jay.

"Not everyone appreciates your kind of art," said Grampa.

"I know. Don't tell Mom, please," said Jay.

"Since you like painting so much you can give this old garage a fresh coat," said Grampa.

"I don't like that kind of painting," said Jay.

"What if I paid you?" asked Grampa.

"How much?" asked Jay.

"$2.00 an hour," said Grampa.

"Ouch…" Jay clutched his chest. "I'm wounded. Seriously, I can get $8 an hour for babysitting or delivering papers."

"Not around here you can't. How about $5 an hour?" countered Grampa.

"OK, you've got a deal. Will it count for my community service? I don't want to disappoint Mrs. Thornton," said Jay, rolling his eyes.

"We won't tell her you are being paid. Speaking of Mrs. Thornton have you ever heard of the Cannibal Ogress?" asked Grampa.

"No, sounds cool," said Jay.

"A long time ago in this very village, a group of children heard about an ogress who lived down the stream. Their parents told them never to go near her because she liked to eat children. But the children were curious and they set off to get a look at her. Along the way the children caught fish to eat. They each took turns eating the heads and bodies but they always gave the tail to the boy with the crooked back. He didn't like the tail but if he didn't eat it they would leave him behind. Soon they were close to where the ogress lived. They hid behind the rocks and watched as she poured water into a giant clamshell on top of a fire.

She added many roots and herbs to the soup. The children could smell the wonderful aroma. Then she went into the forest to collect more wood for the fire.

All the children crept closer to taste what was in the giant clamshell, except the boy with the crooked back. He was too afraid. As the children leaned in to take a sip the ogress snuck up, pushed them in and slammed the clamshell shut.

(Grampa clapped his hands and Jay jumped.)

The boy was too late to warn his friends so he called to the ogress.

"Hey, don't you want to eat me, too?"

"Mmm yes, I do," she said, licking her lips.

"Open the clam shell and I'll hop in."

The greedy ogress opened the clamshell. The children pulled her into the steaming water as they jumped out. The boy with the crooked back closed the clam shell on the ogress and in the evening he didn't have to eat the tail of the fish."

"How old is that story?" said Jay, "It sounds a lot like Hansel and Gretel."

"That story is from way before the Europeans came here. I know it's similar. When you get right down to it people just have different ways of being the same," said Grampa.

As Jay rifled through yet another box of junk something silver glinted in the sunlight. He lifted it out of the box and studied its 'Y' shape. The rubber band had come undone on one side of the 'Y' but otherwise it felt solid and heavy in his hand. Jay re-attached the surgical quality band. He stretched the rubber back towards him and let it go. Jay smiled at the satisfying sound of the snap. It was the answer he had been looking for to rid his life of at least one problem.

"Does this thing work?" Jay asked.

"Don't know. Haven't seen it in years," said Grampa.

Jay held up the metal sling shot and stretched the rubber band.

"Do you know how to use it?" asked Grampa.

"I think so," said Jay.

"Here, put those cans on the fence." Grampa pointed to a cobwebbed corner of the garage.

Jay placed the cans side by side on the rickety fence. The names, Cowboy Coffee, Mountain Bird Seed, and Supreme Biscuits, were faded from years of exposure.

"Grab some marbles from the jar," said Grampa as he pointed to a pickle jar.

It took Jay a while to pick out a handful as the jar also housed a collection of nuts, bolts, and buttons.

"Put the marble in the rubber band, pull back as hard as you can and let it go," said Grampa.

Jay did as instructed. It sounded simple enough. On the first try the marble refused to stay in place. It dropped to the ground in a cloud of dust leaving a small crater.

"Try it again," said Grampa.

"Oww!" Jay yelled, as the rubber band stung his wrist.

"Like this." Grandpa took the sling shot, put a marble in the rubber band, pulled back in one smooth motion and released the rubber band.

SNAP! PING! The first can jumped off the fence, did a back flip and rolled along the ground.

"Wow! Nice shot," said Jay.

"You try," said Grampa.

Jay tried several times but the marbles only pelted the fence.

"Get closer," instructed Grampa. "Each time you hit one, take a step back."

After a while Jay could hit the cans from about ten feet. Imagining Miles' face on them didn't hurt either.

"Now you are getting the hang of it. We should keep going on the garage before we lose any more light," said Grampa. Single clouds marched across the sky as though late for a meeting.

Together Jay and Grampa sorted the contents of each box into three piles; one for the dump, one for keeping, and one for the charity thrift shop. Most of it ended up in the first pile.

"We'll make a dump run tomorrow," said Grampa.

Jay was surprised to hear that garbage trucks don't come around. If people in remote areas wanted their garbage taken away they had to do it themselves.

As the sky turned denim blue Grampa winked at Jay. "OK, enough for today. I'll see you tomorrow."

"Can I borrow the sling shot, Grampa?" asked Jay.

"Go ahead. Keep it if you want," said Grampa.

Jay took the sling shot home and hid it under his bed along with a bag of marbles.

"This time I'm ready," Jay said to himself before shutting off the light.

Chapter 11

CAW! CAW! CAW!

Jay sprung out of bed like it was Christmas morning. He grabbed the sling shot and a marble and eased open the window. With one eye closed, Jay lined up the biggest crow and let it rip.

SNAP!

CAW!

"I hit it! I hit it!" shouted Jay.

A cloud of black feathers hung in the air.

"Oh, no! I hit it," Jay whispered to himself.

"What if it's dead? What am I going to do?"

Jay thought about it for a minute.

"…Can't leave it there. I'll have to bury it."

Jay grabbed a rag and a shovel from the small garden shed in the backyard. The Martins had no use for garden tools in the city and had left the shed fully stocked.

"Jay, where are you going with that shovel?" asked Tatla through the kitchen window.

"To bury that stupid crow," said Jay.

"What crow?" asked Tatla now standing at the back door.

At the sound of Jay's footsteps the crow opened its eyes. It flapped its wings, stood on wobbly legs and fell over.

"It's alive!" said Tatla, running down the back stairs in her bare feet.

Jay watched the crow's chest rise and fall in labored breaths.

"I'll just give it a good whack with the shovel to shut it up for good," said Jay.

"No, you won't Jay. What's the matter with you," said Tatla, taking the shovel from Jay's hands and letting it fall to the ground.

She wrapped the crow up in the tea towel she had draped over her shoulder and ran into the house.

"Grab my keys and open the car door. We'll take it to Dr. Two Feathers," said Tatla, slipping on a pair of flip-flops.

The crow was heavy and took up Jay's entire lap. Its body heat radiated through the tea towel. Now that the bird wasn't squawking Jay had a good look at it. The crow was larger than he originally thought. The glossy feathers layered one on top of the other. The shortest feathers lay at the head and shoulders like scales; the longer feathers became the wings and tail. When it blinked, charcoal grey skin slid across its eyes reminding Jay of the alien in his dream. One foot stuck out from under the towel; a shriveled, cracked claw with three toes in the front and one in the back. The sharp nails looked like black plastic. The chalky grey skin looked dead and decaying.

Jay thought the claw looked wicked.

"If you don't make it can I have your claw for a key chain?" Jay said aloud.

"Did you say something?" asked Tatla.

"No. How long will it take to get there?" asked Jay.

"About ten minutes," said Tatla. Jay knew he was getting the silent treatment which suited him fine. Soon a barrage of words like "I can't believe you did this!" or "What am I going to do with you?" would come down on him. Or, heavy sighs along with one raised eyebrow, rapid blinking followed by the rolling of the eyes in combination with shaking of the head awaited him; a command performance from the police station.

They drove down the uneven road, jolted every few feet by a pothole.

"They must save a fortune in speed bumps," said Jay.

Tatla was in no mood to respond. She concentrated on driving, doing her best to avoid the road craters or at least aim for the shallow ones.

She drove over the bridge and then turned right onto the paved road that used to be the main highway until the new four lane highway was built. The village was split when they saw the expansion on the map. The plans showed the highway completely bypassing the village further isolating them. Some tribe members were happy about this, wanting to protect their privacy but others thought they were missing the opportunity to draw visitors to the village to sell firewood for the campers or fishing lures to the fishermen, Jay learned later.

The road paralleled the river. Jay watched as the swells disappeared into whirlpools and foamy waves dissolved into the round stones bordering the shore. A division between dark stones and light stones indicated the water line.

Ten minutes past town they pulled into the semi circular pea gravel driveway of a yellow, two story Queen Anne style house. It had a wrap around veranda with a blue porch swing and a small hanging sign said "Dr. Amelie Two Feathers, DVM".

"Her name is Dr. Two Feathers, and she's a vet. Indians have funny names," said Jay.

"I used to have a dentist named Dr. Chu and an eye doctor named Dr. Beattie, as in beady eyes," said Tatla, rolling up her window and pulling on the emergency brake.

Jay got out, holding the crow carefully, and closed the door with his hip.

Tatla leaned over and locked the door from the inside.

Jay looked around at the deserted parking lot. "Why are you locking the door? Really, who's going to steal it?"

"Habit," answered Tatla.

They sat in the waiting area amongst bags of dog food, collars, leashes and molded plastic pet carriers for sale. A blend of antiseptic, cedar shavings and animal scented the air.

Jay alternated picking and chewing a hang nail on his left thumb until he got a grip on it with his teeth. Then he yanked it hard and spat it out. The pain was excruciating but a good distraction while they waited for Dr. Two Feathers to examine the crow.

"The raven will be fine but I'm keeping it overnight, just to be on the safe side," said Dr. Two Feathers. She had shoulder length hair and her bangs pinned back with a kitty bobby-pin. Her dress was casual with jeans and white running shoes.

"It's not just a crow, it's a raven?" asked Jay.

"Yes, and a strong, healthy one, too. Good thing or he might not have made it," said the veterinarian, peering over her bi-focals at Jay.

Jay wanted to hide in one of the pet carriers to get away from the vet's glare. There was no escaping Tatla when they got back in the car.

"Jay, what were you thinking?" said Tatla.

Here it comes, thought Jay.

"I can't believe you would hurt an animal. And, how much is this going to cost me?" said Jay's mom, shaking her head, and putting her foot to the floor. They had to hurry as the school bell was about to ring. If Jay missed even a single class the principal had orders to inform Mrs. Thornton. Jay stared out the window to avoid eye contact with his mom. He looked down his street and saw the boy who walked alone talking over the fence to the waving lady.

"Jay, are you going to answer me?" asked Tatla.

"Sorry, Mom, but that idiot bird tore up the garbage. Then the kids laughed at me for picking up trash, and it wakes me up every morning," said Jay.

"That's no reason," said Tatla.

"No, it's three reasons," said Jay. Tatla raised her eyebrow at him then rolled her eyes.

They neared the school. The dog pack was running in the field, a yellow Lab in the lead. It had something in its mouth the others were trying to get but the retriever dodged and weaved causing his pursuers to trip each other up.

"And it crapped all over your car. You should be thanking me," said Jay as the car pulled up to the school in time to hear the second bell. He opened the door before the car had come to a complete stop, anxious to get away.

"We're not finished talking about this," said Tatla as the car door slammed.

Chapter 12

Jay spent another day at school avoiding people as much as possible. He noticed Miles and his gang sitting in the hallway with their legs stretched out in front of them; four kids on one side and four kids on the other side leaving a narrow gap for only one person to pass through at a time.

The girls navigated the Nike minefield unscathed. The boys, however, accepted their fate and soldiered on. Some made it, some didn't. The kid who walked to school alone was not one of the lucky ones. He stumbled and landed on two of the boys. They called him a klutz and pushed him off. The boy picked himself up and kept going like nothing had happened.

Jay managed to get past most of the denim clad speed bumps. He was almost in the clear when he felt his right foot hooked from behind. Jay lurched forward. His right elbow skidded across the thread bare orange carpet causing a nasty burn. The backpack he carried maintained it's momentum and struck Jay in the head. He lay in the hallway and listened to the snickers. A disgusting smell of feet rose from the carpet.

"You're as clumsy in the hallway as you are in the gym," said someone. Jay didn't have to look up to know it was Miles.

Jay pushed himself up and rubbed his elbow to stop the sting. The heat coming from his face could have melted marshmallows. Jay considered kicking Miles in the head when Principal Williams yelled down the hall.

"What's going on here?" he bellowed.

Immediately sixteen feet disappeared under bent knees.

"Nothing, sir, we're just testing Newton's apple theory on gravity. He was right after all, apples do fall at the same rate as other objects," said Miles. The other kids nodded in agreement.

The principal grunted and carried on toward the staff room. Miles high-fived the other boys as Jay stood in disbelief.

After school Jay went directly to Grampa's and found him working in the garage.

"Hey, Grampa," said Jay, laying his backpack in the doorway. He was slightly out of breath because this time the lady in the window came out of her house to chase Jay down.

Can't she take a hint? Jay remembered thinking. He had picked up the pace without actually breaking into a run so as not to make it too obvious.

"Hi, Jay. How was your day?" asked Grampa.

"It gets better and better every day. This morning the stupid crows woke me up early again with their noisy squawking so I pelted one with a marble," said Jay.

"Yes, I heard," said Grampa, rummaging through another box of junk. This one was filled with yellow bordered National Geographic magazines. "I hate to throw these out," mumbled Grampa.

"I didn't mean to hit it," said Jay. Grampa didn't say anything.

"Why can't they sing like other birds?" asked Jay after a moment of uncomfortable silence.

"They were singing. Not everyone in life is going to sing your favorite song, you know," said Grampa, flipping through the Mars landing edition circa 1976.

"No kidding. What am I supposed to do though? Just take it?" said Jay.

"I can see you are not a 'do nothing' kind of person," said Grampa. "So far that doesn't seem to be a good thing. Sometimes it is better to do nothing, and sometimes not. I was going to tell you the story about Ghost Lake but now I will tell you the story about the baby mountain goat."

Jay turned over an orange plastic milk crate and sat down.

"Many years ago in a village not far from here a baby mountain goat grazed on the mountainside. He kept his head down and walked and ate and walked and ate without paying attention. When he looked up, his family was nowhere to be seen. He didn't know how to get home. Over in the distance he could see smoke from a village. *Maybe they knew,* he thought.

As he walked through the village a bunch of children came towards him. Some of them poked at him with a stick and some threw rocks as they laughed at the silly little goat. The little goat ran away from them but the children chased him around the village until he was too tired to move. They picked up the little goat and decided to cook him in the fire just like the adults did. The adults let the children do whatever they wanted. It was just an animal after all and kids will be kids. But one man heard the cries of the baby mountain goat and shooed the children away. He took the goat from the fire and brought it home.

He put homemade ointment on the goat's sores and nursed it back to health. Soon the man walked the little goat up the mountainside until he could find his way home.

The little goat told his worried family where he had been and what the mean children had done.

They were shocked only one person had the courage to stand up against the villagers and help one of Great Spirit's favorite creatures. Great Spirit heard their sadness and did not want this to happen to anyone else. The villagers must be punished so he told the goats he would cover the village with mud. As the mountain rumbled and the trees slid down the hill on a wave of mud the little goat called to the man to come back. He turned and walked toward the baby goat as the village disappeared."

Jay was silent. Grampa waited him out.

"Are we cleaning the garage or not? We're almost done," said Jay, feeling a lecture coming on the way you feel the flu coming on; queasy stomach, pounding head and a general dread over your whole body.

"Here, take an end," said Grampa, bending his knees to pick up an antique washing machine. It was round and white with rust along the seams and around the rivets. The washer also had two rollers on top to squeeze the water from the clothes before being hung to dry.

They dragged the washer outside the garage and set it down just beyond the doors. Jay and Grampa both bent over to catch their breath.

"We were the first in the village to have our own washer," said Grampa, wiping his brow.

"It's too bad you have to throw it away," said Jay, happy to be busy again.

"I'm not throwing it away. Gordon on the corner wants it," said Grampa.

"That place is already full of junk. Why does he want this?" said Jay.

"He says he's got plans for it. I don't want it so he may as well have it," said Grampa.

"That's just moving junk from one place to another. How do you stand it?" said Jay, kicking the washer. The washer answered back with a hollow bong.

"That's how he is and it's not my job to change him," said Grampa. "Here he comes now." Approaching the garage was a man about forty years old. He wore Levi jeans covered with oil stains and a black t-shirt with a faded Van Halen logo on it. On his feet were weathered work boots. The laces dragged along the ground and the tongue lolled with each step. His thick black hair was cut short in the front and a little longer in the back. Not quite a mullet but close. In his hand was a can of Pepsi that he sipped from often.

"Hi, Gordon. This is my grandson, Jay," said Grampa.

"Your mom almost ran me over the other day. Nice to meet you," said Gordon and bumped knuckles with Jay. "Is this the washer? How much do you want for it?"

"Nothing, just take it. You're doing me a favor. I need all the room I can get. If you sell it for scrap though, make sure you buy groceries and nothing else," said Grampa. "Since you can't drive I can haul it back in my truck. It's heavier than it looks."

"They caught me with beer in my truck and took away my license for the third time," said Gordon as an explanation to Jay.

"But that won't happen again," said Gordon, sliding an aluminum sleeve off the Pepsi can to reveal a beer underneath. He quickly wrapped it back up in the Pepsi jacket before Grampa noticed. Jay couldn't tell the difference. It looked just like a Pepsi.

"Maybe Jay here could help me. My place is just down the street," said Gordon.

Jay frowned at Gordon. "I can't carry that thing. I almost broke my back getting it out of the garage," Jay said.

"It's OK, kid, I'll do it myself. I know you don't have your man muscles yet," laughed Gordon.

Jay thought Gordon was either crazy or under the illusion of having superhuman strength that comes free with every six pack of beer.

"Gordon, you'll put your back out. Why don't we use my truck?" said Grampa.

"Looks like you got a full load already. I wouldn't want to be responsible for putting your old truck out of its misery. I got it covered," said Gordon as he grabbed the washer, tilted it sideways to the ground and rolled it down the street, drinking his Pepsi-beer.

Jay and Grampa looked at each other and laughed.

"Come on. Let's go to the dump," said Grampa.

"What's Gordon got against your truck?" asked Jay as he climbed in and slid across the dark brown vinyl seat.

"Nothing, he just likes to tease me. I think he secretly wants my truck," said Grampa. He put the key in the ignition and the engine rumbled to life.

"How old is it?" asked Jay. Little did Jay know that this one question would spark such passion from his reserved grandfather.

"She's a 1977 Ford F100 Club Cab. Bought her off a farmer about twenty years ago just when she was broken in," said Grampa. He revved the engine.

"Hear that? That's a 400 V8. Sounds good doesn't it?" said Grampa. He didn't expect an answer. It was clear Grampa considered this melodious. "Best truck in the world. Never gave me any problems which is more than I can say for a lot of things. People included."

They maneuvered through the potholes. Grampa seemed to know most of them by heart and avoided the ones that had reached crater status. Once on the highway, Grampa shifted the truck several times, jerking Jay's head forward with each gear. The truck had no headrest and Jay bonked his head on the rear glass, going from second to third.

The drive took twenty minutes. Grampa slowed once for cattle guard but otherwise he sped down the road in fifth gear. Jay kept his eyes on the road; Grampa may have walked and talked at an unhurried pace but driving unleashed the inner racer in him.

Jay's foot hit the invisible brakes a few times; his right hand gripped the arm rest on the sharper curves as Grampa drove the truck down the middle of the road.

"Why don't you drive in our lane? You're going to kill us," said Jay, imagining an over loaded logging truck coming around the corner.

"This is the safest place," said Grampa.

"Of course, drive in the middle of the road. It's safer. I'll have to remember that when I take my driver's test," said Jay. As he finished his sentence Grampa slammed on the brakes and swerved to the left, missing a deer and her fawn by a foot.

Jay watched in awe, struck by the deer's beauty, with its enormous brown eyes outlined by cream colored fur and elegant face tipped by a black nose. As big as its eyes were its ears were even bigger, the best defense against predators. The fawn flanked its mom waiting for a cue. The doe paused, flicked an ear and then bounded into the cedar forest with the fawn at her heels. Jay tried to track it but it vanished into the black and green tartan of the forest. A split second encounter Jay relived in his mind over and over again.

"That's why we drive in the middle of the road," said Grampa. Grampa put the truck in gear and steered it back onto the highway.

"When you do get your license, if a deer jumps out in front of you, remember to hit your brakes but then let them go if it's too late to avoid the deer. That way the car won't be thrusting downward when you hit it. Does that make sense?" asked Grampa. Jay's head jerked forward and back as Grampa pressed on the brake to demonstrate.

"I think so. If the car is still braking then the nose will point downward. The deer will be scooped up by the car and end up through the front windshield," said Jay.

"By gulch and by gulley, you may survive out here yet," said Grampa.

Chapter 13

The next day Jay and his mom picked up the raven from the vet.

"The total comes to one hundred and sixty dollars," said Dr. Two Feathers.

"What? I can't afford to pay a hundred and sixty dollars," Tatla said.

"You should have let me whack it with the shovel," said Jay.

The two women glared at him.

"Not many of my clients can afford to pay me. I try to keep my costs down as much as possible. I don't even have a receptionist," she explained.

"Why don't you open an office in town?" asked Tatla.

"I like it here and I know everyone. Plus the place would be overrun with dogs in no time if I didn't fix them for free. I'm not doing too badly with the business I get from the local ranchers but things could always be better. Pay me what you can now and pay the rest later," she said.

"Thanks so much. No one would ever do that in the city," said Tatla.

"It's nice to have you back, Tatla," said Dr. Two Feathers.

They brought the raven home and kept an eye on it. Jay studied the bird as it lay on a folded towel in the corner of the cardboard carrying box. The blue-black feathers were so shiny he could almost see himself. The raven, still groggy from the medication, moved very little.

The doorbell rang and Tatla answered it.

"Mrs. Thornton, what a surprise. Come in. Yes, Jay is back there," said Tatla, gesturing toward the kitchen.

Mrs. Thornton started to remove her shoes then looked at the stained carpet and changed her mind.

"How was the drive?" asked Tatla, trying to make conversation.

"I should get danger pay. I nearly went off a cliff. The alignment in my car is probably off after driving through those potholes. It's a good thing I was going slowly or else those mangy dogs would be visiting Dr. Two Feathers," said Mrs. Thornton.

"I'm glad I asked," said Tatla.

Mrs. Thornton blinked twice then turned her attention to Jay who stood in front of the box to create a barricade between her and the raven.

"So this is the crow you maimed," said Mrs. Thornton trying to see past Jay. "May I see it?" she asked. She pressed Jay's shoulder until he stepped aside.

"How did you know about the crow?" asked Tatla.

"It's a raven," said Jay.

The two women ignored him.

"You know how small towns are. You lived here long enough," smirked Mrs. Thornton. She adjusted the tight bun attached to the back of her head, making her ears wiggle.

Mrs. Thornton leaned forward and put her face closer to the raven. A vision of the Cannibal Ogress being pushed into the boiling water popped into Jay's head.

"What a disgusting bird. They carry all kinds of diseases and viruses. It really shouldn't be in the house," said Mrs. Thornton.

Jay wished the raven would jump up and bite her nose.

"Dr. Two Feathers assured us it was perfectly safe as long as we wash our hands after touching it," said Tatla.

"It seems you find trouble wherever you go, Jay. You know there haven't been any more rat days at the school since you left. Perhaps your grandfather is not keeping you busy enough. I'm sure Dr. Two Feathers could use some help around her office, washing out cages and such. I'll set something up before I leave," said Mrs. Thornton with a smile.

"You can't do that," said Jay.

"I can do a lot more than that. If you step out of line again, Jay, you'll be spending time in the detention center. Do what you are told. Trust me - obedience will lead to a happy, productive life," said Mrs. Thornton.

"Obedience is for dogs," spouted Jay.

"We'll see," said Mrs. Thornton, narrowing her eyes.

With that she turned on her heel and showed herself out.

"I should have finished you off while I had the chance," Jay spat at the crow.

Mrs. Thornton made good on her promise. Dr. Two Feathers had Jay clean out the cages, sweep the floor, take out the garbage and exercise the dogs that she boarded in the kennel out back. The only part he didn't like was drying the dog's muddy paws after a walk in the rain. Otherwise the work was easy and Jay liked the animals. They were always happy to see him and never judged him or called him names. Living in an apartment his whole life Jay was never allowed to keep a pet, unless cockroaches counted.

"I know you don't want to be here but it has really been a God-send having your help," said Dr. Two Feathers. "My niece Courtney helps when she can get a ride over."

85

"How come you don't live closer to everyone else?" asked Jay, although he was starting to enjoy the bumpy ride there and back. Grampa's 1977 Ford F100 Club Cab had a springy bench seat that bounced them along. It was more like a carnival ride except when Jay's head hit the ceiling. No wonder Gordon preferred the truck bed if Grampa happened to be going in the same direction.

"I can't have my own business on reservation land. The bank won't give me a mortgage so I bought this place," said Dr. Two Feathers.

"That doesn't seem fair," said Jay.

"It's our land but it's not our land. It's complicated although it shouldn't be," said Dr. Two Feathers. "I get to do what I love near the people I love."

Jay saw how much she loved the animals. Each one was cared for as if it were hers.

A rancher came in the front entrance one afternoon while Jay was mopping the floor with pine disinfectant.

"Where's Dr. Two Feathers?" the rancher asked. He was dressed in dusty jeans, black cowboy boots with worn toes and a straw cowboy hat.

Jay wanted to ask the rancher if he was trick or treating, until the worried look on his face told Jay this was no time for jokes.

"My Collie's hurt her paw," said the rancher.

"I'll go get the doctor," said Jay. He dropped the mop into the metal bucket and went behind the counter to the back room.

"Hi, Ronald, something happen to Lucy?" said Dr. Two Feathers, restocking the overhead shelves.

"Yep, she cut her paw. Can't walk on it," said Ronald. "I'll bring her in."

Ronald returned a minute later carrying Lucy. She was a black and white Border Collie and squirmed in Ronald's arms; not happy to be at the vet. Jay figured dogs hated vet clinics as much as Grampa hated hospitals.

"Bring her into the examining room, please," said Dr. Two Feathers. The room looked similar to a doctor's office - glass jars with cotton balls on a side counter, a small sink with pink liquid soap in a pump dispenser, poster size drawings of dogs and cats showing internal organs, bones and muscles. The examining table was taller than the counter, made from stainless steel and about 2 ½ feet by 3 feet. One short side was secured to the wall and the other short side was held up by a steel pole making it look like a table without chairs.

Jay watched through the open door as Ronald gently placed Lucy on the stainless steel counter. The dog tried to stand up but couldn't get any traction on the smooth surface.

"It's OK, Lucy, just lie down and let me look at your paw," said Dr. Two Feathers reaching for the dog's bloodied hind leg. Lucy growled and snapped at the vet.

"Now, Lucy, you know Dr. Two Feathers. She's going to make your paw all better," said Ronald.

Jay almost laughed when he heard the rugged rancher speak to his dog like it was a child with a skinned knee.

"Jay, come give us a hand in here, please," said Dr. Two Feathers.

Jay froze. *What can I do? I don't know anything about dogs.*

Before Jay could find an excuse or duck out the back door, Dr. Two Feathers barked, "Hurry up."

Jay entered the room. It felt cramped now with three people and a dog.

"Here, hold your hand out and let her sniff you. Don't be afraid," said Dr. Two Feathers. "Talk to her in nice soothing tones."

"Her name's Lucy. I'm Ronald," said the rancher, nodding his head to dip his hat. Both hands were holding Lucy down. Her breathing was quick and shallow.

"Keep her still while I get the needle ready," said Dr. Two Feathers. She scrubbed up and stretched chalky white surgical gloves over her hands.

Jay held Lucy's shoulder down and stroked the silky fur. She had black ears and a white blaze down her face that ran down her chest and her front legs. Everything else was black except the tip of her tail looked like it had been dipped in white paint.

She fixed her gaze on Jay. "It's OK girl. Nice girl. Won't be long. Dr. Two Feathers just wants to put a band-aid on your foot," said Jay, mimicking the rancher. He felt stupid at first until he realized that it was working. The dog calmed down. Instead of rapid panting the dog breathed normally.

Jay looked down at the dog's leg. It was crusted with blood. Red smears streaked the table.

Dr. Two Feathers swabbed around the cut with yellow-red iodine. It looked almost worse than the blood. She shaved the fur exposing the two inch gash.

"Good girl," cooed Jay.

"Such a brave dog," murmured the rancher. "We'll have you back at work in no time."

"Your dog has a job?" asked Jay.

"Sure, she's one of my best employees. Without her the cattle would never find their way back to the barn," said the rancher.

"It's going to be a few weeks," said Dr. Two Feathers. She laced up a needle and stitched the gash.

Jay made the mistake of watching the first stitch and nearly blacked out. Lucy strained to get up when she felt the needle but Jay and Ronald held her down.

"A few weeks? She'll go stir crazy," said Ronald. "This is the dog that ran around the above ground pool until there was a one foot moat."

"What can I tell you? The cut must be kept clean and dry. She'll have to stay off it or the stitches will come out. All done," said Dr. Two Feathers. She snapped off her gloves and tossed them in the garbage.

Jay looked down at Lucy's paw wrapped neatly in white gauze. Ronald picked her up and set her on the floor. She tried putting weight on her foot but yelped at the pain.

Jay bent down and scratched her behind the ears. She licked his hand and Jay noticed that she had a brown eye and a blue eye.

"Cool eyes," said Jay.

"Limit her physical activity and place this cone on her neck if she starts licking the wound," said Dr. Two Feathers. She handed Ronald an opaque plastic cone that looked like a loud speaker.

Ronald handed it back to her and said he had one at home they used after Lucy was spayed.

He paid by credit card and helped Lucy into his pick up truck.

"You were very good in there," said Dr. Two Feathers. "Animals can tell the good people from the bad."

"Thanks. Lucy's a cool dog," said Jay. He picked up the mop and finished the waiting area. His last chore was to spray down the examining table and wipe it clean with paper towels.

Before he went home Dr. Two Feathers gave Jay more formula for the raven to get its strength up and to keep any infection away.

"I'm not sure I want it to get better. It will keep waking me up or going through the garbage," said Jay.

"It's probably the dogs that got into the garbage first. I do what I can to keep them from breeding but unless people bring in their pets there's no time for me to collect them and also take care of them later. I just don't have the room," said Dr. Two Feathers.

"I still think it's a stupid bird," said Jay.

"Ravens are very important to our culture," said Dr. Two Feathers.

"Whatever," said Jay. He reached for the trash to take outside.

Dr. Two Feathers forced a breath out of her nose. A sound Jay had heard many times from his mom.

"Not 'whatever'," said Dr. Two Feathers. "I want to show you something."

She went through the back room where a few cats, a guinea pig, a rabbit and a white curly haired poodle named Polar were curled up in their cages waiting for their owners to rescue them. Jay followed her out the back door and down the stairs. She pulled a couple of dog treats from her pocket then took off her lab coat. Not the usual doctor's coat in starch white but a baby blue one with different types of cats and dogs all over it.

She held up the dog biscuit and walked about thirty feet to the storage shed in the back corner. Then she walked back.

Jay had no idea what she was doing.

"So," said Jay.

"Wait. You are very impatient," said Dr. Two Feathers. She put the lab coat back on. Again she started walking toward the shed.

Out of nowhere a raven appeared. It circled overhead and followed Dr. Two Feathers to the shed. It landed on the peaked roof and squawked that awful screeching call Jay hated so much.

"Should I get my sling shot?" called Jay.

Dr. Two Feathers gave him a dirty look. She held up the dog biscuit and kept walking.

The raven glided through the air and snatched the biscuit from her hand.

"Meet Coal," said Dr. Two Feathers. "Ravens are one of the smartest animals on Earth. They have adapted well to their environment. I know you think they are a menace but they actually do more to clean up the garbage than any other animal, including raccoons."

"Here, put on my lab coat," she shrugged it off and held it up for Jay to put his arms in. "Take out a biscuit and walk across the yard."

Jay did as she said. He had taken not more than three steps when Coal put the reverse thrusters on his wings and with claws first, grabbed the biscuit.

"Take off the lab coat and try it again," instructed the doctor.

This time Jay made it to the shed and back.

"Why didn't he take the biscuit?" asked Jay.

"Because he associates the lab coat with food," said Dr. Two Feathers.

"That's stupid. He should just take the food when he can," said Jay.

"Pass me the lab coat," said Dr. Two Feathers. She put the lab coat back on and sat at the picnic table, painted yellow to match the house.

The raven flew from the hydro wire it was perched on and circled overhead. It's wings stretched wide splaying single feathers at the tips like fingers.

Coal spiraled down and landed on the bench seat across from Dr. Two Feathers. It jumped up onto the table and hopped towards her. She reached out and stroked it with her index and middle finger. It opened its beak slightly. She continued to stroke it for a few more minutes until it saw Jay move. Quickly, it flew back to the power lines.

"Wow, you are like the crow whisperer or something," said Jay.

"No, I'm not," said Dr. Two Feathers as she laughed. "Ravens are intelligent and social birds. They adapt well to people and other birds. That's why you see so many of them in the city."

The sound of tires crunching on gravel announced Grampa's arrival. He rolled down the window and chatted with Dr. Two Feathers before driving Jay home.

Every morning and evening for the next few days Jay took an eye dropper and fed the raven the medicine from Dr. Two Feathers. He tried to help it to its feet but the bird lay still most of the time. Jay didn't think it would ever get better.

"Are you ever going to leave or are you doing this to bug me? Grampa told me ravens are mischievous. I'll bet you are just faking it," said Jay. The raven blinked a lash-less, black eye.

The following morning Jay found the crow hopping around, squawking and flapping its wings, trying to get out of the box. The skritchy sound of claws on cardboard made Jay's fillings hurt.

"Jay, I think it's time to let the crow go," said Tatla, rummaging through her purse for her car keys.

"I think it needs more rest, Mom, maybe one more day," said Jay.

"It needs fresh air and blue sky. If it can't fly then we'll keep it longer. I don't want one of May-Belle's cats getting it," said Tatla.

They took the cardboard box outside and pulled back the flaps. The raven hopped out of the box, stretched its wings and soared into the trees.

"Go on, get out of here," said Jay.

When Jay took the garbage out after dinner, a silver metal sling shot went out too.

In the morning Jay awoke to silence.

"I guess that dumb crow learned its lesson," said Jay to the ceiling tiles.

Chapter 14

On his way to school, Jay saw the kid who was tripped in the hallway. The boy was scrawnier and shorter than Jay. He wore a brown ball-cap over black hair that stuck out around the rim. His well worn camouflage pants hung loosely off his hips and did not go past his ankles.

Jay picked up his pace. The boy also picked up his pace. Jay fell into a slow jog and was almost even with the boy when two dogs bounded up beside him. One was the muscular yellow Lab from the field the other day and the other was a smaller black Lab. The dogs sandwiched Jay in between themselves and sniffed him. Jay brushed them aside and kept walking. The yellow Lab trotted to the roadside and picked up a stick. He returned and laid the stick at Jay's feet.

Jay walked around and was swatted by the thick cordlike tail of the yellow dog. The boy was twice as far ahead now. Jay continued down the sidewalk and almost tripped over the yellow Lab as it dropped the stick at Jay's feet, again. It stood with its tail wagging and its soulful brown eyes looking hopeful.

"Do you want me to throw the stick? Is that it?" Jay asked the Lab. The two dogs danced and jumped. They spun circles around each other and bowed to Jay.

"Will you leave me alone if I do?" asked Jay. The dogs barked.

Jay bent down and picked up the stick. They posed, ready to run, tail toward Jay but head turned to keep an eye on the stick. Jay waved the stick. The dogs were wound so tight they bucked like rodeo bulls. Jay cocked his arm back then froze when someone yelled, "Stop, don't do it!"

Jay relaxed his arm. The yellow dog came over to tug the stick from Jay's hand. Jay pulled the stick away and held it out of reach. He looked up to see who yelled.

The boy approached Jay. "Why not?" asked Jay.

"That's Dillon and Jody. If you throw it once they'll never leave you alone. They will follow you to school and expect you to throw that stupid stick or rock or whatever they can find. One time it was a Barbie doll," said the boy.

Jay laughed. "That's dumb."

"Go ahead, laugh now, but don't say I didn't warn you," said the boy. He turned and headed back up the sidewalk.

"I'm not doing what you say. They just want to play," said Jay. He threw the stick.

The dogs scrambled after it at full speed. The black Lab overshot it and careened into a chain link fence. The yellow Lab skidded on its back paws and clutched the stick in its mouth. They immediately returned to Jay and dropped the stick at his feet.

"OK, that's enough guys. Go on home now," said Jay. He stepped over the stick.

The yellow Lab snatched it up, caught up with Jay and dropped it at his feet.

"I said 'Go home,'" said Jay. His voice sounded stern. The Labs were oblivious. They looked up. Their eyebrows cocked back and forth as they watched Jay then the stick.

Again Jay stepped over the stick. Again the yellow Lab snatched it up, rounded Jay and dropped the stick at his feet.

"Once more and that's it," said Jay. This time he picked up the stick and threw it hard in the other direction. The dogs raced after the stick. Their tails propelled them forward, oscillating like an old plane. Within seconds they were back.

"No, forget it. That's it. No more," said Jay. The dogs whined but Jay held his ground. He was going to be late for school.

Jay caught up with the boy. The dogs leaped up and down. "You were right. How do I get rid of them?" said Jay

"You can't. You're stuck with them," said the boy. Along the way they had collected other dogs; a Duck Toller with red fur and piercing blue eyes, a goofy Lab-Shepherd cross that kept lying down on the sidewalk to wait for a belly scratch and a white Husky with a fluffy grey tail. "That's Maggie, Grommet and Shiloh."

"Doesn't anyone leash their dogs?" asked Jay.

"Only the vicious ones and even then not usually," said the boy.

"Hi, I'm Jay."

"I know. You're the 'apple'," said the kid.

"Why does everyone keep calling me that?" asked Jay.

"Red on the outside and white on the inside," replied the kid. "Red 'cause you're Indian and white 'cause you're from the city."

"Really? Huh. OK if I walk with you?" asked Jay.

"Whatever," said the kid.

"So much for country people being friendly," said Jay.

"Most city kids like you think you're better than us trailer trash," said the kid. He pulled up his hoodie as the rain started to fall.

"If I was better than you I wouldn't be here in the first place. It doesn't matter, I'm leaving as soon as school ends," said Jay, hoping that was true.

The whole village knew Jay had been sent here as punishment. They didn't know all the details and Jay wanted to keep it that way.

96

"Why wait? Just drop out or run away like half the other kids," said the kid.

"The thought has crossed my mind," said Jay. "I saw you trip in the hall the other day."

"I saw you, too," said the kid.

"How come the principal doesn't do anything?" asked Jay.

"He doesn't care. He's waiting to retire. When he does punish the kids they just take off. If any more leave he won't have a school to run. I'm Jackson, by the way."

The dogs kept up, peeing on fences, dandelions, wild daisies, and car tires.

Jackson waved at the lady standing in the window of her bungalow. The same lady who had waved to Jay nearly every day since he arrived but Jay never waved back. He thought she was creepy. He had made a conscious effort to look the other way when passing her busy yard. Jay assumed it was just another cluttered mess. No avoiding it now that Jackson had breached the silent code.

Jay discovered her yard was filled with stuff but in an organized way. Her front lawn had gnomes standing guard along the fence exactly six feet from each other. In another corner she had a collection of pot bellied stoves complete with cast iron frying pans and kettles. The perimeter of the house had ceramic pigs, cows, horses, and geese mulling about on lava rocks. On the outside wall were three gigantic butterflies, one bigger than the next, with their wings cocked upwards. In the window perched a white cat.

"Who is that lady?" asked Jay.

"That's May-Belle," said Jackson. "Want to meet her?"

"No way. We have to get to school," said Jay.

"Come on. It'll take two minutes. Trust me it'll be worth it," said Jackson, holding the gate open.

"Hurry, here come the dogs," said Jackson barring the dogs with his body. "Believe me; we don't want the dogs getting in here."

Jay squeezed passed Jackson. He quickly closed the gate. The dogs looked insulted and then gamboled over to bother some other kids.

When May-Belle heard the gate creak she opened the door and called to the boys. Her pink hockey jersey and purple sweat pants made her look younger than Jay first thought but he figured she was about the same age as Grampa.

As Jay reached the front step May-Belle swooped in. She gave him a huge hug before Jay knew what was happening. Jackson got the same treatment. She led the boys into the house and closed the door.

"You look exactly like your grandfather did at your age; so handsome. I can't tell you what it means to him to have you here," she said to Jay. Her smile made her nose crinkle.

Jay smiled back uncomfortably. He looked to Jackson as if to say 'let's get out of here'. Jay backed up to reach for the door knob and almost stepped on a cat. He moved to the side to avoid it but there was another cat to take its place. He looked down and saw May-Belle picking up yet another cat. The grey tabby squirmed out of her arms, balanced on her right shoulder and sprung to the top of a bookcase.

"Jackson, you are just in time," said May-Belle. "I'm frying up a fresh batch of bannock. Go wait in the living room and I'll bring you some."

"Can we get those to go, please, Grandmother," called Jackson.

"Sure, no problem," replied May-Belle. She briskly walked into the kitchen, her thick silver braid bounced against her back spurring her on.

"Wayne, Sydney and Bobby, you come with me," she said to the three cats weaving in and out of the boys legs.

"She loves hockey so much she named her cats after her favorite players," said Jackson.

"The one on the bookshelf is Mario Le Mew," said Jackson.

Jay and Jackson turned to their right and entered the living room. The sound of the oven door slamming and the rattle of pots and pans came from the kitchen. An aroma, similar to the Rise 'n Shine Bakery where Jay often stopped in the morning for an egg sandwich called 'Breakfast in Bread', followed him into the living room.

May-Belle's living-room was the same organized clutter as her front yard. Jay went to the window to pet the fluffy, white cat, perched on the sill. He stroked the soft fur and the cat fell over, rolling to Jay's feet. Its glassy eyes stared up at Jay. Jay stumbled back and Jackson howled in laughter. The feline felt stiff in Jay's hands as he hurried to put it back in the window before May-Belle returned.

"It's dead," said Jay.

"No kidding. They're all dead," said Jackson. Jay scanned the room and counted about five other cats in various positions; an orange tabby on an old electric organ, a yellow-eyed black one on the back of a gold crushed velvet couch, its tail wrapped around its paws, a Siamese curled up on a chair under the dining table and a white one with black patches like a cow, posed sphinx style in front of the white brick fireplace.

"What a house of horrors," said Jay.

"And this is just the living room," said Jackson.

"Did she kill them all?" whispered Jay.

"Nah, these were her pets. She kept every one. The thought of burying them was too much for her so she had them stuffed. She even stuffed some of the birds they'd catch," said Jackson.

"What a freak," said Jay. He was about to poke the orange tabby when it opened its eyes.

Jay nearly jumped out of his skin. "I thought you said they were all dead!" The cat stretched its jaw and had a tongue-curling yawn.

"I can't keep track," said Jackson, laughing.

"This is too bizarre. Let's get out of here," said Jay.

"She's a super nice lady, just lonely. Her only son died of a drug overdose when he was twenty and her husband died of diabetes," said Jackson.

"Are they here, too?" said Jay, half joking, half serious.

Before Jackson could answer May-Belle came out holding two packages.

"Here you go, boys," she said. Jay and Jackson held their hands out as May-Belle placed a wad of toilet paper in their palms. It was warm. Jay flinched and dropped his on the floor.

"Sorry," said Jay as he stooped to pick up the wad with his thumb and index finger as though it was dog crap.

"That's OK," said May-Belle. "Just don't eat too much or you won't poop for a week." Laughing and slapping Jackson on the back.

Jackson unwound the toilet paper and steam rose out. As he leaned in to take a bite Jay lunged forward to swat it out of his hand, but Jackson pulled it close to his body and kept eating.

"Delicious bannock," said Jackson.

"Sorry, there's no jam. I have to wait for your mom and grandmother to bring me my groceries and hopefully some paper towels before I also run out of toilet paper. I don't know what I'd do without those two," said May-Belle.

Jay slowly pulled the toilet paper off his bannock and dared a small bite. It was soft, sweet and tasty.

"That's really good," said Jay. "What is it?"

"It's bannock, flat bread we learned to cook from the Scottish immigrants. About the only thing the Europeans were good for," said May-Belle. She smiled and winked at the boys.

"We better get to school. Thanks, Grandmother," said Jackson to show respect.

"Thanks," said Jay. He looked around the living one more time at all the cats and then followed Jackson back to the road, now polka dotted with puddles as the rain fell.

"You were right, Jackson. That was totally worth it," said Jay.

"I knew you'd like May-Belle's bannock," said Jackson. But that's not what Jay meant.

"So why are you here?" asked Jackson, his mouth full of bannock.

"I got busted for tagging," said Jay. It was partly true.

"Oh, you're a painter," said Jackson.

"Sort of. Hey, if the rain ever stops, do you want to help me paint my grandpa's garage?" asked Jay. The puddles blew bubbles as the rain drops grew larger.

"Why would I want to do that?" asked Jackson, peeling greasy toilet paper away from the bannock.

"I'll give you two bucks an hour," said Jay.

101

Jackson stuffed the last piece of bannock in his mouth and said, "Really? OK."

"Cool, meet me at my house after school. I live…"

Jackson cut him off, "I know where you live."

"Small town," said Jay.

"You got that right," said Jackson.

Chapter 15

"You any good at lifting boxes, Jackson?" asked Grampa. Jay had done the introductions even though Grampa and Jackson already knew each other.

"I think so," said Jackson.

"Good, you and Jay can start in the corner." Grampa waved toward the yellow plastic milk crates stacked against the wall.

"Jay, how's the raven?" asked Grampa.

"I let him go yesterday morning. I think he'll be alright but I haven't seen him since. He's probably plotting his revenge to turn me into a goat or something," said Jay.

Jackson gave him a funny look.

"It's a story Grampa told me. You got any other stories?" asked Jay.

"Come with me," said Grampa. He stood outside the garage and held his hands out, palms up, open to the sky. "Good, the rain has stopped."

"Where are we going?" asked Jay.

"Yeah, what about painting the garage? I need the money," said Jackson.

"What money?" asked Grampa.

"Jay's going to pay me two bucks an hour," said Jackson.

"Is he now?" said Grampa as he raised his eye-brows at Jay.

Grampa shuffled behind the garage turning right past his house to a path bordered by bramble bushes on the left and the back of houses, including Jay's, on the right. The path was mushy like soggy cereal. Water dripped from leaves, the last rain drops to reach the ground.

"This story is about totem poles. Do you know what a totem pole is?" asked Grampa.

"It's some religious thing the Indians worshipped to make it rain," said Jay.

Jackson laughed.

"What are you laughing at?" said Jay.

"Oh, you were serious," said Jackson.

They reached an algae covered, wooden bridge that crossed over a rushing creek. The boys stopped to lean over the cracked handrails. Jay spat. Jackson copied.

"Many people think that, but a totem pole is really like a family tree," said Grampa.

"Makes sense, since it's made from a tree," said Jackson.

"Yes, from the cedar tree. Only the Coastal First Nations have totem poles. You can't find them anywhere else in the world," continued Grampa.

"I thought all Indians had them," said Jay.

"No, they are unique to our people. We live where the trees are tall enough and thick enough to make a totem pole. How many giant trees do you see in the prairies?" asked Grampa.

The path led them to a forest of tall cedars. Jay took a deep breath. It smelled like the live Christmas tree lot they set up around the corner from his apartment, in early December. He had played 'hide and seek' there with his friends until the owner kicked them out for knocking over a whole row of blue spruce.

"Wow, look how big this tree is," said Jay. He looked straight up and felt slightly dizzy. The sheer height gave the sensation of the tree falling on top of him. A drop of water hit him square in the forehead.

"Guess how old it is," said Grampa.

"Fifty years old," said Jay, wiping away the water.

"Older, much older," said Grampa.

"One hundred years old. That's an antique," said Jackson.

"No. Sorry Jackson, not even close. This tree has a diameter of six feet and is about seven hundred years old," said Grampa. "Before even Christopher Columbus sailed to America."

"Whoa," said Jay.

"If the three of us held hands and circled the tree we couldn't close the gap," said Grampa.

Jackson reached out for Jay's hand.

Jay looked down and said, "Not in this lifetime."

Jackson put his hands in his pockets and continued down the trail.

"We also use the totem pole to honor the tree itself. The trees gave our ancestors so many things, like logs to build longhouses for shelter, bark to make baskets, mats and clothes, and wood for fire. Trees are also the oldest living things on Earth and unlike today's cultures we honored our elders. Tribe members built the totems and erected them at a special ceremony called a potlatch," said Grampa.

"What's a potlatch?" asked Jay.

"It is a great feast and celebration put on by the whole village. Everyone had to bring something - food, baskets, blankets, mats or small carvings to give as presents to guests from other villages. The chief conducted any legal business such as sharing of property when someone died, presiding over births and marriages, and he blessed the new totem pole. Then the traditional dancing began and lasted the whole night," said Grampa.

"Sounds like fun. When is the next potlatch?" asked Jay.

"There hasn't been a potlatch since your mom was little. Most people don't remember the dances or songs," said Grampa.

"That sucks," said Jay.

"Each totem pole is different. It is made up of symbols, usually animals that represent the family like a family crest," said Grampa.

"How do they know what animal?" asked Jay.

"It's an animal they feel connected to. The animal will show itself but you must be willing to see it. Each animal has traits you may identify with. This is called your 'totem animal'," said Grampa.

"What's my 'totem animal'?" asked Jay.

"No one can tell you. It is something you must discover for yourself," said Grampa.

"What's your totem animal?" asked Jackson.

"Mine is the wolf. It symbolizes strength, leadership and family," said Grampa.

"What about you, Jackson? Do you know your 'totem animal'?" asked Grampa.

"No, I never really thought about it," said Jackson.

"Don't they teach you kids anything in school?" asked Grampa.

"Math, English, and Social Studies," said Jackson.

"I guess you need those, too," said Grampa. "I know your grandmother must have mentioned totem animals to you."

"Probably, but she talks so much I forget to listen half the time," said Jackson.

Jay continued to check out the trees looking for the biggest one. Some of the trees grew on top of the stumps of other trees. Some shared the same ground but split into two trees about ten feet up. One tree grew straight for six feet then veered right for eight feet and then went straight up about fifty feet. The ferns thrived in the flat area making the tree look like it had a horse's mane.

"Hey, raspberries," said Jay. He reached up and plucked a huge red-orange berry from the bush growing close to the creek, full from the day's rain.

"Those are salmon berries," said Jackson.

"Can we eat them?" asked Jay.

"Sure, my mom makes jam out of them," said Jackson.

Jay grabbed the biggest one. It easily slid off the stem. He popped it in his mouth and waited for his taste buds to tell him what this new flavor was.

"It doesn't taste like salmon at all," announced Jay, surprised at the sweetness. He stretched to reach one from an upper branch. "It's crunchy, too."

"You must have got one with a bug inside," said Jackson. Jay stuck out his tongue and pretended to spit it out. Jackson placed a berry on the end of each finger and waved his hand around groaning, "My finger tips have been cut off in a horrible mill accident. Now I am left with these bloody stumps."

"You're weird," said Jay. Jackson didn't care and popped one berry after another into his mouth.

"Don't eat the ones below your knees," warned Grampa. "Dog pee."

"How come they call them salmon berries?" asked Jay.

"I am not sure, maybe because they grow near salmon streams," offered Grampa. "They are also a favorite of the black bears so watch out if you come down here alone."

"Bears! Really? Cool!" said Jay.

They continued down the path. Jay stared intently into the trees in search of a bear but among the giant trunks he saw only a myriad of vegetation; healthy ferns people would pay big bucks for at the garden shop, thick carpets of ivy and hostas covered the ground, but what struck Jay the most was the moss.

Plush springy moss grew everywhere and on everything. It knew no boundaries. Rocks, nothing grows on rocks, there's no dirt. Didn't matter; moss loved rocks. Granite boulders with lime green toupees cropped up along the way. Tree trunks wrapped in moss fifteen feet high like fuzzy socks. Arched branches from fallen trees clothed in moss so bright compared to the other browns and greens it took on a yellowish tinge. One mossy branch starting where another one ended like some sort of piping system.

"I thought moss only grew on the north side of trees," said Jay. He had circled another tree to find the moss thriving equally around the circumference.

"Old wives tale. Not enough sunlight in here to stop the moss from growing anywhere it wants," said Grampa.

Grampa veered off the path and held back some branches.

"Through here," said Grampa.

Jay ducked under the bramble with Jackson close behind. When they emerged from the trail Jay stopped in his tracks. Black eyes peered down, nostrils flared, and sharp teeth grinned hungrily as four inch claws reached for Jay.

Face to face with a bear, Jay breathed a sigh of relief when he realized it was a totem pole. Three totems in total towered as tall as trees. On top of the first one was a large bird. Its right wing was missing.

Jay circled the totem poles, one by one, stroking the features of each carving as though reading them, like a blind person memorizing a face by touch. Up close, the notches and grooves from the many strokes of a long dead carver's tool were visible.

"Awesome," whispered Jay.

"These totem poles are over one hundred years old. They hold the stories of our ancestors. The building behind us is the longhouse. It hasn't been used in years, but boy did we have some good potlatches in there," said Grampa. The building was about a hundred feet long and made from overlapping split cedar logs attached by heavy rope. Green powdery algae grew on all sides. A blanket of moss covered the roof along with cedar cones and twigs.

Grampa pointed to the tallest totem pole. "Do you see the eagle at the top?"

"Yes," said Jay and Jackson.

"He's called Thunderbird. He saved the people from a killer whale that ate all the salmon while the villagers starved. See how he has the whale in his claws?"

The boys nodded.

"Where is his other wing?" asked Jay. The totem pole was showing its age. One of the wings was missing and the other wing sagged slightly like Thunderbird had tired of flying in circles.

"A group of kids came up here to camp for a graduation party. When they left they took a wing as a souvenir I guess. Shameful," said Grampa.

"I always thought it was pointing left," said Jackson, his head tilted back. He stood with his right hand on his hip and his left arm extended.

"Maybe it's left-handed," said Jay.

"Like me," said Jay and Grampa at the same time.

"You're left-handed?" asked Jay.

"Yup," said Grampa.

"That's weird," said Jay.

Grampa smiled then continued, "Do you see Wolf?"

"The second one down?" said Jay, pointing.

"No, he is Bear, you can tell by the flat ears and the tongue. Wolves have pointed ears," said Grampa.

"Here's the wolf, the one on the bottom," said Jackson.

"Wolf is our family crest," said Grampa.

"Figures we are the 'low man on the totem pole'," snickered Jay.

"The 'low man on the totem pole' is the most important part of the totem. Everything is built on the shoulders of the bottom symbol. Many people worked hard to carve each totem pole but only the master carver worked on the base. It was too important to leave to the apprentices," said Grampa.

"Really?" said Jay, going in for a better look. He looked at each feature of the totem pole. Symmetrical shapes like ovals, circles, shark tooth, whale tail and crescent moons combined to bring the animals to life. No hard edges. Even the square teeth on the bottom row of the snarling Wolf mouth were rounded on the corners.

"How did they do all this without chainsaws?" asked Jay.

"Do you know which one is my family totem?" asked Jackson.

"I know," said Jay. "It's this one with the slimy frog." The frog faced downward as though crawling to the ground.

"No, it's not," complained Jackson.

"I think Jay is right. You are from the Frog Clan. Frogs are said to bring great wealth," said Grampa.

"Wow, I'm gonna be rich one day," said Jackson.

"Dream on, Frog boy. Your only chance of being rich is to get a girl to kiss you and turn you into a prince," joked Jay.

"What's this one with the scales?" asked Jay.

"That one is very important. It is Salmon which represents instinct, persistence and determination," said Grampa.

"Do you have a favorite?" asked Jackson.

"I like Otter. It is symbolic of laughter, curiosity, grace and empathy. In fact, I married an otter," said Grampa. "You remind me of her, Jay."

"Do you think my totem animal is the otter?" asked Jay.

"It doesn't matter what I think. It's what you think, what you feel connects you to nature, that counts," said Grampa.

Jay rolled his eyes. "How come adults never really answer your questions? They always want you to figure it out for yourself," said Jay to Jackson.

"Yeah, and then they get all mad at you when you don't do it the way they would do it," agreed Jackson.

"Right, Grampa?" said Jay.

"Why don't you figure it out for yourself," said Grampa. All three chuckled.

After Grampa explained what the other animals and their symbols were they started to walk back.

"We also believe our 'totem animal' is our 'guardian spirit'," said Grampa.

"I don't believe in ghosts or spirits," said Jay.

"Have you ever been alone but thought you saw someone out of the corner of your eye?" asked Grampa.

"I have," said Jackson.

"Yeah, a couple of times," admitted Jay.

"That is your guardian spirit," said Grampa.

The boys furrowed their eyebrows, taking in what Grampa had said.

Jay pushed aside the bushes that led to the trail. He didn't hear the snap of twigs behind him and turned to find out why. Grampa and Jackson had gone in the opposite direction.

"Why are we going this way?" asked Jay, jogging to catch up.

"Shorter," said Grampa.

"Why didn't we take the shortcut in the first place?" asked Jackson.

"For Jay's first time I wanted him to see the totem poles as they were before the roads and the phone lines," replied Grampa.

They walked across a gravel parking lot overgrown with weeds and onto Grampa's street. Dillon and Jody bounded over to escort them back to the garage. Grampa threw a stick for them. It landed in the creek and picked up speed. Jody chased it from the edge of the creek but Dillon dove in and lunged for the stick. He almost had it but the speed of the current floated the stick easily over the weirs until it was gone. Dillon returned to Grampa and the boys. He shook the water from his fur like it was acid and sprayed the three of them.

"Thanks a lot, Dillon," said Jay.

"It's just a little dog rain," said Grampa. Dillon bowed. Grampa snapped a dog biscuit in two and threw a piece to Dillon and Jody.

"Here you go, last box," said Grampa. They had arrived back at the garage in half the time.

"Old photos. Who are these people?" asked Jay, looking at the stacks of sepia colored snap shots.

"They are our ancestors. This is a picture of a potlatch inside the longhouse. See the dancers dressed in their regalia? Against the wall, beside each door, are story totem poles; smaller totem poles to signify a certain event or family," said Grampa.

"I see Thunderbird on top, then the whale and the one with the big square teeth. Is it a beaver?" asked Jay pointing to one of the totem poles.

"Yes. Beaver is a good spirit. It works hard cutting down trees and building homes, like we do. Now you are seeing the symbols and reading the totem poles," said Grampa.

"My grandmother has a picture like that. She usually cries after looking at it though so we don't bring it out too often," said Jackson.

"Here is a photo taken outside the longhouse. The house is painted with the sign of Grizzly Bear, our brother," said Grampa. "Looks different now, eh?"

Grampa passed the picture to Jay. The front of the longhouse was covered, ground to roof with the First Nations symbol of a grizzly bear face.

"Wow, now that was some graffiti artist," said Jay.

Chapter 16

Jay and Jackson painted the garage all day Saturday and half of Sunday and were almost done. The sun rose high in the sky eliminating all shade.

"I need a break," said Jay, rubbing the pale grey paint into his knuckles.

"Good idea. Let's go to the store and get Popsicles," suggested Jackson. He climbed down the wooden ladder with paint can in hand. His right hand carried a paint roller that left a trail as he stepped from rung to rung.

"Where's the store?" asked Jay, pounding the lid onto the paint can.

"Down the street. Well, it's not much of a store, but you can buy Popsicles there," said Jackson.

"I'm not supposed to leave the yard," said Jay.

"Why not?" asked Jackson.

"I don't know. I'm just not," said Jay.

"It's just down the street. We'll be back in five minutes," said Jackson.

Jay did not want to look like an idiot in front of his friend. A five minute walk to the store wouldn't hurt. He was pretty sure Mrs. Thornton wasn't lurking in the woods.

It was so hot even the dogs couldn't be bothered to move. Jay and Jackson passed Dillon and Jody panting under a cherry tree that shaded the whole yard two doors down from Jay's house.

The two boys traversed the dusty lane leaping over potholes lined with cracked mud.

"First one to fall in buys the Popsicles," said Jackson.

Grasshoppers clicked and clacked in erratic flight patterns to avoid being stepped on. The sound reminded Jay of typing on his mom's IBM Selectric she later replaced with her lap top computer. A car drove by sending up a swarm worthy of Ethiopia. Jackson waved 'hello' to the driver. Jay waved too after the car passed. Not to say 'hello' but to ward off the cloud of dust and insects.

A blue flame caught the attention of Jay as they reached the end of the street. Gordon was inside his carport welding something. Jay couldn't make out what it was as up-ended furniture, cardboard boxes and stacks of newspapers blocked the view.

"What's he doing?" asked Jay.

"Who, Johnny Walker?" asked Jackson.

"No, Gordon," said Jay.

"No one calls him Gordon, except a few elders. We call him 'Johnny Walker'," said Jackson.

"Why do you call him that?" asked Jay.

"Because he's always getting his driver's license taken away. He's probably cutting up scrap metal to sell for beer money. He used to be some kind of artist, then his wife took the kids and left. Now he just drinks," said Jackson.

The boys walked on. Sweat ran slow then fast between Jay's shoulder blades.

"I thought you said it was only five minutes," said Jay. He wiped his face with the bottom of his t-shirt. Not a good day to wear AC-DC Back in Black Tour, but better than baring his skinny chest. They had already walked past the school to the other corner of town.

"We are almost there," said Jackson.

115

Jackson led the way to the store; a thirty foot trailer with a plywood room built off one side. A hand painted board, leaning against the wall outside read 'Sadie's Genral Store'. The second 'e' in "General" was missing and that's how everyone pronounced it.

They climbed a cement cinder block step to enter the plywood store. It was even hotter inside. The heat prickled Jay's nostrils when he breathed.

Not much to choose from, thought Jay as he checked out the sparsely filled racks. No hot dogs sweating on a Ferris wheel, no coffee island, no slushy machine. Only a few loaves of bread, two types of potato chips, canned soup, one rack with outdated videos for rent, an avocado green fridge and a long, white deep freeze all crammed into about one hundred square feet of space. The fan blowing on top of the fridge was wasting its breath.

A plump, brown hand pushed aside the curtain separating the trailer from the store. A short, portly lady came out wiping the sweat from her forehead. Toddling behind her was a girl with pig tails and big, brown eyes clutching a 'Bratz' doll.

"Hey Jackson," she greeted him. "Who's your friend here?"

"Hi Sadie, this is Jay," said Jackson.

"Oh yeah, I heard you moved back. How's your mom?" asked Sadie.

"She's OK, I guess," said Jay, disturbed that she knew him. Anonymity was fiercely protected in the city.

"We used to go to school together, you know," said Sadie. A bead of sweat ran down her temple.

"Oh yea," said Jay surprised at how much older Sadie looked than his mom. Maybe it was her thick, black-frame eyeglasses.

"What can I get for you?" asked Sadie. She seemed slightly out of breath like the heat had sapped all her energy.

"Popsicles. I'll have root beer," said Jackson.

"Me, too," said Jay.

Sadie opened the freezer; the sound of the rubber strip peeling away from the edge made their mouths water. Mist erupted, surrounding Sadie as she reached in and pulled out two Popsicles. Not the short kind with two sticks but the round, foot-long ones.

Jay and Jackson paid Sadie and rushed out of the stifling trailer. They sat on the hood of a gutted Chrysler Cordova carcass parked under a trio of cedar trees.

"If I had a blow torch like Gordon's, er I mean, Johnny Walker's, I could do all kinds of things to this piece of junk," said Jay, patting the roof; sprinkles of rust fell onto the front seat.

"Like what?" asked Jackson.

"Take the top off and turn it into a convertible or remove the trunk and make it into a pick up truck," said Jay.

"Or put in a swimming pool," said Jackson, wide-eyed.

Jay rolled his eyes and shook his head.

"How come you don't have any friends?" asked Jay.

It wasn't meant to be mean but Jackson scowled anyway.

"You know, besides me, 'the apple'," said Jay.

"I used the hang out with Mitchell and Donny, they're brothers. They had to move up north to the oil patch when their dad lost his job," said Jackson.

"That bites," said Jay.

"Yup," said Jackson.

"Hey, I bet I can make my Popsicle last longer than you can," said Jackson, changing the subject.

The brown ice started to melt before they had even removed the wrappers. To stop it from dripping down their arms they held the wooden sticks high above their heads like slurping sword swallowers.

Jay and Jackson steadied the last morsel on the stick into their mouths and spied five or six kids from school entering Sadie's. They came out a few minutes later with packs of cigarettes and cans of pop. The tallest kid opened the cigarettes and passed them around.

"Hey Apple, come here," called the boy. It was Miles.

"Nah, it's too hot," said Jay.

"Don't, Jay. You better go," said Jackson, sliding off the car, his shorts riding up his legs.

"I wanna ask you something. Come on," said Miles.

Jay sauntered over with Jackson at his heels.

"We're going to party down by the creek. You want to come?" said Miles. He placed his cigarette between his lips and lifted his tank top to reveal a bottle of vodka stuffed into the waist band of his cut-off shorts.

"We even got mix. Let's go before it gets warm," said one of the boys. He had a shaved head and wore a brown t-shirt with a faded screen print.

"No, I've got to finish painting my grandpa's garage," said Jay.

"Cool, paint fumes," said one of the scruffier kids in the back. His blue and green striped shirt covered his head and most of his face providing shade to his head but exposing his back to the sun.

Jay just looked at him and shook his head.

118

"You should come, Jay, it'll be a blast. Your grandfather won't care," said Miles putting his arm around Jay. The cigarette hanging off his bottom lip bobbed up and down as he spoke.

"Get lost," said Jay, shrugging off the arm.

Jackson's eyes went wide.

"Let's go with them, Jay. I'll show you the rope swing and we can put our feet in the creek," said Jackson.

"Who said you could come?" sneered Miles.

"Uh…I…uh..I just thought," stuttered Jackson.

"Well don't just uh…," Miles stuttered back. The kids laughed at Mile's imitation.

"Maybe some other time," said Jay, as he stepped past Miles.

"NO! Now!" said Miles.

"Sounds just like my mom," said Jay under his breath to Jackson.

"What did you say?" asked Miles. He grabbed Jay's t-shirt in his fist and twisted the fabric, pinching Jay's skin.

"Nothing," said Jay, inches from Miles face.

"Jackson, what did he say?" asked Miles.

"I don't know," mumbled Jackson. He looked at the ground and shrugged his shoulders.

"Tell me or you'll get it next," said Miles, still holding Jay by the shirt.

Jackson looked at Jay.

"I said you sound like my mom," said Jay. He pulled at Mile's hand. The t-shirt stretched until a ripping sound was heard.

"But I act like my dad," snarled Miles through clenched teeth.

He pushed Jay back and then took a swing at him. Jay lifted his arm and blocked the shot. Mile's fist connected with Jay's elbow. The crunch of cracking knuckles spurred the crowd to yell 'ouch'. Miles came at Jay again. Jay considered running but the kids had formed a circle around them.

To protect his face, Jay put his hands up. Miles punched him in the gut instead. Jay doubled over as the air vomited from his lungs. Miles laid an upper cut on Jay's chin and everything went black for a second. Jay dropped to the dirt and stayed down. The rusty taste of blood filled his mouth. He turned over onto his stomach to push himself up. Miles kicked him in the ribs, collapsing Jay into the fetal position.

Jackson ran inside the store to get Sadie but two boys grabbed him.

Miles picked Jay up and dragged him to the side of the trailer toward an old refrigerator. Jay tried to get his feet under him but they just helped Miles to move faster. With one hand, Miles pulled the chrome handle of the antique refrigerator door like it was a slot machine. The cream colored fridge had rounded corners and only one door. The freezer was housed in the upper left hand corner of the fridge. Separate doors for freezers came later. No racks or drawers were left, only black mould around the edges.

Jay knew what was coming. He kicked and thrashed, pulling at Mile's hands. Jay managed to scratch Miles but that only made him more determined. He shoved Jay in the fridge and kicked at Jay until he pulled his legs inside. When Miles stuffed Jay's hands in Jay's legs would come out making it impossible to shut the door.

"Let me go, you moron," shouted Jay.

"Give me a hand, will you," said Miles to the boy with the shaved head.

"Don't," cried Jackson. "It's dark in there."

"Oh, are you afraid of the dark?" said Miles in the same tone as a six year old girl.

"Stop, this isn't funny. Let me out," said Jay. He was feeling panicked. He'd been locked in a locker at school but this was different. No air slits.

"You are afraid of the dark. Here this will help," said Miles. He motioned for one of the boys to come closer. Taking the lit cigarette from the boy's fingers Miles threw the 'Export A' into the fridge. The door sealed shut with a click.

Jay kicked and screamed. The fridge rocked slightly but the door held fast. The smoke from the cigarette burned his nostrils. He reached for the cigarette but grabbed the wrong end, scorching his finger tips. He tried again, this time he had the filter. The smoke was filling his lungs.

Put the cigarette out, dummy.

It's the only light you have, dummy.

Jay argued with himself while he continued to kick at the door.

The glowing ember of the cherry was not enough to illuminate the door latch but it was better than pitch black.

He held his t-shirt over his mouth to stop the smoke but it was still hard to breathe.

Jay kicked as hard at the door as he could. His knees were up around his chin taking away most of his leverage. The cigarette burned down to the filter singeing his fingers. He let go. The cigarette rolled in a semi circle under Jay's leg. He pressed himself up against one side of the fridge, twisting to find the cigarette. He banged his head on the corner of the freezer. His heart raced as claustrophobia set in. Clawing at the fridge in an attempt to open it from the inside, Jay felt tears stinging his eyes from smoke and fear.

I am going to die. The oxygen is almost gone. It's black. Jackson can't save me. I'm going to die, thought Jay.

"Let me out. Let me out. I can't breathe," screamed Jay. It sounded to Jay like he was yelling into a pillow. He knew no one could hear him.

He banged on the door again.

Finally the door swung open. Light and fresh air filled the fridge. Jay dove into the sunlight, rolled over and lay coughing with his forearm covering his eyes.

When the coughing ceased, he sat up. Sadie hovered over him.

Satisfied he was OK she turned to the group of boys. "Kids have died playing in fridges like this. You all ought to know better. Now, clear off. I don't want any trouble around here. Don't forget, I know your parents," she warned.

"Kids and their games," she muttered as she closed the fridge door, pressing on it with her ample hip until the chrome latch clicked into place.

Miles and his gang did as they were told and backed away from Jay and Jackson.

"Next time someone invites you to a party you should have the manners to accept. We can finish this tomorrow after school. Jackson, you comin'?" said Miles as he and his buddies headed towards the creek.

"No, maybe next time," said Jackson.

"That's what I thought. More for me," shouted Miles. Jay and Jackson listened to the laughter fade away in the shadows of the trees.

"Damn heat makes everyone crazy. Are you alright?" asked Sadie. She attempted to help Jay to his feet but he waved her away.

"Yeah, just great," said Jay as he dusted himself off and rubbed his aching chin.

"I'm sorry, Jay. I tried to stop them. Look at the bruises on my arms," said Jackson. He pushed up his sleeves to reveal red marks on his upper arms.

Jay stayed silent until they reached his front yard.

"I don't feel like painting anymore today, Jackson. I'll see you tomorrow," said Jay.

"Those guys are jerks," called Jackson as Jay disappeared into the house.

Chapter 17

"Knock, knock," said Tatla from the hallway.

Jay didn't answer. Instead he turned up the volume on a "Chili Peppers" song playing on his obsolete boom box.

"Knock, knock," she called again much louder this time. "Is everything OK?"

"I'm doing homework," said Jay. He sat on his bed, staring at the pictures from Grampa's garage.

"Can I come in, please?" she asked.

"No," said Jay.

Jay turned his back to her when she entered the room anyway.

"I heard you got in a fight," said Tatla. She twisted the volume button to the left.

"It's no big deal, just some guy from school being an idiot," said Jay.

"Do you want me to talk to his parents?" asked Tatla.

"NO!" Jay said, horrified at the notion.

"You weren't raised to solve problems with violence and neither was I," said Tatla.

There was no way he could tell her he'd been locked in a fridge or that he had to fight the village bully tomorrow.

"I guess he wasn't raised the same way. It's over. I don't want to talk about it," said Jay.

"Have you been smoking?" asked Tatla.

Jay shook his head.

"You smell like cigarettes," said Tatla.

"I wasn't smoking," said Jay, the irritation building in his voice.

"Ok, I'm sorry," she said.

"What have you got in your hand?" asked Tatla. She sat beside Jay on the bed.

"Some old pictures from Grampa's garage," said Jay. He handed a photo to his mom.

"I haven't seen these for years. Here is the longhouse, and the totem poles. Have you seen the totem poles at the end of the street?" asked Tatla.

"Grampa took me and Jackson when you were at work," said Jay.

"I'm glad you made a new friend. This is the potlatch. Those were so fun," said Tatla, studying the cracked photo.

"You've been to a potlatch?" said Jay, as if his mom had done time travel.

"Sure, the whole village went. I dressed up in regalia made of buck skin and turquoise beads with feathers around the cuffs. My shoes had jingly things on them. We listened to the old stories, ate tons of food and danced around the fire all night," said Tatla staring at the ceiling as if viewing the potlatch on a big screen TV.

"Why don't they have them anymore?" asked Jay.

"I don't know. A lot of people have moved away and many elders have passed on. Chief George has enough on his plate, trying to keep the village employed, and dealing with the land treaties. Potlatches are a celebration and there's not much to celebrate lately," sighed Tatla.

"There's a chief?" said Jay.

125

"Yes, Chief George; elected about three years ago according to your Grampa," said Tatla.

"Next you'll tell me there's a village witch doctor," said Jay.

"No, not even a regular doctor," said Tatla. She slapped Jay on the knee. "I should check on dinner. Are you sure you are OK?"

"I'm fine," said Jay, even though he wasn't. He wanted to tell her he hated this stupid village and that he'd almost died today and wished they were back in their apartment. Jay knew it was pointless. He touched the goose egg on his head from the freezer and winced.

"Are you sure you're OK?" asked Tatla.

"I banged my head," said Jay.

"Here, let me take a look," said Tatla.

Jay swatted her hand away. "Leave me alone. I'm fine."

"OK, OK. Grampa is coming for dinner tonight, by the way," said Tatla.

"What are we having?" asked Jay.

"Spaghetti," Tatla said over her shoulder.

Spaghetti? Maybe today won't be the worst day of my life. Oh yea, I'm saving that day for tomorrow. If I'm going to have a last meal this is the one.

Jay loved his mom's spaghetti. It was about the only dish she prepared from scratch, browning the meat, chopping up onions, celery and carrots and adding a nasty amount of fresh garlic. However, it usually came with strings attached and not of the noodle variety. Last time she made spaghetti Jay found out she had quit her job and started her own business that meant a lot of traveling. She didn't even discuss it with him first.

"I heard there was a bit of a scuffle at Sadie's this afternoon," said Grampa, pulling up a chair to the oak table. He didn't mention the fact that Jay had broken Mrs. Thornton's rules.

"You heard right," said Jay, hoping Grampa would drop it.

"Who was it?" asked Grampa.

"A guy," said Jay.

"Miles?" said Grampa.

"How did you know?" asked Jay.

"He is always causing trouble. The boy is like a hermit crab," said Grampa.

"Why, because he's so shellfish," Jay tried to laugh but his jaw hurt too much.

"No jokes, listen," said Grampa. "He is like a hermit crab because he is big on the outside but small on the inside. He lugs around a heavy shell to protect himself. It is a tiresome burden to carry."

"I think his dad hits him sometimes," said Tatla.

"I am sure his dad has his reasons," said Jay lifting a glass of chocolate milk to his mouth. The coldness soothed his lips.

"I am tired of people blaming others for their own foolish actions. Miles has got a brain in his head, although they did keep him back a grade. That makes him bigger than the other kids. He uses his size to intimidate everyone," said Grampa shaking his head.

"He pushes the kids around to impress his friends," piped in Tatla as she strained the noodles.

"He also gets booze and cigarettes to impress them. Why do so many kids drink and smoke around here?" said Jay.

"Bored dumb," said Grampa.

127

"Don't you mean 'boredom'?" said Jay.

"No, I mean 'bored dumb'. The kids don't know what to do with themselves. They are bored and do dumb things like smoke and drink," said Grampa.

"Another thing we can thank the government for; cheap booze and cigarettes. Give it to us tax free so we will drink and smoke ourselves to death," said Tatla. She ladled chunky sauce onto steaming noodles.

"Don't blame others for our problems. We have the ability and opportunity to fix them. You did OK. You never smoked or drank," said Grampa.

"You and Mom kept me busy doing chores," said Tatla. "Maybe that's where I went wrong with you, Jay."

"I'm making up for it now," said Jay.

"The garage is coming along nicely. You are an excellent painter. How is school going?" asked Grampa.

"I have one presentation to do on Friday about Coastal First Nations. I think Mrs. Thornton must have bribed the teacher. And then no more school for the whole summer," said Jay. *And no more Miles.*

"It's good they are teaching about our own people. If we don't understand ourselves we can't move forward," said Grampa.

"I borrowed some stuff from the garage. I hope that's alright," said Jay.

"Me garage es su garage," said Grampa.

"What does that mean?" asked Jay.

"It's Spanish. It means my garage is your garage," said Grampa.

Tatla placed the plates of spaghetti on the table. The symphony of twirling forks and noodles slapping chins began.

"So what's the bad news?" Jay asked his mom.

She frowned at him.

"You always make spaghetti when you have something bad to tell me," explained Jay.

"I do?" said Tatla, sprinkling parmesan cheese from a green plastic container onto her spaghetti.

"Yeah, like when you promised to get tickets for "Slam Jam" skateboard competition but you forgot and then they were sold out," said Jay.

"You are never going to let me forget that, are you?" said Tatla.

"Uh, uh," said Jay, licking sauce from the corner of his mouth.

"I guess I made spaghetti because it's your favorite. I knew you had a bad day so I thought this might cheer you up," said Tatla.

"It's my favorite, too. I thought you made it for me," said Grampa, pretending to be hurt.

"I made it for you too, Dad," said Tatla.

Grampa smiled. Jay noticed his mom and Grampa were getting along much better. The common goal of keeping Jay out of trouble knocked down the walls they had put up between each other.

"Grampa you have sauce on your chin," said Jay.

"That's OK. I'm sure there'll be more in a minute. I'll get them all at the end," said Grampa.

"What are your plans for the summer?" asked Grampa, mid bite.

To be as far from here as possible, thought Jay.

"Jay?" said Tatla.

"Um, Jackson's dad said he would take us salmon fishing before all the seal ice kills them off," said Jay. "What the heck is seal ice?"

"Sea lice," corrected Tatla, passing the parmesan to Jay.

"Lice? Gross," said Jay drowning his spaghetti with crumbly cheese.

"They think this lice is from the fish farms," said Grampa, gesturing for the parmesan cheese and then also dousing his plate with the yellow powder.

"One day there might not be any wild salmon," said Tatla.

"Back in the old days our people ate salmon just about every day," said Grampa.

"Jay showed me the picture of the potlatch," said Tatla.

"What would a potlatch be without smoked salmon and seaweed?" said Grampa, licking his lips.

Jay screwed up his nose. "Seaweed? Really?"

"I'll get some for you to try. It'll put hair on your toes," said Grampa as he rose from the table.

"I'll only eat it if it gives me powers of invisibility," said Jay.

"I haven't seen it do that yet, but you never know," said Grampa.

Jay replied. "You wouldn't see it because..."

"It'd be invisible," said Jay and Grampa at the same time. They all had a good laugh.

"I'm off to a meeting with the elders," said Grampa. He picked up a white paper napkin and scoured his face removing all traces of spaghetti sauce. "Thanks for dinner. See you tomorrow, Jay." Grampa kissed Tatla on the cheek and left via the back door.

Maybe not, thought Jay, *if Miles gets his way.*

Chapter 18

Jay lay on his bed, fingers linked behind his head, thinking of a way to deal with Miles.

If I leave I'll get thrown in juvy but if I stay I'm dead.

Jay dumped his homework on the floor. He stuffed a hoodie, a pair of jeans, socks and boxer shorts into his backpack. His skateboard beckoned but he knew it would hold him back. The window resisted then slid open. Jay threw his backpack out first, aiming for the corner of the house so as not to alert Tatla. He climbed on his desk and swung his leg over the sill. He twisted over onto his forearms banging his elbow against the window frame. The pain of his bruised ribs was excruciating as he doubled over the sill. He lowered himself by his fingertips and dropped five feet, suppressing a groan. Picking up his backpack he forced himself to walk at a casual pace.

The deserted road looked like the best route to the highway. Most people were having dinner in their backyards. The smell of barbequed hamburgers filled the air.

Splashing and squealing came from the house with the pool inside the garage. A yellow, white and red beach ball rolled across jagged gravel.

Four heads popped up and peered over the side of the blue plastic; three girls and one boy about nine or ten years old. Sleek black hair clung to their faces and shoulders like liquid satin.

Jay picked up the ball and carried it over to the kids.

"You wanna come swimming?" asked the boy, taking the ball from Jay.

"Hey, it's 'apple'. Yeah, come swimming. We can play bob for 'apple'," said one of the girls. The three girls squealed, and then dunked underwater to hide their embarrassment.

"No, I don't swim in garages. Why don't you guys put your pool out in the yard like normal people?" said Jay. He knew it was mean to say but after the 'apple' comment he didn't feel like being nice. Besides he'd never see them again.

"The pool is in the garage because if we put it in the yard we'll spend the whole summer fishing out leaves. Look around," said the same girl, enunciating every word like an English teacher. The house was close to the trail where the wind generously scattered cedar needles that looked like lacey snowflakes, only green and about the size of a hand.

"It's your house. Do what you like. I really don't care," said Jay. "It looks stupid, that's all."

The three girls shot water at Jay through their teeth. The boy bopped one of them on the head with the beach ball. They screamed the high pitch scream of tween girls and went back to their game.

Jay had only gone a few steps when he reached Gordon's on the other side of the street. The blue flame burned again. Gordon looked up and shut the nozzle off.

"Hey, Jay, where ya goin'?" asked Gordon. He reached for a beer, wiped the sweat off his upper lip and took a long guzzle.

"For a walk," said Jay.

"Come 'ere," said Gordon. Jay did as he was told, more out of curiosity than compliance. He maneuvered his way around old lawnmowers, an overturned bathtub, a mildewy truck canopy and several barbeque propane tanks stacked on top of each other like a pyramid.

"You don't like it here much, do ya'?" said Gordon. "They treat ya different. I know. They treat me the same way. I'm not

133

from here either," said Gordon, scratching his stubble with the dirty fingers of a mechanic.

"You're not?" said Jay. Gordon certainly looked like he was and definitely talked like he was from the village.

"Nope, I'm from another village," said Gordon. He crushed the beer can and threw it towards the overflowing garbage can, knocking more cans to the floor as a result.

"Why live here and not in your own village then?" asked Jay.

"This is my wife's home. They'd love it if I left but I don't plan on goin' nowheres," said Gordon. "Living in a small town is like living with a family. They say you're one of them, say you're family but no matter how long you live with them you'll always be an in-law," said Gordon.

He tugged on the handle of a full size fridge. A red metal tool box and a carton of glass canning jars prevented the door from opening wide. "Yawannabeer?" asked Gordon over the racket of the glass jars. "Shut up," he yelled at the box. The box went quiet. Jay and Gordon chuckled.

"No, thanks, I better get going," said Jay. A vision of Sadie's fridge brought the taste of spaghetti to his mouth.

"I am not saying they're all bad. There's lots of good people here, too," said Gordon.

Jay shrugged, adjusted his back pack higher onto his right shoulder and returned to the alley.

"Have a good walk," said Gordon, cracking open a fresh can.

Jay continued toward the highway. Dillon and Jody squeezed under a fence and greeted him.

"How come you guys are so happy?" asked Jay.

134

They wagged their tails hard, beating Jay on the legs. Petting them was impossible. They either wanted to jump up or lick you. Saliva dripped from their tongues.

That's disgusting, thought Jay.

He side stepped them, not wanting anything to slow him down. Talking to Gordon had already used up precious daylight.

A car grumbled up behind him, creeping across the potholes. If someone followed this slowly in the city it meant they either wanted directions or to abduct you. Either way, Jay knew to do an about face and walk the other way. This time he wasn't worried; only one car sounded like that. It was a 1975 Chevy 442, two door, black paint and tan interior. Its engine was throaty. Jay had seen it and heard it around town a few times.

The dogs bounded over to the car, shaking their rear ends, overjoyed to see more people they knew. The yellow Lab stood on his hind legs and hung his front paws inside the window. A spit bridge spanned from his mouth to the sill.

"Get down, Dillon, you're gross," said Courtney. "Cute but gross."

Courtney, the girl in the passenger seat, was in Jay's social studies class. She was in his grade and they had spoken a few times. Nothing deep, just stuff like "How did you do on the test?" or "Mr. Dunbar thinks he's training an army." She was the smartest one in the class but did her best not to show it. She was also Dr. Two Feathers niece but they were never at the office at the same time.

"Where do you think you are going?" said Courtney, in a knowing voice. She dangled a cigarette out the window and tapped it expertly to remove the ash build-up.

"For a walk," said Jay.

"You want a ride to the highway?" asked the driver.

Jay thought his name was Kelly but didn't want to get laughed at so he just said "No, that's OK."

"Are you running away? Because you can't be part of the village unless you run away at least once," said the girl in the back seat, her hands folded across her stomach. She was soggy from the heat. A strand of black hair stuck to her forehead like her face was split in half. Sweat stains wormed their way down the sides of her pink rhinestone tank top. White cotton shorts cut into her thighs. Her smile, however, was dazzling. She radiated joy somehow and Jay liked her immediately.

"Hop in. It's a long way to town. We should know, we've all done the runaway bit," said the guy beside her. He didn't look up but kept his eyes focused on something on his lap.

Jay stood for a moment not knowing what to do. It was a long way to town and it was hot.

Courtney opened the large door. Her ankles were adorned in silver and leather jewelry. She swung the bucket seat around so she was facing him. It swiveled. The seat actually swiveled. It was the coolest thing Jay had ever seen.

The girl in the back scooted over and he hopped in. Courtney swiveled back around. The car accelerated before she had the door closed. They rumbled across the remaining potholes then fish tailed down the street once they hit pavement. Jay felt exhilarated.

Dillon and Jody pursued them but gave up after a few houses.

Courtney did the introductions. "This is my boyfriend, Kelly, his little sister Skye and their cousin Levi."

"How come I haven't seen you at school?" Jay asked Skye.

"I dropped out last month," said Skye.

"Hey, slow down, Kelly," said Levi.

136

Jay looked over at Levi and realized why he was so interested in his lap. Levi had a red plastic notebook with green tobacco on it. Jay watched in fascination as Levi deftly chopped up the chunks of tobacco with a tiny pair of scissors. He sprinkled the tobacco onto a white piece of paper about the size of a Post-it note. Then he pinched the paper between his thumb and two fingers and licked along the edge of the paper like an envelope, rolling it into a skinny cigarette. To finish it off, Levi twisted one end and ran it under his nose like a fine cigar.

Levi dug around in his pocket and pulled out a chrome Zippo lighter with an angry skull engraved on the cap. With his thumb he snapped back the lid and struck the flint wheel across his cut-off jean shorts, igniting the lighter in one fast motion.

Jay was impressed. He'd seen joints being rolled at the skate park and lighters flicked before but not this fast and not this smoothly.

The kid's got skills. Not ones you'd put on a job application, but still, skills, thought Jay.

Levi put the joint to his lips, the flame to the joint and breathed deeply. He coughed as he exhaled and exclaimed what good shit it was. Jay looked out the window, trying not to make eye contact. Levi tapped Jay on the arm and thrust the joint at him.

"No, ladies first," said Jay, smiling at Skye.

"Can't, I'm pregnant," she said and rubbed her belly.

Levi tapped Jay again to take it.

He had tried it once. That was enough. Whatever other people got out of smoking weed did not apply to Jay. He remembered feeling like he was swimming inside his own body, visiting each organ. His heart banged on his ribs demanding to be let out of its bony jail; the liquid in his eyes had vanished to the same place as the saliva in his mouth. Where were the 'munchies'?

Where were the uncontrollable giggles? Jay only felt the elation of relief when the drug had worn off.

"No, thanks anyway," said Jay.

"Come on," said Levi.

"He doesn't want to. Here give it me before it totally burns away," said Courtney. After a few tokes she passed it to Kelly. The pungent smell was not totally unpleasant and much more tolerable than Courtney's cigarette smoke. The three continued to toke up until it burned down to the roach clip. Jay snickered when Levi singed his lips.

"Remember the first time you smoked a joint, Levi?" said Courtney. She had a goofy grin on her face like her cheek muscles were made of silly putty.

"Yeah," said Levi, snorting. Jay could tell the marijuana had worked. Even Levi's eyelids looked relaxed.

"That was so funny," said Skye, rubbing her belly.

"What happened?" asked Jay.

"The joint got stuck to his lips. He tried to pull it off but it wouldn't move. It was burning down closer to his face and he was freaking out. He had to go to the bathroom and run his face under the tap to put it out," said Kelly, laughing so hard he almost drove off the bridge.

"You had a total panic attack," said Courtney, with tears running down her face.

"What a waste of a good joint," said Levi, laughing along with them.

They dropped Jay off at the first exit and wished him luck.

Chapter 19

Real good influences, thought Jay but still in all he thought they were alright. He stuck out his thumb and walked backwards on the narrow gravel shoulder of the road. Not many cars passed and Jay was worried no one would stop.

A boxy semi truck barreled past. The updraft pulled Jay towards the road. The driver blasted his horn sending Jay back several paces to the edge of a twenty foot embankment. He cursed at the truck until he heard the thrum of the engine brakes.

The passenger door opened. Jay hurried in case the trucker changed his mind. Out of breath, Jay climbed up two steps onto the wiggly seat and heaved the door shut. The truck smelled of stale cigarette smoke, onions, sweat and greasy food.

"You're not Johnny Walker?" said the driver.

"You know Gordon?" said Jay.

"Sure, I give him a ride to town all the time and he gives me half price smokes," said the driver as he patted his front left pocket. "Ya' mind if I smoke?"

"I kinda do but since it's you truck I guess I have no say," said Jay. He wound the window down to avoid the acrid odor. The opposite effect happened as the smoke wafted past Jay looking for an exit.

"That's the spirit. Name's Brent," said the trucker. He grabbed the gear shift; a chrome head of a bull dog. The truck droned at a snail's pace, through the first few gears with one jolt after another. Grampa's truck felt like a limo by the time the three hour journey was over.

"I'm Jay. Thanks for stopping," said Jay.

"No problem, it's nice to have company," said Brent. "Sorry about the mess. I pretty much live in my truck."

Wrappers, fast food containers, cigarette butts and coffee cups were strewn about the cab. Receipts were piled up on the dash board and stuck out from the edges of the glove box. Jay resisted the urge to pop the button picturing the tiny squares of paper flying around the cab like the time he and Anthony took the lid off the hot air popcorn popper in mid pop.

"Where are you headed?" asked Brent.

"I'm going back to the city. To my home," said Jay.

"Good for you. Most of the kids I pick up are running away from home. It's nice to see one of you going back for a change," said Brent.

"Yeah," said Jay. He wondered if his mom knew he was even gone yet.

When the engine noise was too loud to talk over, Brent cranked up the country tunes. Jay recognized a song from his alarm clock station and caught himself singing along.

The truck picked up speed as the way to the city was mostly downhill. Jay arrived in the industrial part of town before sundown.

He thanked Brent for the ride. As soon as he hit the ground Jay felt a weight lift from him. He was back. He didn't realize how much he missed the speeding cars on the smooth asphalt, the hissing sound of busses stopping and starting, the homeless guy pushing his over-loaded shopping cart down the alley, or the people with either a coffee or cell phone in hand.

It was crowded, noisy, and dirty. Jay couldn't have been happier. It took another half an hour to reach the bright lights of the skate park. Jay listened to the familiar roll and grind of skateboards against the concrete block edges and steel rails. He regretted leaving his skateboard behind.

"Jay? Hey, Jay, is that you?"

Jay turned to see his friend Anthony. Anthony had blond, baby fine hair, with a face somewhere between Charlie Brown and the man in the moon. His solid stocky build made Anthony the polar opposite to Jay.

"How's it going?" said Jay.

"What are you doing here? You aren't supposed to be back for a couple of months," said Anthony. He rode toward Jay on his skateboard, skidding to a stop. He stepped on the back of the board so the front popped up into his left hand.

"I moved back today," said Jay. They bumped fists.

"Where are you staying?" asked Anthony.

"With you, if that's OK?" asked Jay.

Anthony looked at his friend and frowned. "I guess so. Are you in trouble, dude?"

"Only if they catch me," said Jay. Jay looked around at the park where he had spent so many hours after school. His eyes were immediately drawn to the concrete half pipe where bikers, boarders and inline skaters were taking turns rolling up and down the curved concrete; some achieving air while others abandoned their vehicles mid flight and slid on padded knees down the polished surface.

"Hey, where's my mural?" asked Jay. He had worked out a design combining three of his favorite skateboard logos into one unique graphic.

"It's still there, you just can't see it anymore," said Anthony.

Jay borrowed Anthony's skateboard and cruised over to the half pipe. On closer inspection Jay's mural was still there but barely noticeable. Another tagger had left his mark. Thick black letters covered the wall. "SkH8ters SUCK".

"Sk-haters suck?" said Jay. He couldn't believe someone painted over his mural in such a crude way.

"Yep, not very original," said Anthony who'd ducked and dodged his way through the maze of kids on boards, bikes and blades. "Let's get outta here."

They caught the train back to Anthony's place. Jay smelled the diesel of the trucks and busses and watched the bustle of the city go by at a break-neck pace.

Jay looked up at the glass high-rise buildings to see if any stars shone through. Not one.

"You wanna catch a movie tonight?" asked Anthony as they took the escalator down from the train platform.

"Sounds good," said Jay.

It had been less than a month since Jay left but it felt like years.

They rode the elevator to the 46th floor of Anthony's building. The boys pressed nearly every button before slipping through the closing doors. They roared hysterically and entered the luxury apartment. Anthony's dad was a successful real estate agent and owned several condos in the area. Anthony's mom managed an art gallery.

"I see your mom's been decorating again," said Jay.

"She's addicted to those home reno shows. Something comes on the TV and she simply must have it," said Anthony mimicking his mother's haughty attitude.

"It is umm brown," said Jay.

"Not brown. The couch is 'skinny latte', the drapes are 'double espresso' and the carpet is 'mocha-chino'," corrected Anthony.

"Sounds like you live in a Starbucks menu," remarked Jay.

"Wait 'til you see my room," said Anthony.

Jay followed Anthony down the wide corridor to his bedroom. Anthony opened the door and let Jay enter first.

"It's definitely orange," said Jay.

"Not orange," said Anthony with a glint in his eye.

"Tangerine Frapp," said Anthony.

"More like Tangerine Crap," said Anthony and Jay at the same time.

"Where are your mom and dad?" asked Jay, looking out the window at a hundred other glass buildings.

"Dad's showing homes to some clients and mom's got a new artist she's giving an exhibition for. It's a guy who turns running shoes into masks," said Anthony.

"Who'd want to put someone's stinky shoes on their face?" said Jay.

"I know, it sounds gross, but you know, it's art, anything goes," said Anthony. "You want some mac and cheese here or just grab something at the show?"

"I'll get some popcorn at the show. The only place the truck driver stopped for food was at this greasy spoon called 'The Dogwood'," said Jay.

"Did you eat there?" asked Anthony.

"No, only the 'dog would'," cackled Jay.

"That is so bad. I bet you've been dying to tell me that, saving it, waiting until I fell into your trap. I hope it was worth it," said Anthony.

"Totally worth it," said Jay, feeling more relaxed than he had in a long time.

Jay missed having his friend around, someone who knew his thoughts and could finish his sentences.

Anthony grabbed his backpack and told Jay he had to stop by his mom's gallery to get some money. They weaved in and out of the people on the sidewalks. Jay peeked down one of his favorite alleys to see if his handiwork was still there. The brick wall had been scrubbed clean.

"What a waste," said Jay.

The gallery was on the corner of two busy streets. It pays to have someone in the real estate game; location, location, location. Anthony's mom did quite well and had a knack for picking the next up and coming artist. Opaque glass separated the gallery from the street. They entered the gallery.

Inside, the stark white walls and modern halogen track lighting gave an unfettered back drop to the art work. Jay hung back while Anthony searched for his mom. Jay didn't want her to see him, but she was so focused on greeting the guests she wouldn't have noticed an elephant juggling tiki torches.

A black First Nations mask with bulging white, red rimmed eyes stared at Jay. The mouth, twisted into either song or scream, called to him. Long, straight black hair sparse and straggly, looking ragged and battle worn hung from the back of the mask.

Forgetting he was not supposed to be seen, Jay continued to take in the dark face. It was fierce, wicked, and a master of concealed identity. Jay wanted to be it. Feared and protected at the same time.

"Jay. Jay!" said Anthony but Jay didn't hear him. Finally Anthony tugged on Jay's sleeve and said "Let's go."

"I want to see the running shoe mask," said Jay.

"You are looking at it," said Anthony.

144

Jay's right eyebrow went up. He knew Anthony was smart but even Jay wasn't dumb enough to believe this. "No, this is an Indian mask," said Jay. "It's probably made of wood."

"I'm telling you it's made from running shoes," said Anthony.

Jay stepped closer to the mask and tried to pull the mask apart in his brain. The black, white and red running shoes had been unstitched and reassembled into a native ceremonial mask.

"I can't believe I didn't figure it out. That's amazing," said Jay.

A crowd of people gathered around the mask. Jay squeezed through just in time to see Anthony's mom coming towards them with a glass of champagne in each hand. She smiled at everyone making eye contact with each guest. Anthony pulled Jay behind a tall, gleaming white pedestal that supported another warrior like mask on a stick.

"Who made these?" whispered Jay.

"That guy," said Anthony. He pointed to a man surrounded by dazzling people, women in skinny high heels with their hair swept up to show off their sparkling earrings, men stuffed into suits and ties.

"He's young. And he looks like the people from the village," said Jay. The artist was from a northern First Nations village and beamed as people admired his work. He appeared slightly uncomfortable when their attention shifted directly to him. He did his best to steer the patrons toward the masks and away from himself.

"Why make masks from running shoes? Those are expensive. Why not just use clay or wood?" said Jay.

"Who knows why? It's art," was all Anthony could come up with. "We better go or we'll miss the movie."

145

Jay sat through the movie but didn't see it. His mind made its own movie, revisiting the confinement of the fridge, Mile's smug face, Courtney, Levi, the masks and the artist who made them. He wondered if Grampa knew about the masks.

After the movie Jay and Anthony walked home in the dark. The streets still buzzed with activity.

"Look, another art display," said Anthony. He pointed to a lone running shoe perched on top of a newspaper box. A soiled white canvas cross-trainer with the toe curled up and the lace tied in a double knot like the owner had been snatched in mid-step.

"I'm not really into art but those masks were cool," said Jay.

"Forget about the masks; I've got something for you," said Anthony. He unzipped his backpack.

"Check it out," he said, pulling out a can of spray paint, shaking it so the marble rattled inside. "You can redo your piece at the skate park."

"I haven't painted anything in ages. It's like my fingers are itchin'. I've spotted two dumpsters and a wall in my favorite alley that I'd love to tag," said Jay. "It's the perfect way to get back at everyone who sent me to that stupid village."

"Ok, let's go," urged Anthony.

"You have to do it, too," said Jay.

"Nah, I'm no good at that stuff," said Anthony.

"What's to be good at? You just hold the can up and press the nozzle. Spelling doesn't count. It's easy," said Jay.

"No freakin' way. I'll get caught and sent to juvy," said Anthony.

"But it's OK for me? Did you turn into a serious wuss or what?" said Jay.

"Well, I won't have someone to bail me out and send me for a few weeks in the country. I'll get serious time," said Anthony.

"Thanks a lot," said Jay. He felt like he'd swallowed a stone. The stone turned into a boulder when Jay looked up to see two police officers on bicycles heading their way.

Jay and Anthony turned to each other and said, "Copcycles!"

Anthony stuffed the spray can into his back pack. Without zipping it up the two boys ran across the street not stopping until they knew it was safe.

"That was so close," said Anthony in between panting and laughing.

"Yeah," said Jay with a straight face. "Maybe this isn't such a good idea, my being here."

"You can't go back. They will turn you into one of them," said Anthony. They walked to the McDonalds and ordered soft ice cream cones.

"No they won't. They all hate me. They call me "apple" and this goon named Miles wants to kick the tar out of me," said Jay. They licked the cones on the way back to Anthony's apartment.

"Kick the *tar* out of me?" repeated Anthony. "See, you are starting to talk like them already." He crunched the edge of the cone and tossed the bottom part onto the sidewalk. A group of pigeons swooped in to fight over it.

Anthony snuck Jay into his room. When Anthony's dad came home Jay slid along the hardwood floor and hid under the twin bed furthest from the door.

When the coast was clear Anthony asked Jay what the village was like. Jay told him about the raven, the totem poles and even repeated the stories his grandpa told him.

"A cannibal ogress, she must be related to you," said Anthony. "Do you have any other stories?"

"This isn't a story but it's kinda cool," Jay began. "Coastal Indians must find their 'totem animal'."

After Jay told Anthony about the different animals and their meanings Anthony had an epiphany.

"I bet my totem animal is the pigeon. They're everywhere I go plus I live on the roof of a high rise and I'll eat pretty much anything my mom throws at me," Anthony said as he checked off the things he had in common with pigeons.

"Yeah, maybe, and you like to crap on people," said Jay. He threw a pillow that looked like a baseball at Anthony's head. Anthony deflected it with his white athletic sock covered foot. Jay didn't ask but he was almost positive Anthony never wore the same pair of socks twice. The baseball pillow sailed through the air and crashed on top of the oak desk covered in baseball trophies, team pictures, fake metallic medals on red, white and blue ribbon and the class picture taken last year with Jay and Anthony in the back row.

"Ha ha. Got any more stories?" asked Anthony, leaving the mess on the desk.

"What am I? Mother Goose? Those are all I can remember. But I'll tell you about the potlatches they used to have," said Jay.

When Jay finished Anthony was very excited.

"Next time you have a potlatch I want to come, OK?" said Anthony

"They don't have them anymore," said Jay.

"Why not?" asked Anthony.

"Yeah really. Why not?" Jay asked himself out loud.

A knock came at the door. Jay dove under the bed.

Chapter 20

"Jay, I know you are in there," said Mr. Gardener. Jay heard the door open and saw a pair of brown leather slippers coming towards him.

'Oh my God. It's just like my dream', thought Jay.

"Jay, come on out. I'm driving you home," said Mr. Gardener.

"It's too far. Just put me on a bus or something," said Jay as he climbed out from under the bed, his hair in his eyes, dust bunnies stuck to his socks.

"No, your mom said not to trust you. She is going to meet us half way at The Dogwood Café. Do you know where that is?" he asked.

"Yes," said Jay. "Fine, take me to my death."

"Go to the washroom. It's going to be a long drive,' said Mr. Gardener.

Jay did as told then put on his shoes.

"Maybe it'll be 'rat day' at your school tomorrow," said Anthony, pressing the elevator button.

"No, if a rat showed up at my school we'd have to stop and honor its spirit," said Jay.

"I guess I'll see you around. Send me an email or something," said Anthony. "Here's your backpack."

"You gotta visit me next time," said Jay, entering the elevator. Mr. Gardener reached over and pressed the P1 button.

"Yeah, I'd like to find the cannibal ogress and feed Miles to her," said Anthony before the door closed.

Tatla was pacing the parking lot when the silver, luxury SUV pulled into The Dogwood Cafe. She barely had the where-with-all to thank Mr. Gardener for driving Jay an hour and half in the dark through the mountains. Her focus was getting Jay home.

"Do you know how worried I was about you? Why are you doing this to me?" asked Tatla.

"I didn't do this to you. Maybe you should have sent me to juvy," said Jay.

"Maybe I should have," said Tatla.

"I bet they're still open. Let's go check," said Jay.

Anything but go back to the village.

"Get in the car, Jay," said Tatla. She was in no mood to spar with Jay in front of Mr. Gardener.

"I think the boys just missed each other. We'll bring Anthony out for a visit when school ends," said Mr. Gardener trying to smooth things over.

"Or Anthony can visit Jay in jail instead because that seems to be where he is headed," said Tatla. "Thanks for driving all the way up here. I hope it wasn't too much of an inconvenience." She glared at Jay.

Step right up, folks. Get your ticket; we're going on a guilt trip, thought Jay.

Jay and Tatla argued for the next hour until both were fed up listening to each other. Tatla did most of the talking and Jay didn't want to hear it anymore. At one point, he considered opening the car door and rolling out, landing wherever. It didn't matter as long as it was quiet and he didn't have to listen to his mom rehash all the bad things he had done lately. Relief washed over him when they pulled into the driveway. The light in

151

Grampa's bedroom window was on but went dark as soon as Jay shut the car door.

Tatla woke Jay in the morning. Her eyes were red and she had dark circles under them. Jay thought she looked ten years older.

"I'm not feeling well, Mom," said Jay. He pulled the blankets up under his chin and curled into a ball.

"Too bad, neither am I. I didn't sleep a wink, in case you decided to sneak out again. Honestly Jay, do you want to go to the youth detention center?" she asked.

Jay shook his head 'no' but wondered if he'd be safer there or if youth detention was filled with boys like Miles.

"Then get up for school. I'm driving you today. You can't miss one class. Remember what Mrs. Thornton said."

"Jay had better be in a coma with two broken legs before I get a call he's missed school." Jay mimicked her nasally voice.

Tatla informed Jay she was going to the city on business. She'd return tomorrow unless she careened off the road from exhaustion. Jay rolled his eyes at her exaggeration.

"You nearly gave me a nervous breakdown," said Tatla on the way to school.

"I'm sorry. You don't understand how much I hate it here or how much I hate being cooped up all the time. I guess it was just 'bored dumb'," said Jay.

"I had hoped you'd try to see the good things around here," said Tatla.

"There aren't any good things around here. Isn't that why you left? Isn't that why everyone is leaving?" countered Jay.

"I don't have all the answers, Jay. You have to be here whether you or I like it, so stay put until I get back. Keep an eye on

152

Grampa, too. He had chest pains when we couldn't find you last night," said Tatla.

It never occurred to Jay how much Grampa would worry.

Tatla dropped Jay off in front of the school. The school yard was empty. She didn't leave until the main door closed behind him.

Jay dragged himself from class to class. He didn't get much sleep either and his nerves were frayed. His fingernails were a mess of exposed nail beds surrounded by freshly scabbed over cuticles. The ring finger was singled out for attention. Jay gnawed, picked and pulled at the skin around the nail until the blood and throbbing made him stop. It was the longest and shortest day of his life. He wanted the day to end but dreaded hearing the final bell.

Miles bumped Jay against a locker a few times in the hall while changing classrooms. Miles always had a smart remark like, "Have you made out your will yet?" or "Apples keep better in the fridge." The adrenaline pumped through Jay sending him to the bathroom with nausea.

Jay and Jackson ate lunch together ignoring the stares and whispers. Jackson shared his lunch with Jay as lunch was the last thing on Jay's mind when he left for school. Miles and his buddies stopped by and dropped apple cores on Jay. The cores landed on his head, his lap and the half sandwich he didn't have the stomach to eat.

"Why do you hang out with me, Jackson?" asked Jay, shaking off the apple cores onto the ground. The crows on the rooftop screeched at the sight of food on the ground.

"To see what will happen next," said Jackson. He didn't have to wait long.

The third period bell rang marking the end of lunch time. Jay and Jackson rose from the picnic table and walked across the asphalt in the under cover area toward the rear door. Jay felt the mob of kids move away from him. He turned in time to see Miles with his lacrosse stick raised. He cocked the stick back and lunged forward shooting an object at Jay's head. It wasn't until Jay ducked and the object smashed against the wall that he realized it was an apple. Juice and apple chunks ricocheted onto Jay. It stuck to his hair, his clothes and his friend.

Jay pushed through the mob trying to get at Miles.

"There, now, you smell like an apple, too," yelled Miles, over the top of his buddies, laughing as he entered the school.

When the final bell rang Jay leaped in his seat but was the last one to leave the classroom. He took his time organizing his papers in his binder. He was too tired and too rushed to remember his back pack that morning.

Jackson waited for him in the hallway.

"I've gotta get out of this, Jackson. The whole school knows; maybe home-school for the last couple of days? What do you think? Do you think my mom would go for it?" Jay spewed out the words.

"Sorry, buddy. You can't hide in this town. He'd just come to your house," said Jackson.

"I might as well get it over with, and then he'll leave me alone," said Jay, taking a deep breath.

"Doubt it," said Jackson. They walked down the deserted hallway toward the windowless double exit doors.

"Wait here, I have an idea," said Jay. He hurried back to his locker and grabbed something from his art supplies box and then caught up with Jackson.

Jay pushed down on the metal bar to open the exit door. He spotted Miles where the smokers hang out, referred to as 'the smoke pit'. Most of the school had already congregated.

"What did you get?" asked Jackson.

Jay pulled something from his pocket and showed it to Jackson.

"What are you going to do with that?" asked Jackson.

"I am not sure. It probably won't work but I can't think of anything else." Jay's stomach tied itself into a mess of knots.

Chapter 21

Jay popped the lid off the bottle and kept it hidden in his palm.

On the way across the gravel field he spotted Courtney.

"I didn't think I'd see you today," she said.

"Yeah, me neither. Do you mind if I borrow a couple of cigarettes?" said Jay.

"You don't smoke," she said but handed him two cigarettes anyway. It's hard to refuse the walking dead.

"I need to calm my nerves," said Jay. "Can I borrow your lighter, too?"

"Sure thing," said Courtney. She tossed him the yellow Bic that appeared from inside her overstuffed purse. A dozen or so key chains of fuzzy, cartoon characters hung from the straps.

Jay put the cigarettes in his other hand and walked backward, head down, so only Jackson could see what he was doing.

"What's he doing?" asked one of the boys.

"Saying his prayers," said Miles. Everyone laughed.

Jay turned again and continued toward Miles. The sweat ran down Jay's forehead. He wondered if the cigarette in his hand was getting soaked.

"You look hot. Maybe some time in the refrigerator will cool you off. Ready to be turned into apple sauce, city boy?" said Miles. The boys from Sadie's snickered.

"You mind if I have a smoke first?" said Jay. His heart beat so loud he could hear the blood pounding in his ears.

"Go ahead, you don't have worry about cancer 'cause I'm gonna kill you first," jeered Miles.

An "ooooooohhhhhhh" came up from the crowd.

"You want one?" said Jay holding out the cigarette in his trembling hand.

"Nah, I just had one," said Miles.

"Come on, don't be rude. It may be my last one," said Jay.

"Ok, gimme one," said Miles.

Jay handed Miles the short white tube and flicked the lighter. Miles placed the cigarette in his mouth and leaned in for a light, keeping one eye on Jay.

If this doesn't work I'm a dead man, thought Jay.

Miles puckered his lips and drew in the smoke. The embers crept up the white paper tube. His first two fingers scissored the butt end but as he pulled on the cigarette, it stuck to his lips. Miles pulled harder. His lips stretched out and back with each tug.

"i's stuck!" Miles coughed and sputtered. "Geh i' off! Geh i' off!" begged Miles as smoke burned his nostrils and reddened his eyes.

"I will if you promise not to beat me up," said Jay.

"No frickin' 'ay," said Miles, bent over in a coughing fit. His feet stepped up and down on the spot like a four year old trying to hold it in.

"Ok," said Jay. Miles continued to gag on the smoke.

"OK, OK. I won' 'utch you," said Miles. Tears ran down his face.

"And you'll stop picking on everyone else?" said Jay.

157

"Yeth, yeth, huweey up," pleaded Miles.

Jay grabbed the middle of the cigarette and snapped it in half. Sprinkles of tobacco fell to the ground leaving Miles with just the butt stuck to his lips.

Miles inhaled deeply through his nostrils.

Jay threw the burning cherry down and squashed it under his sneakers. *It worked. I'm not dead.* Jay breathed a sigh of relief. The tension in his body disappeared.

The crowd cheered.

"Right on! Awesome! I can't believe Miles fell for that. What an idiot," said one of the kids.

"Why didn't I think of that?" said Levi to Courtney when Jay returned her lighter.

"Some vinegar will get the rest off," Jay told Miles. "Can we agree to stay away from each other?"

Miles sucked back some drool forming at the corners of his mouth.

"I'll take that as a 'yes'," said Jay.

A few kids followed him home and said, "It was about time."

Jay took the tube of super glue out of his pocket and almost kissed it. Almost.

Chapter 22

"Hi, Jay how was your trip?" said Grampa. Jay climbed the steps to the porch and collapsed in the wicker chair beside Grampa. Dillon and Jody lay at his feet. They banged their tails on the porch in rhythm with Jay's steps.

"Alright, I guess," said Jay, grinning from ear to ear. He scratched Dillon behind the ears and rubbed Jody's belly. Jody stretched to her full length enjoying every minute of it. She was shameless.

"How come you are so happy? You look like the eagle that caught the whale," said Grampa.

"I had a good day at school," said Jay. Dillon nudged Jay's hand when he stopped petting him.

"I'm glad you're back," said Grampa.

"I didn't have much choice," said Jay.

"You always have a choice," said Grampa.

"Are you going to lecture me or tell me one of your stories, like how the skunk ran away so they put on a hex on his tail for causing such a stink," said Jay.

"Not a bad story, but no, I thought the Cannibal Ogress would have been enough," said Grampa.

"Maybe if I was five years old," said Jay.

"No lectures; just don't make me worry about you like that again. I thought those days were over. I have something else for you to do," said Grampa.

"What now, Grampa? This is the last week of school and then I just want to do nothing," said Jay.

"It will count for your community service and could take two months to finish so you'd have to give up most of your summer," said Grampa.

"Sounds great. I can't wait. What is it?" said Jay in a monotone.

"I'll tell you when your mother comes back from her business trip, tomorrow. She had to leave this morning after she dropped you off at school," said Grampa.

"I know. She told me. So what now, do I have to clean up Johnny Walker's yard next? The place is like a permanent garage sale is happening," said Jay.

"It has to do with the project I have been working on with the elders," said Grampa. He rose from the creaking chair and headed toward the garage.

Jay followed him. "Have you seen the raven around?"

"No, he's probably just lying low," said Grampa.

"What project? Just tell me. You are going to punish me for taking off last night, right? It is something so cruel and unusual it will take days to plan," said Jay.

"Cruel - sometimes. Unusual - definitely," said Grampa, strolling around the garage and checking the paint. Dillon and Jody followed as if they too were inspecting the paint. "And it took more than a few months to plan."

"A few months?" Jay was really curious now.

"You and Jackson did a wonderful job on the garage. You have a good work ethic," said Grampa.

"I think it's boring, but it does look better than before," said Jay.

"It's plain but nice," said Grampa. He reached into his back pocket for his wallet. It was a hand-made, tan leather two fold with an embroidered wolf head.

160

He pulled out five, twenty dollar bills and handed them to Jay. "Make sure Jackson gets his cut," said Grampa.

"Nice wallet," said Jay. "Where can I get one?"

"They don't make them like this anymore. The lady who made this passed away about ten years ago and took her skills with her," said Grampa, blinking quickly.

"What's up, Grampa?" asked Jay. He realized he liked spending time with his Grampa. He was a no nonsense guy. Grampa was unlike anyone Jay had ever met. Jay knew he'd miss his Grampa when he returned to the city.

"It's the mill. More layoffs are coming. Mary Joe and her family will have to leave by the end of summer. They've been on this land for at least ten generations," said Grampa. "Let's hope the fishing is good this year."

"Yes," said Jay, thinking about Jackson and his dad.

"Can you do a favor for me and run that box of odds and ends down to Gordon's?" asked Grampa. "I cleaned out my kitchen cupboards last night because I had a hard time falling asleep." Jay got the message.

"Sure Grampa. I'll see you at dinner. Thanks for the money," said Jay.

"Don't go spending it on bus fare, eh," said Grampa. Dillon and Jody bowed to Grampa. He pulled out a plastic bag and threw a couple of treats to them. Jay heard the snap of their jaws as they snatched the treats from the air. The dogs bowed again. Grampa threw a couple more treats to them. The dogs bowed once more.

"No, no that's enough," said Grampa. "These dogs have got me trained, I swear. Here you want one?"

"No, I'll pass on the dog treats," said Jay.

"Not dog treats. It's dried salmon. Jackson's dad brought some over. He's trying to figure out what the elders and I are up to so he's taken to bribing me with Indian candy. This one is teriyaki. Try some," said Grampa. He held out the baggie and Jay grabbed one. It looked like beef jerky. The dogs were drooling and bowing like crazy.

Jay ripped a strip off and let it melt in his mouth. It was smoky and tangy and delicious.

The dogs barked at him and bowed again. Jay threw them each a piece.

"Now, they've got you trained too," said Grampa. He smiled and his eyes crinkled. "Hurry back from Gordon's in case Mrs. Thornton comes around."

Jay grabbed the cardboard box sitting outside Grampa's back door crammed with a chrome toaster from the 1950s, a green metal coffee pot, mix-matched drinking glasses, some with faded gas station logos on them, and a couple of dented aluminum cooking pots.

More junk, thought Jay as he lugged the clinkering contents to Johnny Walker's carport. Johnny was nowhere to be seen. Jay dropped the box at the side door between the house and the carport. He wandered around checking out all the stuff. *Everything but the kitchen sink,* thought Jay. It turned out everything was there including two kitchen sinks; stainless steel and stained porcelain.

The sound of snoring broke the silence.

Jay peered over the back of a ripped couch and found Johnny Walker asleep. A cigarette smoldered in an ashtray, heaped with cigarette butts, on a white plastic patio table.

Jay poked Johnny until he sprang up, startling both of them.

"Jay, buddy, how was your walk?" said Johnny, rubbing his chin and reaching for his smokes.

"It was OK. I brought over some stuff for you from Grampa," said Jay.

"Oh yeah, let's see," said Johnny. He put the cigarette in his mouth and lit the end with the smoldering cigarette.

"It's there by the side door," said Jay.

"Man, this is great," said Johnny, genuinely excited. He pulled out the items and scattered them on the sidewalk. He did not return them to the box but just left them where they lay.

Jay shook his head. "I really don't get why you stay here."

"I gotta be here in case my family comes home," said Johnny.

"Why do you keep all this junk?" asked Jay.

"Some of it I sell to Stan the Scrapman, some of it I fix and resell, like your Grampa's washer. If I can get it working I know an antique shop that will buy it," said Johnny.

"I thought you were an artist. Why don't you do that?" asked Jay.

"Too much pressure, too much traveling from show to show, too many people wanting a piece of me. I was good, ya know. Come and see," said Johnny.

Johnny led Jay into the house. It smelled like a saloon that served bowls of puke to wet dogs who were chain smokers. Jay left the door open.

"It's here somewhere," said Johnny. He heaped newspapers, pizza boxes and beer cans off the couch and onto a chair that matched the couch in the garage. "Here it is."

Johnny handed Jay a scrapbook. The cover was ripped at the seam and dangled as Jay leafed through the pages. Newspaper articles of Johnny standing with official looking people in clean cut suits shaking hands.

"See that sculpture in the background? I made that," said Johnny. It was a forest of cedars with a huge moon rising behind it, made entirely of metal and stood as tall as Johnny.

163

"It's really good," said Jay.

"I've artwork all over the world in fancy shmancy hotels and govment offices. Places that wouldn't even let me in the front door right now, eh," said Johnny poking his tongue through the hole left by a missing tooth.

Jay wondered why Johnny was wasting his time and talent in this hole.

"Too many people wanted my stuff and I couldn't handle it. Drank the wife and kids right out of my life. But one day they'll be back and I'll be here waitin'," said Johnny.

"You might want to clean up before they get here," said Jay, scanning the room.

Jay, Grampa and Jackson had bachelor night dinner; frozen pizza washed down with Pepsi and Cap'n Crunch cereal for dessert. Jay even asked Johnny Walker if he wanted to come. Johnny just grumbled something, fired up his torch and attacked an old ride'em lawnmower. After dinner Grampa had a meeting with the elders leaving Jay and Jackson in the house.

"Don't stay up too late," said Grampa, on his way out.

"I'm really tired. I'll probably be asleep before you get back," said Jay.

Jackson was ecstatic to get the money for painting the garage. It was more money than he'd ever had in his life. Jay decided to split it with him fifty-fifty even though he'd have to wait longer for his iPod.

"My dad said I'd make a ton of money fishing. If you come too we could buy anything we wanted," said Jackson.

"I've almost got enough for an iPod," said Jay. "If I didn't pay my mom back for the raven's vet bill I could have bought it by now."

This was the first year Jackson was old enough to go on the annual salmon catch. Jackson told Jay his family had fished the waters here for hundreds of years.

"Wow, they must be tired," Jay joked.

"Seriously, you're really lucky to know so much about your family. I have no idea where my dad is except that he's in northern Ontario and doesn't give a crap about me," said Jay.

"I'll bet he does, too. I bet he was just a scared kid. Lots of the guys around here have left after knocking up some girl," said Jackson.

"That girl was my mom," said Jay. "This is too weird to talk about." He picked up the remote and flicked through the channels.

"You know that girl Skye? She knows who the father of her baby is but won't say because she knows he'll leave. I can't believe how many people are moving," said Jackson.

"I wish I was one of them. This place really sucks," said Jay.

"It's not the big city but it's still my home. I don't want it to disappear," said Jackson. Tears welled up in his eyes.

"Sorry, dude, but a bull dozer is the best thing that could happen to this place," said Jay. He settled on a reality show about car accidents and high speed chases.

Jackson shrugged.

"If you all care about this place so much why don't you do something to fix it up?" said Jay. "I have seen less car scraps at a junk yard."

"That's how it's always been. Why should we have to change? Why are we the ones who always have to change?" said Jackson, his cheeks turning crimson.

"Whatever. If you don't do something then it will disappear," said Jay, stuffing a handful of dry cereal into his mouth.

"Like what? What are we supposed to do?" asked Jackson. His face was red and he was sweating.

"I don't know. It's not my problem," said Jay.

"What about your grandfather? It's your family's village, too," said Jackson. He pushed himself off the couch and stormed out.

Jay went to his room, crawled under the sheet, and dozed off. When he awoke, the red alarm clock numbers glared at him: one a.m. Jay tossed and turned until two, arguing with an invisible Jackson.

"What's your problem? It's not my fault everyone is leaving. My dad left and you don't see me all curled up in a ball complaining. Deal with it. Move on to something else. My family's village, too? I don't think so," said Jay aloud.

He kicked the sheet off in a rage. His backpack fell to the floor. A familiar sound rattled in the pockets. Anthony had left him a little present; the cans of spray paint from the other night. Jay rolled "wild poppy red" in his hands. The coolness of the metal felt good.

Out of the corner of his eye Jay thought he saw something. He snapped his head around but saw only the shadow of the curtain. *Was that my guardian spirit?* Jay shuddered. *There's no way I can sleep now. Maybe I'll go to Miles' house and leave him a message*, thought Jay. He admired the symbol warning of explosive contents, like black rays of sunshine.

He grabbed the other cans and headed outside into the cool night. The moon watched from behind a grove of cedars.

Chapter 23

"Jay! Jay! Wake up!" Tatla yelled. The table lamp shook as she marched across the bedroom floor.

Cans of spray paint were scattered on the floor. Jay lay sprawled on top of his covers, fully dressed. His shoes, still on his feet, dangled off the side of the bed. Black and red paint covered his fingers.

"Hi Mom, you're back early," said Jay.

The blinds screeched open as Tatla tugged on the cord like a sailor in the America's Cup race.

Jay rolled over and shielded the light with his forearm.

"Don't 'Hi Mom' me. What have you been doing? I thought I could leave you here for one night. Unbelievable," she huffed. "Do you know who is here for a surprise visit?"

"The tooth fairy," said Jay.

"Mrs. Thornton is downstairs waiting to talk to you. She must have found out about your trip to the city, and now this." Tatla picked up an empty can of spray paint and waved it at Jay.

"How am I going to keep this from her?" whispered Tatla when she realized Mrs. Thornton was probably eavesdropping.

"And wait 'til I tell your Grampa. Where is he? Why is he letting you out in the middle of the night to do who knows what?" said Tatla. She scrambled around the room picking up clothes and damp towels.

"No, wait Mom. Hold on." He tried but he couldn't get a word in edge wise. She was not in listening mode. She was in yelling slash cleaning mode.

Jay got up and left the bedroom.

"Come back here. I'm not even close to being done with you," said Tatla through gritted teeth.

Jay didn't stop. He knew she wasn't going to hear anything he said anyway. He bounded down the stairs three at a time and jumped the last four, crashing into Mrs. Thornton.

"Hi, Mrs. Thornton," said Jay. He steadied her as she wobbled, then continued out the front door.

"Jay! Jay, I have to do an assessment on your progress. Some things have been brought to my attention that I need to discuss with you," said Mrs. Thornton doing her best to keep up with Jay. Her ankle buckled as she crossed the gravel driveway in her cream colored dress shoes, a perfect match to her skirt and jacket.

Dillon and Jody trotted over to see who the stranger was. Mrs. Thornton clutched her purse as if they were going to rob her. They followed closely and sniffed her. Jody put her cold nose on Mrs. Thornton's leg. She jumped and swatted at the black dog.

Tatla cut across the yard and yelled, "Jay, come back here and talk to Mrs. Thornton!"

"Dillon! Jody! Leave Mrs. Thornton alone." The dogs turned to face Tatla causing their tails to thrash against Mrs. Thornton's legs. She yelped and put her hand down to protect her exposed knees.

"What's all the shouting about?" asked Grampa. He watched his daughter hound his grandson across the parched front lawn. He watched the hounds harass Mrs. Thornton.

"You were supposed to be watching him," said Tatla when Grampa fell in step beside her. "Now Mrs. Thornton is here and she's going to take him away," whispered Tatla, sounding desperate.

"Mom's got this crazy idea. Come on, Grampa," said Jay.

Dillon and Jody sandwiched Grampa between them, nudging his pockets. Grampa removed his hands from his pockets to show them there weren't any treats.

As they rounded the corner of the house the three adults stopped in their tracks.

The entire front of the garage was sprayed black and red.

A two story tall painted raven stared down at them. Its beak, outlined in thick black, curved downward into a sneaky smile. The intense eyes, black rimmed with red pupils, warned trespassers to enter at the risk of their very souls. The double doors were dark, folded wings to block passage of uninvited guests.

"Wait here," said Jay as he ran through the side door of the garage leaving Grampa and Tatla to decide if they were ever going to close their mouths. Having never seen the garage Mrs. Thornton wondered what the fuss was about. Dillon and Jody sat. Their tails swept leaves and dirt side to side like a pair of windshield wipers.

The double doors creaked open showing the newly painted inside of the doors. At each step the wings of the raven spread wide and majestic, as if taking flight.

Jay stood under the raven mural. No one said a word.

"It took me almost six hours," said Jay, after a moment.

"Jay, it's wonderful," said his mom.

"Six hours, you said?" asked Grampa. "I'm not paying for that," he winked at Jay.

Jay's mom dabbed her eyes.

"Do you still want me to clean it off?" asked Jay.

"No, don't you dare," laughed Jay's mom and hugged him 'til he gasped for breath.

CAW! CAW! CAW!

Jay looked over at the fence. The big, black crow was back.

"I think I found my 'totem animal'," said Jay to Grampa.

Grampa grinned and shook his head. "You are a trickster, a prankster and a transformer."

"I think I've seen all I need to. You are obviously keeping Jay busy and he is learning about his culture. I will recommend to the board that his probation end," said Mrs. Thornton. Dillon bowed to her.

Jay hugged her and Mrs. Thornton managed to squeeze out a smile from her shiny, pinchy face.

"We can go back to the city now, Mom," said Jay. "Isn't that great, Grampa?"

"Great," said Grampa and walked back to his house.

Chapter 24

"Last day of school. Last day of school. Don't be no fool. Don't be so cool. Last day of school," sang Jay in the shower to no particular tune. Jay was euphoric. No more school for two months and they could move back to the city anytime they wanted.

"Jackson is here," called Tatla from the bottom of the stairs. Even though Jay and Jackson walked to school together everyday, Jay wasn't sure if Jackson would show up today.

"I'll be right down," said Jay.

"Hey, Jackson, I'm off probation. I don't have to stay in the yard anymore like a dog. As soon as school is done I'm moving back to the city," said Jay.

"Good for you," said Jackson. He didn't sound thrilled.

"Why is everyone so down?" said Jay. "Come and see what I did to Grampa's garage."

Jay showed Jackson the mural and how the doors spread open the wings.

"That is so cool," said Jackson.

"I know, cooler than the seats in Kelly's 442," said Jay. "Sorry about what I said last night. I had no right to," said Jay.

"No, you're right. This place doesn't have much but I know something it has that the city doesn't," said Jackson.

"What's that? A high percentage of teen drop outs?" said Jay.

"No, we have a lake. As soon as the water warms up we can go swimming. If your grandfather lends us his canoe I can show you the pictographs," said Jackson.

"What are pictographs?" said Jay.

"They are writings from thousands of years ago, left by my ancestors," said Jackson.

"My tags didn't even last a month," said Jay and yawned. He was tired but happy. The sun was shining, the birds were singing and May-Belle handed the boys fresh made bannock, this time with strawberry jam. They managed to eat it in peace without Dillon and Jody bugging them.

"Class, it's time for your assignments on coastal Indians," said Mrs. Scott, the social studies teacher.

One by one, the students made their presentations. Most of the kids talked about the bad things affecting the village; unemployment, fetal alcohol syndrome, poor graduation rates, diabetes and drug abuse. Jay thought he had done the whole thing wrong.

Jay gripped his papers, picked up a small cardboard box, and faced the class.

"Hi," he said. Thirty students gawked at him. A sea of black hair, brown eyes and tanned skin. Not at all like his old school where every nationality seemed to be represented.

"I grew up in the city so I don't know much about living in a First Nations village.

My mom grew up here and so did my grandparents and great grandparents. I've been talking to my grandfather a lot lately about what it means to be a coastal Indian today. He told me, to understand who the coastal Indians are today we need to know who they were in the beginning.

Coastal Indians have been on this land for centuries. They were great survivors. By hunting, fishing, and gathering berries there was always lots of food. By respecting the animals, taking only what they needed and wasting nothing there was always plenty of meat. By using trees to make longhouses for shelter, and bark to make baskets, mats and clothing they always had a roof over their heads and clothes on their backs. They also had time for honing their skills as artists."

Jay held up one of the tools from the garage.

"This is an adze. It was used to carve totem poles. The totem poles were made from the old growth trees in the forest; some were over 700 years old. The tribes-people used fire to slowly burn away the bottom of the tree until they could chop it down with hand made tools of stone and wood. It took months or years to carve the totem pole but they were not afraid of the work or the time and effort to make it. While the craftsmen carved the totem pole the entire village prepared for the potlatch. This was a huge celebration with food, dancing and giving of gifts. Other tribes and special guests were also invited."

Jay held up the picture of the potlatch.

"Kids didn't have school but they were taught many things by their elders. Things like carving, painting, hunting, fishing, and making blankets. Some of the current artists today can sell their masks and blankets for thousands of dollars."

The class perked up at this bit of news.

"The elders also told them stories, like how Raven brought the light to the world, how the first beavers and otters were created and why there are so many mosquitoes. I believe being a coastal Indian today means getting in touch with the past. Coastal Indians can again be proud artists, story tellers, and good family providers. And, let's not forget they knew how to throw a great party."

As Jay headed back to his seat the whole class applauded. No one else got applause. Even Miles yelled out, "Party!"

Afterward some of the kids stuck around to look at the faded picture of the potlatch and to examine the carver's tools.

"These are awesome," Jay heard over and over.

"You guys probably have stuff like this in your attics or basements, too," said Jay.

"Want to come to my house and help me look?" said Courtney. "Kelly and I aren't seeing each other anymore."

"I can't. I have to help my Grampa with something," explained Jay as he felt his cheeks burn. Today was the day Grampa promised to tell him what the next project would be. Jay was curious even though he knew he'd be leaving soon.

"So what's the secret project?" asked Jay. He had discarded his back pack on the porch, thankful to be rid of it for the summer.

"Look in the garage," said Grampa. "I had them bring it while you were at school. No easy feat."

Jay ran towards the garage, thoughts of cars, boats and motorcycles flashed in his brain. He flung the door open and flicked on the lights. The fluorescent tubes struggled to life, illuminating the cavernous room.

"Grampa, it's a telephone pole. Why'd you get a telephone pole?" asked Jay.

"It's not a telephone pole. It's going to be a totem pole. After meeting with the elders, we decided on a design to honor our people. I want you to help me carve it," said Grampa, his eyes sparkled.

"Really, Grampa? But we're supposed to move back to the city after I go fishing with Jackson," said Jay.

"I thought we could carve it together. I could show you how to carve a totem pole like our ancestors did. You could teach your children and keep up our traditions," said Grampa, hope shining in his fierce brown eyes.

"I'm not having kids," said Jay. He felt a stab of regret when Grampa hung his head.

"This isn't going to save the village," mumbled Jay.

174

"Maybe not. Some of the elders are against it. Said it is a waste of time and money but maybe it will save my family," said Grampa. "You think about it, eh," said Grampa leaving Jay alone in the garage with the cedar log.

Chapter 25

"You ready to go to the lake? Did your grandfather say we could use his canoe?" asked Jackson.

"Yes, it's around the side," said Jay.

"What's this?" asked Jackson, looking inside the garage.

"It's a log, what does it look like?" said Jay.

"What's it for?" asked Jackson. He went inside the garage and ran his fingers across the rough sewn rings. The wood was fresh and slightly damp.

"Grampa wants me to carve it into a totem pole," said Jay.

"Right now?" asked Jackson.

"No, of course not, it'll take all summer," said Jay.

"Is this the secret project?" asked Jackson. "Wait until I tell my dad. He's been bugging grandmother to tell him but she wouldn't. Hey, what about fishing this summer?" asked Jackson.

"I don't know. Let's get the canoe," said Jay. He hadn't made up his mind yet. He mulled it over and over; a whole summer working on a totem pole. The village already had three of them. What difference would one more make?

Jackson and Jay lifted the green fiber-glass canoe from the side of Grampa's house. Jay had seen it there while they were painting and figured it was more junk. He didn't realize anyone actually used it.

They lugged the canoe into the trail past the totem poles. Jay looked at a fifty foot cedar nearby and then back at the totem poles. *How did it get from a tree to a totem pole,* he wondered.

176

When they reached the end of the trail Jackson turned left and led the way up to a skinnier less defined path. It was a steep climb over loose dirt, slippery muddy sections and tree roots. Woodpeckers knocked, chicades peeped and two ravens called back and forth across the forest ceiling. A silver squirrel ran up a tree and then leaped to the next tree, risking a sixty foot drop. Otherwise the boys had the woods to themselves to smell the scent of cedar and pine needles made stronger by the warmth of the day. So strong the aroma seemed man made.

"Hey, did you bring the paddles?" asked Jackson when they were about half way there.

"Paddles? What paddles?" asked Jay.

The boys dropped the canoe. The sound of fiber-glass slamming the ground echoed through the forest, disturbing the birds. Exhausted and frustrated, Jay climbed inside to sit on the molded plastic bench seat, Jackson did the same. They sat in disbelief listening to the symphony of birds scolding them for the disruption. From the corner of his eye Jay saw trees and rocks pass by at a slow pace. He realized they were moving. As the canoe inched forward the boys reached out to get a hold of something. Jay's finger tips brushed a fern. He stretched to grasp a tree root exposed by run off after many rainy days, but he couldn't get a grip.

Jay and Jackson hollered as the canoe gathered speed. Rocks and tree roots battered and bumped the boat as it careened down the path. Jackson ducked down and waited for the ride to end. Jay hung over the side flailing his arms. Branches scratched his hands and whipped his face. The trail turned sharply not fifty feet away. Jay leaped from the canoe. He rolled onto his side banging his elbow on a jagged chunk of granite before stopping face down in a carpet of moss. When he looked up, the canoe was airborne; sailing like it had never sailed before. It sliced through the salmon berry bushes and wedged itself between two giant cedars with a thunk.

Jay ran down the trail, sliding on loose dirt and looked inside. Jackson, who started at the back of the canoe, had slid fifteen feet to the front. He stared, bug-eyed at Jay as if to ask "Am I alive? Is it over? Can I move now?"

After letting out a deep breath, Jackson and Jay started laughing and couldn't stop.

"Whew, that was some ride," said Jackson, his breath ragged.

"Yeah," said Jay. "Let's go again." His heart beat faster than normal from the rush of adrenaline.

"Get in. I'll give you a push," said Jackson.

"Maybe next time," said Jay.

They dislodged the canoe and headed home.

"Thanks for bailing on me," said Jackson.

"What are friends for?" said Jay. "You want to come over for dinner?"

"No, my cousin, Emily, is visiting from the city," said Jackson. "I hope she doesn't want to French braid my hair and put make-up on me again."

"Sure you do," teased Jay.

They returned the canoe to the side of the garage.

"See ya'," said Jackson. "Next time remember the paddles."

"Next time - tell me," said Jay.

Chapter 26

Jay walked past the giant log lying like a body in an open casket. He entered the garage. The fresh cedar aroma filled his lungs. He stepped to the side of the log and wrapped his arms around the circumference; barely half of the way round. He continued to circle the log. At one end Jay grasped the sides like a boat captain at the helm and stood looking down the length of the mighty log.

He pressed the heel of his hand against the rippled wood then let go and viewed the dimples it left on his skin. Sap wept from between the rings, stopping mid stream. Jay poked at a drop. It had a hard sugary crust and a soft gooey center. The cedar tar oozed onto Jay's finger. He rolled it around on his thumb and forefinger hoping to flick it off but it spread like honey.

He struggled to pull his finger and thumb apart making strands of sappy angel hair. It reminded him of kindergarten and the amber glue that came in the clear bottle with the red rubber cap. Scraping his finger then thumb across the rough bark was the only way to remove the sticky substance. A trace still remained. Jay put his finger up to his nose and inhaled.

That's probably about the best thing I've ever smelled, thought Jay.

"So how do we carve a totem pole, Grampa?" asked Jay during dinner. Grampa's eyes lit up and then turned serious.

"You're sure you want to spend your whole summer cooped up in the garage?" asked Grampa.

"I didn't spend hours cleaning it up for nothing," said Jay. "I figured I'd see what summer is like here and then go back to the city when school starts. Anyway Mom said we are on a couple of waiting lists for apartments."

"What about Anthony? I thought you two were going to hang out this summer," asked Grampa.

"I doubt he'd want to carve a totem pole, plus he's going to Europe with his mom on some art expedition. So how do you carve a totem pole?" Jay was growing impatient.

"First we peel off the bark, then we cut the general shape and then we carve the wood," exclaimed Grampa, waving his hands in the air to show how it's done.

"Oh is that all," said Jay. "Sounds easy enough. What's it going to look like?"

"You'll see. I've got it all up here," said Grampa, tapping his temple with his index finger.

After dinner Jay and Grampa went to the garage. The log was propped up at both ends by wooden saw horses plus one in the middle to prevent sagging. The saw horses looked too skinny to support the future totem pole. It swayed slightly when Jay rocked the log.

Grampa bent over one end of the log. He touched the wood, his lips moving slightly.

"What are you…" Jay tried to ask but was cut off.

"Shhh," said Grampa.

"…doing?" finished Jay.

Grampa stayed focused.

After a few minutes he stood up and announced, "Three hundred."

"Three hundred what?" asked Jay.

"Three hundred years old," said Grampa.

"Did the tree tell you?" asked Jay.

"No, I counted the rings. Trees get a ring every year," said Grampa.

Jay whistled. "Whoa, a ring every year. That's a lot of bling."

"Not that kind of ring. See here, the rings start off small in the middle and get bigger towards the outside, like rippling water. The fat rings were good years for growth," said Grampa.

"And there are three hundred? You cut down a three hundred year old tree to make a totem pole. That doesn't seem right," said Jay.

"It is not a sad thing, Jay. This tree is fulfilling its destiny. I didn't find the tree, the tree found me. I roamed the forest and when I came upon this tree I heard the call of Raven, the howl of Wolf and the scream of Eagle."

Jay looked skeptical.

"When we felled the tree, the seeds were returned to the earth to become a new part of the forest. The branches will feed the existing plants and seedlings for the next generation of trees. We are grateful to the cedar and honour it by carving a totem pole that will be the rebirth of the tree and maybe the rebirth of our family."

Jay didn't want to disappoint his Grampa but he just couldn't imagine living here forever.

"That's a pretty tall order," sighed Jay.

"Eighteen feet tall," said Grampa.

"Where do we start?" asked Jay.

"First we peel away the bark. Take the chisel; place it under the bark and push," said Grampa.

Jay grabbed the wooden handle. He placed the metal blade on the bark and pushed. It didn't move. Jay pushed harder, wiggling the tool until it slipped off the log. He lunged forward almost falling on his face.

"Here, let me show you. First always use two hands. Get behind the tree, find the place between the bark and the dark red ring, put your weight into it and push."

As he did, the bark split and lifted upwards revealing moist strands the color of strong tea before it's muddied by milk. Grampa broke the piece off. "Sounds like my knees cracking first thing in the morning."

"The bark is like a layer of armor, protecting the secrets and dreams of the tree. Once it is removed we can see the grain of the wood. The inner beauty of what makes the wood unique. It is no longer hidden behind a crusty exterior," said Grampa.

"Like you were when I first got here?" said Jay.

"Me? Well, you had a chip on your shoulder, remember?" countered Grampa.

Jay shoved the chisel under the bark then pulled up on the handle, using it as a pry. Once he got it started the pieces came off in larger and larger chunks. Ribbons of red cedar clung from the log to the bark like the string left behind when peeling a banana. Jay hung on to a chunk of bark with both hands and yanked the ribbon away from the log. After an hour of bark peeling Jay's hands were already sore.

"Hey, Grandpa, how many blisters you got?" asked Jay.

He held his hands out, palm side up to show the blisters and splinters.

"What am I thinking? Sorry Jay, it's been a while since I worked with wood like this. I'll get some gloves," said Grampa.

"That's OK. I like the blisters. Shows I am working like a real man," growled Jay. "Did your ancestors use gloves?"

"No," said Grandpa.

"Then I don't want to either. I'm going 'old school'," said Jay.

"If our ancestors had gloves I am sure they would have worn them," said Grandpa. "Change and progress doesn't have to be bad; without it you wouldn't have things like that eye patch you keep talking about."

"What eye patch? Oh you mean iPod," said Jay and realized he was being teased. "Ok, give me the gloves."

"What about the knots in the wood?" asked Jay, afraid the sculpture would be imperfect.

"We work around the knots. The so called imperfections of the wood are what give it character. Perfect is boring, don't you think?"

Jay nodded in agreement.

Jackson and his dad came by to see how things were going.

"Stone, nice to see you," said Grampa.

"Jay, this is my dad," said Jackson.

"Nice to meet you, Mr. David," said Jay.

"Please, just call me Stone," said Jackson's dad. "So this is the secret project. Where are you going to put her?"

"She'll be over with the other totem poles. The new kid on the block," said Grampa. He smiled and patted the log.

Jay continued to chisel the bark away, letting the chunks fall to the ground.

"Can I have a try?" asked Jackson after watching Jay for a few minutes.

"Sure," said Jay.

Jackson picked up the chisel and figured it out right away. "Look at the size of this piece," said Jackson holding a piece up three feet long and curved to the same degree as the tree. He put it on the ground and rocked it like a cradle with his toe. Jay let Jackson work the bark for as long as he wanted.

Grampa and Stone were deep in conversation and Jay moved closer to hear what they were saying.

"Why didn't you just have the mill skin her? They could have done it in two minutes," said Stone.

"Then the whole village and the next town over would have known," said Grampa.

"I am amazed you were able to pull this off without hardly anyone knowing," said Stone.

"It wasn't easy. We sure got some stubborn elders. And the paperwork to get it approved by the government was a nightmare," said Grampa.

"I wish the politicians would leave us alone and let us take care of ourselves. We certainly couldn't do a worse job than them," said Stone.

"Well, we got the log here and that's the main thing," said Grampa.

"Why did you keep it a secret?" asked Jay.

"The elders were afraid it would cause a rift in the village. They said I was wasting my time. And they said that the government and the environmentalists would never agree. I spent many meetings defending the right to continue my ancestors' tradition," said Grampa.

"How long did it take to get them to agree?" asked Jay.

"Over a year," said Grampa.

"You started this before you even knew I was coming here?" asked Jay.

"Yes, I had a dream I found a tree very much like this one. The tree opened its branches and pulled me into its arms. Then it dropped me to the ground and I felt the wind knocked out of me. The roots grabbed me and squeezed me like the tree was hanging on to me to keep from drowning. I felt myself become a beaver and used my teeth to get free from the roots. Then I gnawed my way through the bark. I stopped, afraid the tree would grab me again but its branches relaxed and the sun shone on my fur. I felt warm and loved," said Grampa. The serene look on his face told Jay this was something his grandpa experienced in a life changing way.

"I knew I had to do this. One way or another, with help or without," said Grampa.

"Well, it seems like you will have help," said Stone. "Come on Jackson. We have to get to the marine shop or we'll never have the boat ready for fishing humpies."

"Humpies?" Jay said with a huge grin on his face.

"Humpies are pinks," said Stone.

Jay continued to grin.

"Pink salmon, you goof," said Jackson.

"Are you coming out with us Jay?" asked Stone.

"No, I'm going to stay here and help Grampa," said Jay. Jackson looked disappointed for a moment. Stone started talking about what was needed for the trip and Jackson's face lit up.

Jay felt a pang of jealousy that he didn't have a dad to take him fishing.

"I know you wanted to go fishing. Maybe you still can. We'll see how far we get," said Grampa. "The totem pole is important but it is also important that you have some fun this summer. I pushed hard to get the totem pole approved but I don't

185

think I realized why it was so important until you came here. The truth is I wanted something to show for being on Earth and a member of this tribe. When I lost touch with your mom I thought I had wasted my life. My legacy was to carve this totem pole for the village. To show our ancestors' that their lives and their skills live on I had to do something unforgettable. I see now that my legacy is you."

"Can you walk your legacies over here and help me with this knot?" said Jay. The conversation was getting too intense. He understood what his Grampa was saying but didn't want to analyze why or why not they were carving a totem pole.

Grampa grabbed a hammer and banged the end of the chisel. On the third tap the stubby protrusion gave way.

The garage floor was a carpet of thick, rough bark. The smell of cedar clung to Jay's hair and clothes.

"You smell like a sauna, Jay," said Tatla as he entered the house. "How long will you be at it tonight?"

"A couple more hours and then we have to spray water on the log to keep it from cracking," said Jay, reaching into the fridge for a cold drink.

"It'll be past ten o'clock by then," said Tatla.

"I can't help it if your dad won't stop. Anyway, it will still be light out," said Jay. The northern latitude kept the sun in the sky longer as the equinox approached.

Chapter 27

Jay got an early start the next day. He was in the garage alone. Clouds paraded in front of the sun making the garage dark then bright like a child playing with a light switch.

"Hey, Jay."

Jay stopped chiseling and turned around. It was Courtney. She was dressed in Wrangler jeans, running shoes, a white t-shirt and a yellow hoodie zipped halfway up. She wore a pink baseball cap with her hair in a pony tail pulled through the hole in the hat. She took off her sunglasses and parked them on the hat's visor.

"Hi, Courtney," said Jay. He wiped his sweaty forehead with the back of his arm. Another shadow crossed the garage.

"So this is the totem pole?" asked Courtney breaking the silence. She walked closer to Jay and ran her fingers across the bark.

"Not yet," said Jay.

"Ever carved a totem pole before?" asked Courtney.

"No, I've never even carved a turkey," said Jay. Courtney laughed. Jay smiled.

"Let's see you carve something," said Courtney.

"I have to remove all the bark before we actually do any carving," said Jay.

"Well then let me try," said Courtney.

She reached across Jay and snatched the chisel from his hands. With one hand she poked at the bark. Jay felt the blood fill every pore in his neck and face.

187

"It's not working," said Courtney. Jay was pretty sure she was toying with him but decided to play along.

"You have to use two hands," said Jay.

"Why don't you show me?" asked Courtney like this was the greatest idea ever imagined.

Jay grabbed the handle on the chisel but Courtney refused to let go. They stared eye to eye. The sun lit up the garage again. Jay thought everyone in the village had brown eyes. Now he saw that Courtney's eyes were the color of amber with specks of green. Jay tried to speak but nothing came out. He tried to swallow but his tongue forgot how.

"Teach me," said Courtney. She stood in front of the log where the clean wood and the bark met, chisel in hand and looked back at Jay.

Jay took off his gloves and wiped his hands on his brown Nickelback t-shirt. He took a deep breath and exhaled. Standing behind and to the side of Courtney he placed her left hand on top of her right hand. He leaned in and put his hands on top of Courtney's. She turned and smiled at him. She smelled like mint toothpaste and wildberry shampoo.

"Ok, now, lean into it," said Jay. He guided her hands as they nudged the chisel under the bark. A piece flew off and shot across the garage. Jay fell forward pinning Courtney to the log.

"Sorry," said Jay. "I guess we pushed too hard." He stepped back.

"That's OK. I think we pushed exactly right," said Courtney. She moved closer to Jay about to say something when the sound of footsteps on crushed gravel stopped her.

"Getting an early start? Good for you," said Grampa, a cup of coffee in his hand. His cheeks fought hard to keep his lips from forming a full on smile.

Jay wanted to dissolve into the pile of bark and wood shavings.

"Well, I should get going. I am off to the ranch. Dr. Two Feathers got me a summer job cleaning stalls and grooming the horses. It doesn't pay much but I get to ride the horses, too," said Courtney.

"Say 'Hi' to Ronald and Lucy," said Jay.

"Ok, I will," said Courtney.

Courtney cut through Jay's yard and headed down the road. Jay saw her skipping when she was a few houses away.

Grampa cleared his throat.

Jay looked at his grandfather as if to say "Don't say a word."

It was another full day of de-barking the tree. Jay's muscles ached but he slept great. When the sun shone through the slits in the blinds Jay did not hesitate to get out of bed.

"You're up early," said Tatla. She was at her desk with a cup of coffee. File folders piled up on the floor; a sign that her business was doing well.

"Once I finish skinning the tree we can start the actual carving. That's what I'm looking forward to," said Jay.

Jay shoved his feet into his sneakers, the laces already tied, and stepped outside. The sun had not made it past the mountains yet and a golden glow filled the air. A few chicades sent out their message. "Chick a dee dee dee dee. Chick a dee dee dee dee."

Loud voices came from the garage.

"It's here now. I'm carving this totem pole with my grandson whether you like it or not, Fred," said Grampa.

Jay stopped in his tracks and listened.

189

"What a waste of time. You should be helping Chief George with the treaties," said Fred.

"I have helped him as much as I can. When he needs my help again I'll be there for him," said Grampa.

Fred raised his voice. "You are selfish. You are doing this for yourself. When your daughter went to the city and your wife died you had nothing. Carving a totem pole was just to keep you busy so you wouldn't have to think about being alone."

"What's wrong with that?" said Grampa.

"We don't need another totem pole. We need jobs," said Fred. "You are going to set us back. This is a distraction. The village needs to focus on moving forward, not staying in the past."

"We can do both. Right now the village is not moving forward or backward. We are stuck. I don't know how to change the village. I can only do what I feel is the right thing for me," said Grampa. "Maybe I did start out carving the totem pole for myself but now I have my grandson here. I am not carving it out of loneliness; I am carving it to teach Jay about his culture. Now if you'll excuse me I have to get started."

Jay quietly walked to the doorway of the garage. Grampa crossed the garage to the tools and selected a medium sized chisel.

Fred met him at the tool box and grabbed the chisel in Grampa's hands. The two men clutched at the metal hand tool battling over it in a tug-o-war. Grampa gave one good tug and snatched the chisel from Fred. Both men reeled backward. Fred tripped over the leg of the sawhorse and fell into a mound of bark chips.

Grampa stretched out his hand to Fred. Without looking Grampa in the eye, Fred pushed himself up, brushed the wood chips off his jeans and exited the garage.

"What's his problem?" asked Jay.

"His father was a master carver. He carved many things, like flutes and totems and knew how to make drums. It must be very painful for him to think about the past," said Grampa. "I should have been kinder to old Fred. He was laid off from the mill a few months ago. Five years away from collecting a pension and now he doesn't know what will happen to him and his wife. Their son and his wife live with them and he has three granddaughters. You know the Stewart girls?"

"Yes, I've seen them around," said Jay. The kids were nice, polite and clean. Their clothes were obviously hand me downs from other kids but they didn't seem to mind.

"Fred's under a lot of stress. He knows it's just a matter of time before his son takes his family away to find work," said Grampa. "I'm sorry for him and if I could do something to help, I would."

"I know," said Jay.

"Are you ready to start carving?" asked Grampa.

"Yes, finally, we get to carve. Where do we start? Which tool do we use?" asked Jay. He headed over to where the tools were laid out on a thick wooden table about chest high to Jay.

"This one," said Grampa. He handed Jay a shovel. It was the same height as Jay with a blond wooden handle and a square shaped loader.

"We can't carve with this," said Jay, confused.

"First we need to take the bark away," said Grampa. He reached for a snow shovel and slid it along the ground, collecting a large amount of wood chips.

They scooped and shoveled the bark into a wheel barrow and dumped them beside the wood pile. The bark looked like chunks of chocolate.

Several wheel barrow trips later, Grampa said, "That will make good kindling for the wood stove in the winter."

Jay was so hot from shoveling he couldn't imagine lighting a fire anytime soon.

"There's the two hardest working boys in the village," a voice came from across the yard.

"Hi, Mary," said Grampa. "How are you feeling? Looks like your hip surgery was a success."

"It's getting there. Want to see me do a cartwheel?" said Mary to Jay. She smiled her toothless grin. She was wearing a shawl again. This one was red, orange and yellow and not as heavy as the wooly one worn on the night she invaded Jay's kitchen.

"No," said Jay. He pictured her doing a cartwheel and all her bones shattering one by one; first her arms snapping, then her back, then her legs into a twisted mound.

"What brings you by?" asked Grampa.

"I heard about some shenanigans here this morning," said Mary.

"Just Fred letting off some steam; he was against making the totem pole," said Grampa.

"I remember from the meetings. He's still upset about it, eh?" asked Mary.

"Yes," said Grampa.

"We're just about to start," said Jay.

"No, you can't start yet," said Mary.

"What now?" huffed Jay.

"Jay!" said Grampa.

"It's OK. Youth, they are so impatient. I understand," said Mary. "Can you wait ten more minutes, Jay?"

"I guess so," said Jay.

Mary placed a woven cedar bag on the ground. She pulled out an abalone shell about five inches long, a plastic bag with crumbled leaves and some matches. She placed the abalone shell on the work bench with the carving tools and then sprinkled the silvery green leaves into the shell.

The bench was much taller than her. She stretched like a child at a kitchen counter pouring a bowl of cereal. Carefully, she took the shell from the bench and placed it on the ground. She struck a match and held it to the leaves, lightly blowing to ignite the contents. She then withdrew the match and waved it until the flame disappeared. Jay smelled a combination of burnt matches and sweet smoke.

At first he thought she was toking up, and then she pulled out a bird's wing from her bag. The wing was 8" long and thick with layers of brown feathers speckled with black and white spots. With the shell still smoking she walked around the garage wafting the smoke over the log with the bird's wing, chanting a low melody. She stopped to relight the leaves, giving Grampa a knowing look.

When she finished with the log she asked Grampa for the tool from the morning scuffle.

Grampa picked up the chisel he and Fred had struggled over.

"Pass it through the smoke," instructed Mary.

Grampa did as he was told. Holding the tip of the tool and the butt end of the handle between the palms of his hands, he moved the chisel across the smoke. Halfway across the shell, the leaves flared up, startling Grampa.

Mary did not flinch, as though she was expecting this.

"Lots of negative energy in here, especially the chisel," said Mary. "Do you want a cleanse?" she asked Grampa.

"Please, I think that's a good idea," said Grampa.

She took the shell and started at Grampa's feet. The bird's wing flapped and the smoke circled around Grampa's legs. Mary continued to chant. She worked the smoke up Grampa's body. Grampa held his arms outstretched to each side, palms up. Mary allowed the smoke to rise up to Grampa's arms and hands. Grampa bent his knees as Mary covered his head in white air.

When she was done, Grampa raised his palms in the air to give thanks.

"That's wonderful, Mary. I'm grateful to you," said Grampa. Mary and Grampa looked at Jay.

"You aren't doing that to me," said Jay. He had watched in fascination, worried about his Grampa having a voodoo spell cast over him.

"Don't worry, Jay. We don't smudge children unless it's an emergency," said Mary. "The spirits of the young are generally pure but still developing. We don't smudge them in case we remove the good along with the bad."

"Jay, did you notice that I had to light the sage leaves more than once?" asked Mary.

Jay nodded.

"And did you see how the sweet grass - that's another name for dried sage - flared up when we passed the tool through?" asked Mary.

"Those show how much negative energy was stored in here. I'll let you get to your carving now. The garage, the cedar and the tools should be back in balance," said Mary as she placed her sage leaves, shell, matches and pheasant wing into her bag.

"Are you off to see Fred now?" asked Grampa.

"How did you know?" said Mary. She floated out of the garage with her shawl dragging behind her. "Don't forget Theresa is coming over for the strands."

"What was that all about?" asked Jay.

"It was a smudge. A cleanse of sage leaves. The smoke purifies the person or object taking away the negative energies. It is a powerful ceremony and can only be done by an experienced medicine man or woman," said Grampa. "I feel refreshed. Let's get started."

"Grab an end." Grampa picked at the red wood until the first layer peeled back. He pinched it between his thumb and forefinger and pulled back until the strip was above his head. Then he walked the length of the log, the strand getting longer and longer.

"We have to peel the first few layers off before we can get to the wood. These ribbons are good for making baskets, mats, clothing etc. but too soft for carving. The hard wood is underneath."

"So we aren't carving yet?" said Jay, wondering what other interruptions might occur.

"The sooner we peel the sooner we can carve," said Grampa.

Jay picked at a piece and reefed on it. The strand broke after two feet and Jay threw it to the ground. Jay kicked at it on its slow descent.

"Jay, take it easy," Grampa was on his third strip. He placed each strip side by side on the ground a few feet away from the log. "Going slower will actually get the job done faster."

Jay blew the hair out of his eyes and picked at another piece. The cedar stained the tips of his fingers red. After a few strands Jay started to enjoy himself, challenging his Grampa to a

195

competition to see who could go the longest without breaking a strand.

"This is more fun than peeling the skin off Anthony's back when he got burnt to a crisp at summer camp last year," said Jay.

Grampa was right. It didn't take long at all. The log was smoother; the yellow wood revealed.

Theresa came by and collected the strands. She was about forty five years old dressed in Hawaiian printed shorts with a light blue golf shirt tucked in emphasizing her stomach rolls. Jay had seen her when he picked up the mail. The mailman didn't come door to door. Instead the bills and letters went into each family's compartment of a free standing stainless steel box, five feet high by six feet long. Condo's for mail. Three condo's in total. Theresa never looked Jay in the eye; if Jay said 'Hi' she cast her eyes down, mumbled 'Hi', gathered her mail and speed walked down the street. Often she didn't have anything in her box.

"Hi, Theresa. How are you?" asked Grampa.

"I'm good. It's nice and cool in here," she said, only looking at Grampa. Jay felt invisible.

"What do you think?" asked Grampa, pointing at the cedar tresses.

When she saw the lengths of cedar lying on the ground she gasped. "Oh, they are perfect. Just lovely," she said. Her eyes had tears in them. "Thank you so much." Her voice was child like.

She wound them up like a garden hose, leaving a little extra at the end to wrap around the coil to stop it from unwinding.

"Ok, I'm done," said Theresa.

"What are you going to do now?" asked Grampa.

"I've got myself a Mr. Turtle pool so I can soak them for a few days. Then I can start making baskets. Grandmother promised to show me how. I believe Anna knows how to as well."

196

"Who's your grandmother?" asked Jay. He already knew Anna was Jackson's grandmother.

"Mary," she said. This time she looked Jay in the eye. He realized she was not forty-five but probably only about twenty four.

"Can we start now?" asked Jay. Another day had almost come and gone.

"Ok," said Grampa.

With a pencil they marked the four sections where each totem symbol would appear. The knives, awls, adzes and chisels had been sharpened previously by Grampa while Jay was still in school. Grampa used the chisel and hammer to dig into the wood, chipping away piece by piece to make an indentation in the log three feet from the top and mid way down the left side. He handed the chisel and hammer to Jay.

"Keep working it. We need a hole deep enough to put a cantaloupe in," said Grampa.

"A cantaloupe?" asked Jay.

"Well, I don't know how else to explain it. Watch, listen and do as I say," said Grampa.

Jay knew Grampa was saying this with purpose. He didn't want Jay messing around. Carving a totem pole took time, patience and effort. Jay realized the tension he felt was also present in his Grampa. Grampa hadn't carved a totem in decades and never one this size.

"What if I screw it up? It's not like we can pop out to the totem depot and get another one," said Jay.

"Don't screw it up then," said Grampa. "It's going to be great no matter what."

"Hammer the chisel in and then pull up. Move to the next spot. Keep going," said Grampa.

It was awkward at first but Jay got the hang of it. He learned not to do too much at once. Taking it a step at a time, he fell into a rhythm.

"Should I do the same on the other side?" Jay asked when the indentation had passed inspection. He liked the feel of the chisel going inside the wood. Going with the grain, the wood was soft and easier to carve than Jay had imagined.

"Yes," said Grampa. "Then work your way around the top to make a big circle."

"What is it that I'm carving exactly?" asked Jay.

"The moon," said Grampa.

Jay carved the outline of a circle. Grampa started on the other side of the log and they met at the top.

"This isn't as hard as I thought," said Jay.

"This is the easy part. It gets much harder when it comes to the detailed work," said Grampa.

"Who's hungry?" called a voice from the doorway.

Chapter 28

It was May-Belle. She was wearing another hockey jersey; vintage, from one of the original six NHL teams with a matching baseball cap to cover her silver hair. In her left hand she carried a plate with a red checkered dish towel over the top and in her right hand was a red and white plastic Thermos; jug size.

"Guess what I brought?" she sang.

"Bannock," said Grampa and Jay at the same time.

"No." She put the Thermos on a milk crate and pulled back the dish towel. "Peanut butter and homemade strawberry jam sandwiches."

Jay's stomach squeezed itself. "What time is it?" asked Jay. He couldn't be hungry already. He just had breakfast.

"It's 2 p.m," said May-Belle.

"Your timing is perfect. I'm starving," said Grampa.

Jay wondered where the morning had gone.

May-Belle scrutinized the log. "She is magnificent. I knew when I saw her in the forest she'd be perfect."

"You helped pick her out?" said Jay.

"No, your Grampa knew exactly which one to choose. I came for the blessing and to watch them fall the tree. What a mighty crack she made when the trunk split. The Great Spirit brought us a real blessing," said May-Belle. She poured out three glasses of lemonade and passed around the sandwiches.

"Fred doesn't agree but hopefully he'll come around," said Grampa. He took a bite of sandwich and washed it down with ice cold lemonade; delicious.

"Well, you can't blame him. He resents his upbringing. Not everyone has been able to put the past behind them. He had it particularly tough," said May-Belle.

"I thought his dad was a master carver. He should be happy about this. He should be helping us," said Jay, helping himself to a second sandwich.

"Fred's dad never got to show his son how to carve. They took Fred away along with a lot of the other children in the village and put them in residential schools. It was a terrible thing. The children cried, the parents cried. Nothing could be done to stop them. If they tried they were arrested. It was for their own good, the government said," said May-Belle.

"How can taking children away from their parents be good," said Jay.

"The children were to learn English and if they used any words from their own culture they were rapped on the knuckles with a stick. They were supposed to forget their savage ways and become good respectable Christians. I am a Christian myself and let me tell you I would never allow children to be taken from good, caring homes. These were different times. In their own way the missionaries believed they were doing the right thing. Poor Fred lived in a residential school for three years and never saw his family once. The missionaries wouldn't allow it. When he returned home his father had died," said May-Belle. "Probably from a broken heart."

"Your great-uncles and aunts were sent away, too. I was too young. Thank goodness," said Grampa. "It took a toll on them." May-Belle refilled his glass.

"I think that is partly why so many of us old folks never want to leave the village. We feel it's our right to be born here and die here. Leaving feels like we aren't honoring the ones who were forced to leave," said May-Belle.

"I know what it's like to be taken from your home and put some place you don't want to be," said Jay.

"It's not the same thing, Jay. I think you know that. I hope you know that. But maybe the experience will help you to understand why people are so reluctant to leave their homes even if the homes are falling apart," said Grampa.

"Jay, I'm going to bring you some stuff from my house tomorrow," said May-Belle.

"Not one of your cats I hope," said Jay. Grampa gave him 'the look' but May-Belle laughed.

She gathered up the plate, the plastic glasses and the Thermos. "Is your mom home?" she asked Jay.

"She's in her office, working," replied Jay.

"I'll see you tomorrow," said May-Belle. She crossed the yard, went up the stairs, and let herself into the house.

Jay shook his head about to mention the audacity of the older ladies who enter a house without knocking, when he was startled by the loud roar of a chainsaw.

He turned around to see Grampa gunning the chainsaw; a big grin on his face. Blue smoke poured from the engine. He slid the goggles on his forehead down over his eyes. The chainsaw cut a wedge at the bottom of the moon and then from the top Grampa moved through the wood like butter keeping the blade parallel to the log. The chainsaw stopped. Grampa pulled the machine from the gap and handed the curved hump to Jay.

"Isn't that cheating?" said Jay, feeling the weight of the mound.

"Go get the Totem Pole Carvers rule book and show me where it says chainsaws aren't allowed," said Grampa.

"Very funny," said Jay. He picked up the piece of wood and put it in the pile with the bark.

201

They spent the rest of the afternoon planing the surface of the moon until it was almost even with the earlier indentations.

Jackson came by with his dad to say good bye before they went on their fishing trip. They were driving at night because it was cooler and there was less traffic. The journey took a good six hours to get to the coastal area where their fishing license was valid.

After a cold dinner of chicken and potato salad Jay took a cool shower and crawled into bed. He left the window open and the morning sunrise woke him up. The days were getting longer and hotter. He dressed in khaki cargo shorts and a black tank top and strode to the garage meeting Grampa midway.

When they entered the garage May-Belle was there with a cardboard box sitting beside her. "I brought you some of my family's things," she said.

Grampa crossed the garage and peered inside the box. He lifted out a wood hoop 18" in diameter and octagonal like an eight sided stop sign.

"It's for a drum," said May-Belle. "I thought you could make one."

"I don't know how to make a drum," said Jay. He felt bad for her. She wanted so much to be a part of what was going on in the garage.

She looked deflated. She took the hoop from Grampa and put it in the box.

"I'm sorry. You are busy with the totem pole. I don't know what I was thinking. It's time I threw this junk out," said May-Belle. She carried the box out of the garage and into the sunlight.

"She has been so lonely since her husband and son died. The summer is really hard because there are no hockey games to watch. Have you met her cats?" asked Grampa.

"Yes, Mario Le Mew, Sidney Pawsby and Peter Fursberg," said Jay, chuckling. They sharpened the chisels and set to work on the totem pole. They had begun the eyes of the moon when Levi blasted into the garage practically impaling him on the totem pole.

"Have you seen May-Belle?" asked Levi, talking louder than necessary. His voice echoed in the garage. With wide eyes he repeated the question. "Do you know where she is? We need her. Skye is about to have her baby."

"She left about 10 minutes ago. I think she was going to the dump," said Grampa. "Here get in the truck. We'll find her."

The three of them hopped into Grampa's truck and went in the same direction as May-Belle. They caught up with her about a block from the bridge.

When she saw Levi in the truck she knew exactly what was happening. Jay jumped down and took the cardboard box from her. He threw it in the back and climbed in after it. Levi climbed in the back, too.

"Were you walking to the dump?" asked Grampa once May-Belle was in the truck.

"No, I was going to see if Fred or Gordon or someone else wanted it first," said May-Belle.

They arrived at Skye's place in five minutes. The house was a bungalow with green glass stucco and chipped white cedar siding. One of the original houses built over fifty years ago. A rusty mattress skeleton lay against the wall along the side with bramble growing through the springs. Stacked in the carport were boxes, lamps, vacuum cleaners and a brown velvet recliner.

Levi leaped over the side of the truck and ran up the stairs. May-Belle took her time. She opened the door and asked Grampa to fetch her bag from the front hall closet of her house. Levi's feet kept moving, up and down on the spot as he waited for May-Belle to ascend the steps.

He looks like he has to go the bathroom, thought Jay.

May-Belle told Levi to relax. "You'll only make it worse if don't calm down. We don't want the baby to be greeted by a bunch of uptight worry-warts." A scream came from within the house. May-Belle moved into action.

Grampa and Jay drove the few blocks to May-Belle's house. Grampa kept the motor running while Jay flung open the gate of the white picket fence and in the front door. He narrowly prevented two cats from escaping. He found the black leather satchel and slammed the closet door.

"I think I locked one of her cats in the closet," said Jay, breathless.

"I'm sure it will survive. And if it doesn't then she can stuff it," said Grampa. He realized what he'd said and they both laughed. "I must be nervous. Don't tell May-Belle what I said. She'll never bring me bannock again."

They parked on the road. Jay brought the bag up the stairs. A blood curdling scream pierced their ears. Levi grabbed the bag and disappeared inside. Jay was grateful Levi didn't invite him in. The sound of Skye screaming was more than Jay could take. He wanted to get as far away as possible.

"Don't leave," said Levi. He headed them off at the truck. "I can't wait inside. It's too loud. Wait with me, please."

"Shouldn't we get Skye to the hospital?" asked Jay.

"May-Belle will deliver the baby," said Grampa. Levi covered his ears as another scream came from the house.

"She will? Is she allowed?" asked Jay.

"She is a certified mid-wife. She delivered Levi and Skye," said Grampa. "Unless the birth has the potential for complications most women in the village prefer home births."

Another scream. Levi looked like a wreck. "I could use a cigarette," said Levi. "But I don't smoke." He took out his lighter and flicked it on then snapped the lid shut. Repeating this over and over until Grampa reached out and took it. He closed the lid and returned it to Levi. Levi got the message and put the lighter in his pocket.

"Let's have a look in the box May-Belle left," said Grampa, hoping to create a distraction. He pulled out the wooden hoop.

"It's a frame for making a drum," Jay explained to Levi.

Another scream. This one brought the neighbors out of their houses. Fred and his three granddaughters came over to the side of the truck. The three girls, ages six, seven and eight years old were dressed in identical t-shirts and shorts but different colors; yellow for the youngest, hot pink for the middle girl and lavender for the oldest. The oldest girl climbed on the back bumper of the truck then helped her sisters up, hanging on the tail gate like three sparrows perched on a wire.

"What's happening in there? Someone gettin' killed?" asked Fred.

"No, Skye's having her baby," said Levi.

"Hello, girls," said Grampa. They smiled shyly and said "Hi", revealing their baby teeth minus one or two. "This is my grandson Jay. These are Fred's granddaughters Diana, Donna, and Deanna."

"Wow, 3D," said Jay.

Fred laughed. He and Grampa talked like the fight never happened.

"Is that a drum frame?" asked Fred. Levi passed it over the edge of the truck bed. Fred took it and turned it over in his hands. "That's nice wood. You going to make a drum?" Fred asked Grampa.

205

"No, not my area. May-Belle brought this box of stuff over to see if we could do something with it but I got enough on my plate," said Grampa.

"What else she got in there?" asked Fred.

"There is another frame, some needles to sew leather, a leather hole punch, some rawhide strings," said Grampa.

Another scream interrupted them but this one was different, smaller and more urgent. Levi leaped over the side of the truck and sprinted inside. Jay, Grampa, Fred and the girls hurried to the front door. They waited outside to respect Skye and because it was too hot inside.

Jay heard footsteps inside and peeked in the doorway in time for Levi to crash into Jay.

"He's a girl," said Levi, grabbing Jay by the shoulders and shaking him. "I mean *she's* a girl." Levi grinned.

"Congratulations, Uncle Levi," said Grampa.

Chapter 29

Jay and Grampa returned to the coolness of the garage. Jay opened the wings of the Raven mural to let in the air and the light. Direct sunlight had to be kept from hitting the log to prevent cracking. From noon to 2 p.m on sunny days only the side door remained open but a breeze blew in from down the mountain, the air cooled by the constant shade of the dense forest.

"Listen," said Grampa.

Peep, peep, peep.

"Do you hear that?" said Grampa.

Peep, peep, peep.

"I think someone else had their babies today," said Jay. He stood under the swallow's nest. Small fragments of speckled egg shells lay at Jay's feet.

The next day was overcast; perfect carving weather.

Fred and his son pulled up in a red Chevy pick up truck. The truck was newer than Grampa's but the red paint had faded flat making it appear older. The tail gate was lowered and boards of lumber lay in the bed looking comfortable.

The men simultaneously exited and met at the back of the truck. They heaved a thick plank three inches thick and five feet long out of the bed and carried it into the garage.

"We're trying to get rid of wood over here, not collect it," said Grampa. The board entered the garage and leaned on the wall with the help of Fred and his son.

"Jay, this is my son, Billy," said Fred.

"Nice to meet you," said Jay and Billy at the same time. Billy stood 6'2. He was well built and muscular with a slight paunch. In his 20's he was probably into weight lifting but married life, children and a full time job didn't leave much time for working out. His hair was shoulder length and layered. He reminded Jay of a lead singer in a rock band from the eighties.

"What are you doing with the plank?" asked Grampa.

"I wanted to get your opinion. What do you think about me carving this block of cedar to replace the missing wing on the Thunderbird totem?" said Fred. He knocked on the board.

Grampa opened his mouth to speak. Fred held up his hand to keep Grampa from talking. "I know what I said the other day about carving being a waste of time but I had a good talk with Mary. I want to carry on my dad's gift and maybe teach my son how to carve. Being unemployed is not my style. If I sit in front of the TV one more day I'm going to shoot the damn thing with my rifle."

"Since TV hunting season doesn't start for another three weeks I guess you better get carving. I think it's a fantastic idea. Why didn't you think of it?" Grampa asked Jay.

"Do you need any tools or anything?" asked Grampa.

"I found my dad's tools in the attic. A good cleaning and sharpening is all they need. What I need from you is some lessons," said Fred.

"Come by tomorrow. I'd be happy to show you," said Grampa.

When Fred and Billy were gone Jay was silent. "How come you're so quiet?" asked Grampa.

"He's going to slow us down. We need to focus on the totem pole. I don't understand how you can help Fred after the big fight you just had," said Jay.

"Because of the moon," said Grampa. "It was really hard for Fred to come here and ask for my help, especially in front of his son. He's a hard worker; gave his whole life to that saw mill. Provided for his family and has been a good father. How can I turn my back on someone I've known my entire life?" asked Grampa.

For the next few days Grampa showed Fred, Billy and Jay the intricacies of carving. How each tool has its own special job. Fred and Billy practiced their skills until Grampa said they were ready to start on the wing. Jay had drawn a sketch of the other wing so it would match.

Fred's granddaughters hung out in the garage, too. The 3Ds chased each other around the log but when one of them ran under the log Grampa put a stop to the game of tag. He didn't want the log to tip over and roll on top of someone.

"But we're bored," they cried in unison.

"Go outside and play then," said Fred.

"It's too hot," said Donna.

"Well, find something to do that doesn't involve running," said Billy.

The girls sat quietly in the corner. Jay continued to practice notching straight lines in various lengths on a piece of two by four. Totally engrossed, he didn't realize someone was behind him until he felt a tap on his shoulder. Courtney's face flashed in his head. When he turned around to see who it was his surprise erased all disappointment.

The 3Ds had braided their hair together. Donna wove her right braid into Deanna's left braid and Dianna wove her left braid into Deanna's right braid. They stood side by side connected by ropes of glossy black hair thick enough to dock a freighter with.

"We're Siamese twipwets," said Deanna, the youngest.

They turned to show their dad and grandfather, shrieking as one girl pulled the other girls hair by walking too fast or turning too sharp.

Fred, Billy and Grampa bent over laughing. Billy kissed his girls and said they were very smart but a little bit crazy.

"Just like their mom," said Fred, elbowing Grampa in the ribs.

"Hey, I'm telling Sheila you said that," said a voice from the side door.

"Crystal, Anna," said Grampa. "How are Jackson and his dad doing?"

"They called to say the fishing is not as good as it was last year. They are going to keep trying though and see what they can salvage out of the season," said Jackson's mom, Crystal. She was shorter than Jay; slightly plump but slimmer than Sadie. She always had a smile on her face which Jay liked.

Anna was Jackson's grandmother. Her husband had died in a logging accident before Jackson was born and she had lived with them ever since. She wore a black sleeveless dress made from the same jersey fabric as a t-shirt. It stopped at her ankles where she wore pink flip-flops on her feet. Not a fancy outfit except she had also put on a beaded necklace; turquoise, white and black in color, round in shape like a sunburst with two inch rows of beads dangling from the bottom. Her ankles, wrists and ears were adorned in similar fashion. Her silver hair was knotted in a neat but loose bun and a few strands hung around her face. Every time Jay saw her she was wearing a different beaded necklace.

"I came by to see how things were going. Plus I miss my men. It's the first time I've been without both of them," said Crystal.

Dillon and Jody had followed Crystal and Anna into the garage. They made the usual rounds sniffing everyone and bowing for biscuits.

When Grampa caught sight of them he yelled, "Get out of here."

Dillon and Jody carried on pretending not to hear him. Grampa tried to round them up and shoo them out the door. It's not that he didn't like them. He did in fact enjoy having the Labs come over and keep him company. He said they were his rent-a-dogs; the best of both worlds; company when you need it but no vet bills or dog food to buy. At the moment, the Labs were a danger to themselves and the people in the garage. Grampa feared the dogs might hurt their paws on a sharp tool or else jump up on the log and knock it down.

Grampa chased Jody until she took the hint and left out the side door. Dillon, however, needed more coaxing. Now, it was a game. Grampa ran after Dillon circling the log.

"Hey, you said no running in the garage," said Jay.

He winked at the girls. The 3Ds giggled with delight. The giggles soon turned to wails of pain as Dillon ran in between Dianna and Deanna making each girl run in a different direction before being yanked back to collide with the other. A nasty conk sounded in the garage as their noggins cracked together.

"Ouch," howled the girls. All three held onto their braids and stayed as close to each other as possible.

Dillon, bothered by the high pitched squeals, darted in between legs and out the door. Grampa sat down with his head between his knees to catch his breath.

Crystal and Anna ran to the girls.

Crystal spoke first. "What have you girls done to your hair?"

"We were bored," said Donna.

"Well, let's see if we can get you out of this mess," said Anna, suppressing the urge to chuckle.

Crystal started on Donna and Deanna's braid. "You sure did a good job of braiding them together. I'm not sure if I can get them apart." She worked at the knots with her fingers. Then she tried using her teeth. "I think you may be stuck like this for good."

The girls looked horrified.

"I know how to get them apart," said Fred. He reached for Grampa's garden shears hanging by a couple of nails on the wall. He pushed and pulled the handles to open and close the scissor like blades as he crept closer and closer to the girls. The sound of metal on metal emphasized the superior slicing power.

"No, Grandfather, please don't," cried the girls. Deanna broke into sobs.

"Put those down, you old fool. Don't you know little girls love their hair more than nearly anything?" said Anna.

"They should have thought about that before they went and tied themselves together," said Fred.

"Come on now. They didn't mean to. They were just playing," said Crystal.

"Here let me try," said Anna. She wiped Deanna's eyes with the bottom of her skirt and started to unwind their hair. Deanna played with Anna's necklace while she worked the knots.

"That's pretty," said Donna.

"Thank you," said Anna. "I made it, you know."

"Really? Can you make me one?" asked Dianna.

"No, but I can show you how to make your own if you like," said Anna.

"Yes, yes, yes," said the girls jumping up and down with Anna still holding onto their hair. She freed them within a few minutes.

"Thank you, Grandmother," each said.

"Fred, Billy, is it alright if we make necklaces?" asked Anna.

"Yes, keep them busy at all costs, but whatever you do – don't give them gum," said Billy.

"Come on, hummingbirds," said Anna. The three girls followed Anna out the door. They returned fifteen minutes later carrying plastic margarine tubs. The contents shook like maracas.

"Ok if we make the necklaces here? It's much cooler than our place," said Crystal.

"Sure, no problem, make one for me, eh," said Grampa.

At the end of the day Anna, Crystal and the 3Ds made a pledge to meet every day at the garage for a few hours of beading.

Teresa arrived at the garage a few days later with a beautiful cedar mat. It had a diamond design in the middle and zigzag stripes on either end.

"How did you do that?" asked Anna. "It's amazing."

"Grandmother Mary showed me how," said Teresa. She hid half her face behind the mat.

"Don't hide back there," said Anna. She reached out and took the mat away from Teresa. "It's exquisite. You should be very proud of yourself. That's good work."

"I'd love to make a basket. Do you think you could show me how?" asked Crystal.

"I don't know," said Teresa, her hands covering her mouth.

"I know you can. I bet the girls would like to learn too. Right girls?" asked Anna.

The girls nodded their heads. Teresa was good to her word and brought the coils of cedar back to the garage. Mary dragged a lawn chair into the garage and helped Teresa teach the art of weaving mats and baskets. Deanna and Dianna hands were too small to hold the strands so they braided cedar ropes and made beaded anklets and bracelets.

Tatla had a few days off and joined in on the craft making. She even brought out Jay's boom box and played some CD's of First Nations singers and musicians.

Jay overheard Grampa and Anna singing along to some of the tunes they claimed they hadn't heard in years. Tatla got up and did a jingle dance. Fred and Billy did a dance of the deer hunt.

The sound of drums reverberated in the village. Miles' buddies stopped to see what the noise was on their way to the lake. Jay wished they would keep walking. He knew Miles must be nearby.

"Ricky, Matt, Thomas, and Colin come over here," said Grampa. "Have a look at what your cousins are doing."

The boys gathered around Fred and Billy. The Thunderbird wing was coming along nicely. Billy and Fred made sure their wing was the same as the other side by climbing a ladder and measuring the left wing.

The boys left the garage but not before Mary insisted on a hug. She whispered something in each of their ears. They returned the next day carrying rust freckled tools, colorful woven blankets half finished, celebration regalia in need of minor repair and armfuls of rawhide.

Mary gave them the eye as the four boys hovered near Jay. They hung back but Jay felt them watching him. It was like school all over again.

Why don't they just piss off? This is my garage, thought Jay.

Ricky came closer to Jay.

One more step and I'll slice him with my adze, thought Jay.

Grampa watched from the sides of his eyes and kept planing the totem.

"Sorry about all that 'apple' stuff," said Ricky.

"Sorry about the fridge," said Matt.

"Yeah, sorry," said Thomas and Colin.

Jay looked at Colin. His face had more potholes than the road. An easy target but Jay decided against it. He wasn't ready to forgive and forget like Grampa had with Fred, but being civil couldn't hurt.

"Where's Miles?" Jay asked.

"He's at lacrosse camp," said Ricky.

"How can R.J. and Linda afford that?" asked Crystal.

"He got a sponsor from the University to pay for it. If he does well he might even go to college on a scholarship," said Ricky. "Miles a college boy; what a joke."

Grampa's face reddened. "You kids, every one of you, can go to college or do whatever you want if you're not afraid of the work."

"We ain't got no chance of going to college. Face it," said Ricky. "Come on guys. Let's go to the creek or something. I'm not spending my summer hanging out with old folks and babies."

The boys filed out of the garage.

Chapter 30

Grampa dropped his planer and followed them out. "Show me what you brought over first," said Grampa. His voice softened.

They gave their stuff to Grampa to examine. "You know I might have something you can do with this raw-hide. Matt, get the box in the back of my truck, please."

Matt hiked up his cut off jean shorts - homemade and too big with loose threads hanging down - and jogged across the driveway to Grampa's truck.

Jay had forgotten all about May-Belle's box; apparently, so had May-Belle.

Matt brought the box in. Grampa lifted up the drum frame in one hand and the square of raw-hide in the other. "I think this goes with this," said Grampa.

"Cool," said Matt. "We can make our own drums."

"Yeah, we can start a band," said Ricky. "I can play at least as good as the music on the boom box."

"How do we turn this into a drum?" asked Thomas. He was the smallest of the bunch and Jay could tell Thomas only hung out with them so he wouldn't get picked on.

"I don't know," said Grampa. "Anybody else know?"

"No," was the reply from everyone in the garage.

"Any other ideas?" said Grampa.

"It's May-Belle's stuff. We should ask her," said Jay.

"Good idea," said Fred.

The boys headed over to May-Belle's. They returned ten minutes later with bannock in hand for everyone but no further ahead on drum making.

"What about Chief George? He'll know," said Anna.

"He's not back from the Chief's national conference for a few more days," said Mary. "He was taking a side trip to some of the other territories to see what they are doing about the unemployment."

"Ok, here we go - how to make a drum." It was May-Belle. She waved a sheet of white paper in each hand.

"You found instructions in Ken's things?" said Grampa.

"No, of course not, I gave you all his stuff," said May-Belle.

"Then how did you get the instructions?" asked Jay.

"I Googled them," said May-Belle. The entire garage pealed with laughter.

"Teresa, it's good to see you out and about," said May-Belle. "She's just getting over a nasty divorce," explained May-Belle to Jay.

"You were married?" Jay said, expressing his surprise. Tatla shot him one of her patented looks.

"Yes, for about six months," said Teresa.

"Good thing it wasn't any longer. You did the right thing," said Anna.

The beaded necklaces, anklets and bracelets were starting to pile up. The 3Ds no longer sat on the concrete floor but now had lovely smooth cedar mats to sit on. Their friends from school had joined them and now a dozen or so kids came every day and sat at the women's feet making jewelry and weaving cedar strands into works of art. The one person Jay rarely saw was Johnny Walker.

217

Only after everyone had gone home would he come by; Pepsi-beer and cigarette in hand to chat with Grampa.

"Good riddance to Bob," said May-Belle. She had a piece of raw-hide in her lap measuring out where to punch the holes for the string to be laced for the drum.

"You weren't his wife. You were his baby sitter," said Crystal. "Remember when he took you to that party but you had to drive home because he was so drunk?"

"I couldn't wake him up to get him the house so I left him passed out in the car all night," said Teresa.

"He could have died. It got below freezing that night," said Mary.

"That's terrible," said Tatla.

"It's OK," said Teresa. She bent her head down and brought her shoulders up around her ears. A wicked grin filled her face. "I had life insurance."

Anna and Crystal spilled their beads laughing so hard.

The days passed quickly. Stories and music filled the garage. The totem pole was coming to life but much still needed to be done.

Fred and Billy had finished the Thunderbird wing and divided their time between making drum frames and cooking hamburgers or hot dogs on the grill they'd brought over. When they ran out of hot dogs one afternoon Fred went to Sadie's to get more. He returned ten minutes later with the news that Sadie only had frozen wieners.

"Cook 'em slow. They'll be fine," advised Mary.

Fred slit open the plastic wrap that hugged the wieners. The sound of crinkling packaging awoke the pack of dogs lying in the shade of the garage. Dillon, Jody and the gang bounded over to

Fred. He held the wieners high and nearly had his hand taken off while placing the hot dogs on the grill.

"Buzz off ya' beggers," said Fred.

"Oh, give them a wiener," said May-Belle. "Don't be so cheap."

"They're still frozen," said Fred.

"It'll cool them off," said Grampa.

"Yea, dog-sicles," said Jay.

"I wonder if dogs get brain freeze," said Thomas. Everyone laughed.

Dillon bowed. When Fred did not deliver the wiener Dillon bowed again, really slowly, keeping eye contact with Fred. Jay had to laugh to himself. It was like Dillon thought Fred was not smart enough to know that bowing meant you give the dog food so Dillon had repeated it slowly and deliberately so Fred could follow along.

"Who taught that mutt to do that?" said Fred, annoyed at being manipulated by a dog.

"Dog's easy to train. You only need to know one thing," said May-Belle.

"What's that?" said Fred; still not sure he wanted give perfectly good food to a bunch of mutts. "What's the one thing?"

"More than the dog," said May-Belle. The garage erupted with laughter and Fred gave in.

The dogs each snatched a wiener and ran off to be alone with their sub-zero treats.

Soon the garage was filled to capacity on a daily basis; people gathered together seeking shade from the sun or shelter from the rain. Jay and Grampa had to step around bodies and over baskets to reach the totem pole. Jay loved the atmosphere.

219

Everyone and everything in the city was so guarded and anonymous; bars on the windows and alarms on the cars. Keep to yourself. Don't look and don't touch.

Jackson came back early from his first fishing trip.

"How come you are back already? I thought you'd be fishing all summer," said Jay. He took an adze and carved into what was to be an eye, gouging out the whites of the eye to make the pupil pop.

"They closed the season early. Not as many fish returned as they had hoped," said Jackson.

"Did you catch anything?" asked Jay.

"I caught a Tyee. That's a salmon that weighs over 30lbs," he said, proudly showing off the picture of himself holding up the huge fish.

"Which one's you?" said Jay. Jackson rolled his eyes.

"Wow, the garage is crowded. What are they doing here?" asked Jackson, pointing at the boys in the corner who were threading their drums. They worked the raw-hide thread through the elk skin pulling it taught then looped the thread in between the frame and through the handle. The end result was a web of leather rope with a wooden handle in the middle strung up like a spider on the back of the drum.

"Grampa let them in," said Jay. He didn't pay any attention to the boys anymore. Without Miles around they were small and harmless.

The garage was becoming a daily meeting place for those who weren't in summer school or at work.

Everybody was doing something; making baskets, weaving blankets, carving small totems, bowls and spoons. Sometimes, if it wasn't too hot, the older men and women would show the kids the traditional dances. A few kids joined in behind them and tried to copy. Some kids just covered their mouths and laughed. One kid did a hip hop routine to the cheers of all the people in Grampa's garage.

"Here you are," said Chief George. He entered the garage one afternoon and circled the totem pole. "I wondered where everyone was. Look at all the wonderful baskets you made. The totem pole is really taking shape. This must be Jay."

He stopped on the opposite side of the totem pole. He and Jay studied each other's face. The chief had a round open face; his hair was short and parted to one side like a news anchor. The hairline crept back enough to give him a generous forehead where his heavy eyebrows floated. The skin between his eyebrows and eyes folded over obscuring his eyelids. He stared at Jay without blinking, his thin lips pressed together. He wore a beige, long sleeved dress shirt and black pleated dress pants; definitely over dressed for the garage.

"Yes, this is my grandson," said Grampa, placing a hand on Jay's shoulder.

The chief extended his hand. Jay shook his hand, embarrassed by the attention and the fact that his hand was sweaty and dirty.

"I am honored you have chosen to make our village your home. And happy to see Tatla again," said the chief. Tatla came over and gave him a big hug.

"It is good to see you again," said Tatla.

"I wish we had this spirit all the time. It is so good to see everyone working together," said Mary. The 3Ds ran over and nearly knocked the chief down in their excitement to show him the colorful jewelry they had made.

"We have a good village here despite the problems," agreed Grampa. "I am sure once the land treaties are settled we'll get back on our feet."

221

"I am doing my best but it is a long process. I found an old picture taken in 1950 of Chief Sophie in land treaty negotiations. It makes me wonder if I'll be around to actually see it happen," said the chief. "I am afraid if something doesn't happen soon there will be no more tribe to carry on the few traditions we have left."

"We don't know how long we'll be able to stay, either," said Jackson's mom, setting down the red-cedar basket she was weaving. "The fishing's not so good this year."

"Don't worry Crystal, the Great Spirit will bless us. We just need to have faith," said the chief. He wandered around the garage saying hello to everyone.

"Well, who have we here?" said Chief George. "Is this the newest member of the band?"

Skye proudly handed Dove over to the chief. He cooed and cuddled her and said she was as beautiful as her mother. The pink bundle wiggled and waved a tiny hand. "May-Belle, you do good work," he called across the garage.

"Thanks Chief," replied May-Belle.

The chief handed Dove back to Skye and said he had lots of work to catch up on but he'd be back later.

I just met an Indian chief, thought Jay. *Cool.*

His thoughts were interrupted.

"Look who's back from lacrosse camp," said Jackson, out of the side of his mouth.

Chapter 31

Miles hovered in the doorway with his lacrosse stick. Jay's stomach did a somersault even though he was sure Miles would keep to himself.

His buddies never looked up from what they were doing.

Miles called over to them, "Hey guys, you want to go to the rope swing?"

"No, thanks," they said. They continued to work on their drums, pulling the skin tight and lacing up the back to the wood frame.

Miles muttered something then turned and shuffled away, throwing his lacrosse ball in the air and catching it with his stick.

Colin caught up with Miles. He withdrew a cigarette from the package - Grampa did not allow anyone to smoke near the garage - and offered one to Miles.

"No, thanks, I quit," said Miles.

The garage went still.

Grampa put down his shaping knife and approached Miles. With an arm around Miles' shoulder Grampa led him into the garage.

Jay and Jackson's eyes went wide. Jackson looked at Jay as if to say, "What is your grandfather doing? He's letting the enemy in." Jay shook his head and shrugged his shoulders.

"Come, sit here." Grampa motioned to Miles to sit on the floor beside his friends. "It is time you learned to beat on something else." Grampa handed Miles a wooden ring with holes drilled around the edge. "Make a drum. When you feel like hitting someone you hit this." Miles accepted the ring and got to work on his drum.

Only once did he stick out his leg as Jay walked by. When the other boys didn't join in Miles quickly retreated.

"Why did you do that?" said Jay, when Grampa returned to carving the totem pole.

"Because of the moon," said Grampa. Jay was about to ask Grampa to explain when the whole garage shook.

Chapter 32

BOOM!

"What was that?" said Jay. All activity stopped.

BOOM!

"Thunder," someone said. Drums, tools and baskets were dropped as everyone in the garage scrambled outside. The sky was pure blue.

BOOM! BOOM! BOOM!

Down the street, like guided missiles, propane tanks rocketed through the air. Fireballs with comet-like tails landed in the school field.

"It's Johnny Walker's place," said Jackson, from the end of the driveway.

"What the heck has that fool done now?" said Mary. "Someone go see if he's OK."

They didn't have to. Johnny was running full speed toward them.

"I can't stop them! I can't stop them!" Johnny yelled as he ran toward the crowd.

BOOM! Another propane tank launched itself toward outer space. NASA would have been proud. Some of the boys hollered and hooted.

"Gordon, what's going on?" asked Grampa.

"I left the torch on near the propane tanks. Good thing I was tinkering with your washer machine or else I'd a gone up with one of them tanks," said Johnny. "Fun on the way up but a bitch coming down," said Johnny Walker, breathless. No one laughed.

"Your place is on fire," said Jay. Flames shot up from Johnny's carport. The fire threatened to spread to his house. A cloud of dense smoke billowed in slow motion. "Call the fire department."

"It's too late. It takes an hour to get a pump truck here," said Grampa. "We'll turn our own hoses on it."

The men scrambled to grab garden hoses while the women collected buckets to fill with water.

Other people who weren't in the garage, such as Mile's dad, came out to watch.

The fire blazed hotter and higher and threatened to jump to the other houses. They were losing the battle. Jay looked around to see what he could do to help.

"Jackson, get some of the kids and come with me," said Jay.

They followed Jay over to the house with the pool inside the double car garage.

"On the count of three; one, two, three," said Jay. He, Jackson and the kids from the garage jumped on the edge of the pool, pulling down the blue poly sides until a waterfall cascaded over. The water rushed across the street flooding Johnny Walker's yard, then his carport and finally his house.

The fire went out immediately and the kids cheered.

They had kept the fire from spreading to Johnny Walker's house, but the carport was a blackened cinder mess. The only thing recognizable was the fridge.

"We should of let it burn down," said Mile's dad. "I always said Johnny was a fire hazard."

"Johnny Walker is just a lazy no good drunk who should go back to his own village," said someone else. Jay didn't want to know who. He looked at Johnny Walker and felt sorry for him. Sorry he had no family and sorry he had lost everything even if it was just junk.

Grampa offered Johnny Walker the spare bedroom while his house dried out, under two conditions: no smoking and no drinking. Grampa hoped Johnny would dry out, too.

Jay often saw Johnny on Grampa's porch smoking a cigarette. Jay invited him to the garage but Johnny always declined saying he was either going to fix up the carport or go to town to get materials. Then down the road he'd walk. Jay was certain that Johnny went somewhere to have a drink.

Another week passed and the totem pole was really taking shape. Grampa and Jay took turns using the tools: the maul, wedge, chisel, adze, hand drill and up to fifty specialty wood carving knives. Jay leaned over the wood with the elbow adze and then switched to the curved carving knife to carefully sculpt the groove of a tooth. His hands were calloused over. Gloves were no longer needed.

Later in the evening the last glimpses of light hung on from the west. The garage was deserted except for Jay and Grampa.

"Once this part is done we can start on the bottom," said Grampa.

Sweat rolled off Grampa's nose and splashed onto the totem pole. The water droplet disappeared into the yellow wood. Jay felt comforted knowing a part of Grampa would be inside the totem pole forever.

Jay brushed some sawdust from his Grampa's long, silver hair. "Nice job, old man, I think you might be getting the hang of it," teased Jay.

"I'm just getting started. Hey, want to hear an old Indian joke?" asked Grampa.

"Sure," said Jay.

"Knock. Knock," said Grampa.

Jay stopped mid carve and raised an eyebrow at Grampa.

"Come on. Knock. Knock," urged Grampa.

"Ok. Who's there?" asked Jay.

"Heron," said Grampa.

"Heron who?" asked Jay.

"Hair-on your face, better go shave," said Grampa.

Jay groaned, "I thought you said it was an old Indian joke?"

"It is – I am an old Indian," said Grampa.

Jay and Grampa whittled away a few more hours, enjoying each other's company with only the sounds of the tools scraping ruts and grooves and wood chips gathering at their feet.

Jay broke the silence saying to Grampa, "At first I thought we were carving your design into the wood. Now it's like the totem pole was inside the tree the whole time. We are just letting it out."

"Yes! Yes!" said Grampa, excited. "We are freeing the spirits alive in the tree for hundreds of years. Soon we will see their faces," said Grampa, but as he gripped the totem pole with one hand, he clutched his chest with the other.

"Grampa? Grampa, what's wrong?" said Jay, hanging on to Grampa's shoulders.

"My chest. I can't breathe," gasped Grampa. "Get your mother."

Jay stood frozen.

"Now!" wheezed Grandpa falling to his knees.

Jay snapped out of his fog and ran. "Mom! Mom, something's wrong with Grampa. Hurry!" he said breathlessly.

Jay's mom was sitting at her desk working on her laptop computer. She rolled back her chair and slammed the lid of the laptop shut.

"Where is he?" she asked.

"In the garage," said Jay. Jay bounded down the stairs three at a time and ran across the yard. He saw Johnny on the step having a smoke. "Johnny, it's Grampa, come and help us," yelled Jay.

"Huh, ah, OK," slurred Johnny. He picked up his can of Pepsi and stumbled toward Jay.

Jay smacked the can out his hand. The cover fell off the 'Pepsi' and rolled away. "Useless drunk," said Jay. He turned and sprinted to catch up with his mom.

Tatla and Jay found Grampa lying in the dust and wood shavings. His skin was a waxy yellow.

Tatla put her ear to his mouth. She checked his breathing. It was faint but it was there.

"Come on, pick him up. We have to take him to the hospital," she told Jay.

"Shouldn't we call 911?" said Jay.

"There is no 911 out here," she hissed. "Pick up his feet," she said. She bent over and grabbed her father under his arms.

After the two managed to lay Grampa in the back seat of the car, Tatla spun the tires, kicking up rocks as she backed out of the driveway.

"How far is it to the nearest hospital?" asked Jay.

"An hour," said Tatla.

"An hour, that's crazy. Isn't there somewhere closer?" asked Jay.

"Don't you think I'd take him there if there was?" she snapped. "In case you hadn't noticed we are in the middle of nowhere."

Jay sulked in his seat as his mother stepped on the gas pedal. Potholes be damned. She'd fix the car later.

They drove the winding mountain highway at illegal speeds.

"Hang on, Grampa. We're almost there. Please hang on," pleaded Jay over the seat.

Grampa took in short shallow breaths. His eyes were closed. Jay didn't know if Grampa had heard him or not.

Pulling into the emergency entrance Tatla ran into the hospital. What seemed like an eternity later, she returned with two ambulance attendants pushing a gurney.

The attendants expertly placed Grampa on the gurney and rolled him inside. Jay told them what happened before Grampa disappeared behind the examining room curtain.

Tatla stared at the floor for the next hour from orange, molded plastic seats welded together in groups of six.

"I'm sorry, honey. I shouldn't have snapped at you in the car. I just wish we had more medical services. We don't even have a clinic, too small and too remote," said Tatla.

Jay did his best to keep busy. He paced the floor, studied the contents of the vending machines, picked up expired magazines and put them down again. He kept one eye on the 'Authorized Personnel' door for any sign of the young doctor who wanted to know if Grampa had been drinking or if he had any allergies.

"Yeah, he's allergic to waiting to see a doctor," said Jay to his mom after the doctor left. Tatla gave her son a small smile.

"Has he been drinking? What kind of question is that? Do you think they ask everyone that?" said Jay.

"I don't know. I am sure it's standard procedure," said Tatla.

Two hours later the emergency room was full. Children bundled in blankets curled up on their mothers' laps, some of whom were well beyond the age and size to do so; an elderly couple leaned against each other but didn't speak, a man dressed in mechanic's overalls held a bloody rag around his hand.

Tatla asked the nurse several times how Mr. Roberts was.

"The doctor will let you know," was the nurse's pat answer.

"When? We've been here for hours," prodded Jay.

"I don't know. Now if you'll excuse me I have other patients to deal with," said the nurse firmly. She turned her attention to the computer screen.

"You are supposed to help us, not 'deal' with us," said Jay. The nurse never looked up.

"Never mind, honey, I am as frustrated as you are. We just have to wait. Grampa will be OK. He is made of sturdy stuff," said Tatla. She and Jay returned to the crowded waiting room.

After another long hour the doctor emerged.

"Your dad had an angina attack. He needs more tests and will probably be on medication for the rest of his life but he will be OK," said the doctor.

Tatla sank into Jay. "Thank goodness. Can we see him?" she asked.

"He is in there. You can only stay a moment. He needs to rest." The doctor pointed to a pale yellow curtained room.

Gingerly, Jay pulled back the curtain. Grampa lay on the bed with tubes that seemed to go in through his nose and come out from his arms. Electronic machines beeped rhythmically in the background.

"Hi, Grampa," said Jay, his voice cracking. "How are you doing?"

"I'm fine. How are you?" whispered Grampa.

Jay and Tatla looked at each other and smiled.

Tatla took her dad's hand, careful not to pull on the IV. "The doctors are keeping you for a few days to run tests. I'm sure you'll be home soon."

"No, I'm coming home now. I have to check on Gordon and the village is counting on us to finish the totem pole," said Grampa, reaching for the tubes. Tatla stopped him.

"No, Grampa. Johnny Walker is a lost cause. I don't know why you let him move in with you in the first place," said Jay.

"What about the totem pole?" asked Grampa. His voice sounded weak.

"The totem pole can wait until you get better," said Jay.

"Tatla, I need to talk to Jay," said Grampa.

Jay's mom took the hint and left her two men alone.

"Come here," said Grampa.

Jay went in closer.

"I let Johnny, I mean Gordon, move in with me because of the moon. He can stay as long as he wants. As for the totem pole you'll have to finish without me," said Grampa, his voice barely audible.

"No! No! We are finishing it together," Jay protested as the sting of tears blurred his vision.

"You have to do this. Do it for me, please. I know you can," said Grampa. His lips were dry and stuck together when he spoke.

"I don't even know what it's supposed to look like," said Jay.

"Yes you do. I know you have pictured it a thousand times. You are my grandson. You can do this," said Grampa.

"I don't know, Grampa. I'm sure the tribe will understand if it's not done," said Jay.

Grampa motioned Jay closer.

"If you don't finish it for the raising ceremony someone's getting scalped," said Grampa as he tugged on Jay's hair.

"Ouch," said Jay. He scratched his head where Grampa had pulled.

"Promise me you'll keep going," said Grampa. His eyes held Jay's.

"I'll try," Jay said. He escaped to the other side of the curtain, willing away his tears.

The following day was rainy and cloudy. Wind bent the trees back and forth scattering branches over the cars, the rooftops and the roads.

Jay walked past Grampa's house on his way to the garage, half expecting Grampa to open the door and join him. Johnny was nowhere to be seen and Jay could not have cared less. The garage was empty. Most people stayed home when it rained.

He wandered the garage, avoiding the cedar baskets piled against the walls. Raindrops pounded steady and hard on the tin roof. The sound was like bacon sizzling in a pan. Jay slid down a wall and sat on the floor. He stared at the totem pole until he was almost asleep. Jay thought he saw something move in the corner.

233

He snapped his head around to catch it but only a straw broom stared back.

My guardian spirit, thought Jay.

"Making sure I don't screw this up?" he said out loud and chuckled. Peeps from the swallow's nest made him feel less lonely.

Jay stared at the totem pole again. It was getting close to the bottom section; the most important part. Jay was terrified. He knew what had to be done but couldn't bring himself to pick up the adze.

Then something did move in the corner.

Caw, caw, caw.

The raven hopped up and down on a rafter, then swooped down. It landed on the far end of the totem pole.

Caw, caw, caw.

"Ok, I'll get to work," said Jay.

The raven dropped to the ground and skipped out of the garage. Jay had no idea how it got in there. The hole the swallows used was much too small for a raven to fit through.

Jay pictured his Grampa watching him, guiding his hand and correcting his technique. The ancestors, the tree and the people of the village were counting on him.

He picked up the adze and began the last section.

Chapter 33

Tatla and Jay drove to the hospital every day to visit Grampa even though he told them to stay to home and stop wasting gas. During the car ride home Jay asked Tatla if they were still moving back to the city. He had a feeling he already knew the answer but needed to know for sure.

"We can't now," said Tatla.

"Why not?" asked Jay.

"Because of the moon," said Tatla and she smiled to herself.

"Grampa said that to me a couple of times. What does it mean?" asked Jay.

"Your Grampa says we can all learn from the moon. If people were more like the moon then things would be better," said Tatla.

"That really doesn't tell me anything, Mom," said Jay.

"Let me try to explain. The moon always shows his face to us. We never see the back of his head. He doesn't turn his back on us, ever. If we never turned our backs on each other then the world would be a better place. That is Grampa's philosophy. When I left the village I thought your grandpa was invincible. When we came back I thought he was helping you and me but I see he needs us as much if not more. I can't leave him again. I hope you understand. It's not so bad here is it?" asked Tatla.

Jay looked out of the car window. After a few moments he said, "No, it's not so bad."

"And you have Jackson," said Tatla.

"Yeah, I guess," sighed Jay. The rain hit the windshield but up ahead through the tree lined canyon the sun shone down in slanted columns.

"Look, a rainbow," said Tatla. The well defined seven colored bridge spanned across the highway to the other side of the river.

Grampa came home a week later but had to stay in bed. Jay kept him up to date when he could get a turn. Chief George, May-Belle, and Mary were all daily visitors. Johnny Walker still had not returned.

"What do you think?" asked Grampa. He held up the necklace he was wearing. It was a suede pouch attached to a leather strap and adorned with beads.

"What is it?" asked Jay.

"It's a medicine bag filled with healing herbs. The beads are bones from buffalo and deer," said Grampa. "Mary brought it over to help me get better."

"I knew she was a witch," said Jay.

"No, but I do think she has a little magic in her," said Grampa. "I am feeling better already. How is our totem pole?"

"Good. I think it's done," said Jay. He had carved from sun up to sun down and beyond. Fred and Billy offered to help but Jay wanted it to be his and Grampa's.

"Even the paint?" asked Grampa.

"Seriously? We have to paint it?" asked Jay. He blinked rapidly. His face went ashen.

"No, we'll put a varnish on it to protect it, but otherwise we won't paint it," said Grampa, letting Jay off the hook.

"Whew, do you want to give me a heart attack, too?" asked Jay.

"Sorry, couldn't resist. I can't wait to see the totem pole," said Grampa.

"I am sure it's not as good as you would have done. Half the village seemed to be in the garage at any one time. I had to ask Chief George to keep them away. They were in such a panic to get all the baskets, blankets and mats done in time," said Jay.

"In time for what?" asked Grampa.

"Oops," said Jay and covered his mouth realizing he had let it slip out.

"In time for the potlatch," said Chief George. He had let himself in. "We cleaned up the longhouse so everyone could continue with all the wonderful carving and weaving. The elders thought it was time for a celebration."

"We weren't going to tell you until the pole rising," said Jay.

Chief George had agreed with Jay that he needed to focus on the totem pole. The decision to re-open the longhouse put the idea of having a potlatch celebration into everyone's head. They restored the longhouse back to its former glory, scrubbing away years of dust and cobwebs. The broken planks were replaced with new cedar ones bought at a discount from the mill.

"Here, help me up. I want to sit on the porch and get some fresh air. Can't stand being cooped up in here like a rabid dog," said Grampa.

"I know how you feel," said Jay.

Jay handed Grampa his jean jacket which he put on over top of his striped pajamas. Jay supported his grandfather's elbow and led him to the porch. Chief George held the door for them and pulled up a chair for Grampa.

Jackson came over and they whittled sticks with their pocket knives while Grampa watched bark and curled shavings of pale wood gather at their feet.

"Aren't you tired of carving wood?" asked the Chief.

"No way, I'm ready to do another totem pole," said Jay.

"You haven't finished this one," said Grampa.

"Oh crap, I forgot," said Jay. "Hey, Jackson, do you feel like painting some more?"

"I've had enough painting to last me a lifetime," said Jackson.

"Even if it's the totem pole?" asked Jay. His stick was whittled down to a fine point.

"What? Really? You're going to let me work on the totem pole with you?" said Jackson. His blade stuck in the branch.

They found the varnish and hauled out the brushes and rollers, clean except for the grey splatters on the handles.

Jay popped the lid and poured the amber liquid into an aluminum pan. The smell reminded Jay of art class. He ran his hand across the smooth surface of the totem pole letting his fingers outline the grooves and ruts he had painstakingly engraved. The wood was almost white and felt like suede from the hours of sanding Grampa insisted they do. When Jay thought it was good enough Grampa made him sand it again. It seemed a waste to cover the beautiful wood with anything but Jay trusted his grandfather.

They dipped the brushes in the pungent liquid. The consistency of the varnish took them by surprise, expecting it to be thick like paint, instead of watery. As Jay swept the dripping brush across the totem pole, the grain of the wood leaped out at him. Swirls, waves, and ripples patterned the surface.

Jay was mesmerized.

Jackson was terrorized.

The flies buzzed around him and landed on the totem pole sticking like a no-pest strip. The swallows did a great job of keeping the bugs away but they could never get them all.

The boys painted until nightfall and then again the next day. They cleaned the brushes and collapsed on Grampa's porch, giving him an update.

Tatla pushed open the front door, car keys in hand and said, "Ready to go?" She had come over earlier to cook Grampa his low fat, low sodium breakfast which he ate under protest. His blood pressure was still irregular and Tatla's doting was making it worse.

Jay kept his promise and invited Anthony to the potlatch. It was time to pick him up at the bus stop.

Jackson stood up. "I guess I'll see you later." He kicked away some sawdust and walked down the steps.

"Aren't you coming?" asked Jay.

"He's your friend," said Jackson.

"So are you. I thought we could take him up to the lake," said Jay.

"Ok, I call shotgun," said Jackson as he ran to the car.

"Nice try," said Jay. "See you soon, Grampa."

Grampa groaned.

"Mom, Grampa is turning into Grumpa again," said Jay.

"I know. He just found out he's not allowed to have his driver's license back until he goes for another stress test. His entire life he's been independent and self supporting. Now he has to rely on everyone else to get him to the doctor's appointments, bring groceries, and take his garbage to the dump," said Tatla.

Jay, Jackson and Tatla picked Anthony up at the bus stop; a lean-to shelter with a running dog logo painted on the side. Anthony hopped in the backseat beside Jay.

Anthony said hello to Tatla and Jay introduced Jackson.

"Hey," said Anthony.

"Hey," said Jackson.

"How was the bus ride?" asked Tatla.

"A four hour nightmare. The guy beside me took up his seat plus half of mine. He must have sweated the whole time. My window was stuck so I had to smell his disgusting breath," said Anthony.

"Halitosis," said Jay.

"What?" said Anthony.

"Never mind. I'll tell you the secret to riding the bus before you leave," said Jay.

"No way am I getting on any more public transit. My parents will have to come and get me," said Anthony.

Jay could tell by the look on Anthony's face that he wasn't too impressed with the village either. The car bounced over the cracked road. The potholes and ruts were now even deeper from the evening rain storms. Tatla's car had developed an unhealthy squeak.

A car ahead of them kicked up dust. Tatla rolled up the window to keep the dust out but Jay and Jackson didn't want to give up the breeze even for a minute.

"You were right, Jay. There isn't much here," said Anthony. He looked out the car window at the yards surrounded by mangled chain link fences. Plastic toys left out year round along with discarded appliances were so common they were almost considered lawn ornaments.

"Don't worry. We'll try not to totally bore you. Right, Jackson?" said Jay.

"Right, Jay," said Jackson. Jackson sat in the front seat with Tatla and didn't say much.

"There's May-Belle," said Jay. May-Belle waved to them from her window.

"The crazy cat lady?" asked Anthony. Jay had e-mailed Anthony detailed accounts of the village and the people.

"She's not crazy," said Jackson.

"That's your opinion," said Anthony. Jackson scowled.

Jay thought this might be a bad idea. Anthony had on a t-shirt, runners and shorts just like Jay and Jackson only Anthony's clothes didn't come from a big box store. He only wore the trendiest name brands exclusive to the boutique shops on designer row.

They dropped Anthony's bag at Jay's house and headed over to Grampa's. He stirred from his snooze at the sound of footsteps.

"Grampa, this is my friend Anthony," said Jay.

"Anthony, I've heard lots about you. You're here for the totem pole raising?" said Grampa.

"Yep. Can I see it?" asked Anthony.

"No, it is off limits until later," said Jay.

"Come on, just a peek," said Anthony.

"No, sorry, you have to wait," said Jay.

"So what are you kids going to do today?" asked Grampa.

"Jay and Jackson are going to show me some cool graffiti," said Anthony.

"Pardon?" said Grampa, his eyes narrowed with concern.

Chapter 34

"It's OK. I'm taking him to the lake to show him the pictographs. Can we borrow the canoe?" said Jay.

"Sure, but first go inside and bring me the box on my desk," Grampa instructed Jay.

Jay found the inlaid carved box. It had a detailed scene of a wolf pack stalking unknown prey in the forest. He grabbed it and brought it to Grampa.

Grampa removed the lid of the box and pulled out a bag of tobacco.

"Here, take this," he said and handed it to Jay.

Jay looked at Anthony and Jackson as if to say 'I think my Grampa's brain went without oxygen longer than we thought.'

"Thanks Grampa, but none of us smoke," said Jay.

"It is not for you. It is a gift for the Asking Rock," said Grampa.

"The Ass King rock?" snickered Jay.

"No, the Asking Rock. Do you never stop?" said Grampa, shaking his head.

"On your way to the pictographs, stop at the large, grey rock with the hollowed out center. You'll know it when you see it. Place some tobacco in the hole and ask for something. The rock will provide you with protection and answer your question. Sometimes it is not the answer you want to hear but it is always the right answer. You just have to ask," said Grampa.

"What have you asked for?" asked Jay.

"When I was eighteen I asked for a wife. I wanted this wild, beautiful girl who everyone in the village admired. What I got was your Gramma Alice. She turned out to be the most beautiful girl in the village to me. She wasn't wild but she had a giving spirit and made me laugh every day," said Grampa.

"What happened to the other girl?" asked Jackson.

"She ran off with a truck driver. No one has heard from her since," said Grampa. "The Asking Rock gave me exactly what I wanted even though I didn't know it."

"Ok, I'll stop at the Asking Rock. What do you want me to ask?" said Jay.

"You can't ask for me, you have to ask for something for yourself," said Grampa.

"I don't need anything," said Jay. "Except maybe an iPod."

"Think about it on your way to the lake," said Grampa.

Jay, Jackson and Anthony located the canoe at the side of the house. After a few attempts they managed to hoist it above their heads. They scuffled towards the trail like a six legged, olive green, fiber-glass, sci-fi creature. This time they remembered the paddles.

They passed the longhouse where a bustle of activity was taking place. The 3Ds were playing tag around the totem poles. Fred, Billy and Chief George were readying the foundation for the new totem pole. Ronald the rancher and Jackson's dad unloaded folding tables and stackable chairs. Jay had wanted to help but Grampa insisted he take the day off and spend some time with his friends.

Dillon, Jody and three other dogs followed the boys about halfway up then caught the scent of a coyote and took off into the trees. Jay wondered what they'd do if they ever managed to catch one.

The boys traversed their way up the sharp incline. Rocks and tree roots hindered their progress, but the shade of the giant cedars kept the temperature a few degrees cooler than in the village. The sound of crows and ravens in constant chatter accompanied them.

"I see what you mean about those crows. They are annoying," said Anthony.

"Funny, I don't really hear them anymore," said Jay, deep in thought about the Asking Rock.

They reached the clearing between the trail and the lake. Their leg muscles screamed to stop. Their sweaty hands felt fused to the canoe's edges.

"On the count of three, flip the canoe over," directed Jay when they had reached the shore. "One, two, three..."

The boys struggled to lift the canoe off their shoulders but it waffled and fell over, landing hard on the sand. The paddles bounced and banged inside.

"Real smooth," said Anthony.

The lake had warmed since the spring thaw. The water sparkled like sapphire blue glass with patches of emerald green where the fresh water clam beds lay. Jay wondered if the Cannibal Ogress was hiding in the woods.

Then he saw it, the Asking Rock. It was a two story tall boulder, jutting out from the shadows between the cedars. A patina of algae covered the top. Mossy patches and the odd fern grew on the various shelves and ledges. Jay went closer to get a better look. Evidence that other people had been here was clear by the items tucked in the crevices; a Barbie doll, a favorite pen, a pack of cigarettes. A walking stick also leaned against the rock.

A twig snapped behind the rock. Jay backed away. More twigs snapped. The sound of crunching gravel under footsteps made Jay hold his breath.

"Who's there? Is someone there?" asked Jay tentatively.

"It's just me," said Johnny Walker as he came out from behind the rock.

"Johnny Walker! What are you doing here?" asked Jay.

"Walkin' in the forest. Tryin' to get my head clear," said Johnny.

"You've been gone for weeks," said Jay. "Grampa has been worried about you."

"Is he OK?" asked Johnny.

"He's fine, no thanks to you," said Jay.

"Sorry," said Johnny. He stepped past Jay and continued on toward the trail to the village.

"Why doesn't he go back to his own village?" said Jay out loud. He didn't know or care if Johnny Walker heard. "I'm surprised he didn't start a forest fire."

Jay approached the rock still unsure of what to do. He removed the tobacco from the tiny front pocket of his swim shorts and opened the slightly steamy bag. The cherry fragrance of the dried leaves escaped.

Do I close my eyes? Do I say "Dear Rock"? Do I leave the whole bag? Geez, do I feel stupid. What are Anthony and Jackson thinking of me? Ah who cares what they think? Jay lectured himself.

His two friends were too busy throwing stones in the lake to pay attention to him, anyway.

Why am I doing this? It's ridiculous. He reached in and took a small handful of shredded tobacco. If the hole is the rocks' mouth then I should put a bit in its bottom lip. Like the ad says, 'Just a pinch between the cheek and gum'.

As Jay set the tobacco down on the ledge in the hole he decided to ask for something that would never come true. He didn't believe in magic rocks but if Grampa wanted him to ask for something then what could it hurt?

Anthony and Jackson continued to hurl flat stones side arm toward the water. Shoo, shoo, shoo, plunk. The stones skipped across the surface and sank out of sight. Jackson could not come close to Anthony's record of nine skips.

"So what did you wish for?" asked Anthony.

"I didn't wish for anything. I asked for something. And I'm not telling you because it won't happen anyway," said Jay.

"Jay, you mind if I borrow some tobacco?" said Jackson.

"Go ahead," said Jay, handing Jackson the baggie.

Jackson grabbed a handful and ran to the Asking Rock.

Jay took off his t-shirt and wiped his forehead with it.

"Hey, how come you're not a skinny runt anymore? You doing steroids or something?" asked Anthony.

Jay had been so busy with the totem pole he hadn't noticed that his arms and chest had bulked up.

"Steroids, no, just working my ass off, hauling boxes, painting and carving the totem pole twelve hours a day," said Jay.

They watched as Jackson mouthed something quickly, threw the tobacco into the hole like a carnival game, and ran back.

"Are we canoeing or not?" said Anthony. "I didn't lug this thing up here for nothing."

They kicked off their shoes and dragged the canoe halfway into the water. One by one they climbed aboard.

"Keep your body low, walk in the middle and hold on to the edge," instructed Jackson on the finer points of boarding a canoe.

Anthony didn't quite get the concept and teetered several times before plunking down hard on the wooden seat at the bow.

Jay sat in the middle. Jackson pushed off and leaped in as the canoe glided silently across the lake cutting V's into the surface. Jackson and Anthony paddled. The canoe drifted to the right going in a circle.

"Anthony, paddle on the left side," said Jackson. The canoe corrected and headed across the deserted lake. They paddled along the tree-lined shore, the hollow sound of the oars thunked against the side of the canoe as they headed towards the shale and granite cliffs at the south end of the lake. A few misplaced trees jutted impossibly from the steep rock wall. The roots clung to the rocks like an eagle claw.

"It's great to be chauffeured. I could get used to this," said Jay. He leaned back and dragged his fingers across the skin of the water.

"Get used to this," said Jackson. He slapped the water with the paddle and sent an icy wave over Jay.

"Ahhh, feels good," sputtered Jay.

"You can paddle back," said Anthony, sweat dripping down his nose.

The forest reflected black along the edge of the lake.

"Look up there, Anthony," Jay pointed as they rounded a small peninsula with black and white speckled granite towering above them.

"What are those markings?" said Anthony, pointing to red stick figures painted on the side of the rock face.

"Those are pictographs. They are supposed to be over a thousand years old. I'm not the only one who liked to tag walls," grinned Jay. His Grampa had told him of the ancient drawings a few days ago. He felt strangely proud to show them off to his friend.

The figures were simple drawings meant to communicate an event or a significant dream. It is the first writings of our people Grampa had explained. It is not meant to be artwork but a way of telling stories.

"See the four triangles with five lines at the top of each triangle, those must be bear tracks. The animal in the middle is a mountain goat I think, because it looks like it's got horns. There is the plus sign. It is either the four seasons or North, South, East and West," said Jay, recalling Grampa's descriptions.

"Cool. What are those supposed to be?" asked Anthony.

"I don't know. It's hard to tell, they are so faded. Grampa said my Gramma knew them all. Too bad she's not around anymore to tell us," said Jay.

Splash!

Anthony and Jay turned towards the sound, but saw only a ripple.

"Where's Jackson?" they said at the same time.

"Heeeyyyyy, loooosers," called a voice from above.

They looked up to see Jackson perched on a rock about ten feet above the water. He put his arms in front of him and dove in head first.

"I gotta try that," Jay said. He tumbled out of the canoe rocking it so hard it flipped over with Anthony still inside.

Anthony popped his head up a few seconds later looking like one of the otters at the zoo.

"Wow, the water is freaking ccccold," he said.

"Don't be su su such a wu wuss, city boy," stammered Jay through chattering teeth.

"You get used to it," said Jackson, treading water.

"What happened to 'look before you leap'?" said Anthony.

"I've done this tons of times. It's OK," said Jackson.

The glacier fed lake was extremely cold but felt good in the August heat.

Jay climbed the jagged rocks to the top of the cliff. He peered over the edge.

"It's higher than I thought," said Jay.

"That's because it is," said Jackson. "When you're in the lake you see from the water's surface to the top. When you're at the top you see from the top of the cliff to the bottom of the lake so it feels twice as high. It's not as far as you think." Jackson leaped from the edge and canon balled into the crystal water sending up a geyser.

"If he can do it, you can do it," said Anthony.

"Ok, we'll go together, on the count of three," said Jay.

They counted out loud, "One, two, threeeeee." Jay jumped off. His arms flailed like a new bird in freefall. The skin on his arms stung as he slapped the water upon entry. He kicked his legs up to the surface and snorted water from his nose. The sun floated diamonds on the lake.

"That was awesome," shouted Jay, looking around for Anthony who was still on the cliff.

"Anthony, you big chick…"

He didn't get to finish his sentence before Anthony was airborne, crashing into the water beside Jay.

"What a blast," said Anthony when he came to the surface.

The boys hurled their bodies into the water yelling and screaming, until the shadows of the trees stretched across the water and it was time to go back to the village.

"Hey, what's that?" said Jay pointing across the lake. "Is it a dog?" He squinted into the descending sunlight. "No, I think it's a bear."

"Nice try, I'm not falling for that. You're trying to freak me out. Very funny, let's scare the city boy," said Anthony.

"You just want to see a buh bear," stammered Jackson.

The three boys crouched on the cliff and stared at the dark figure as it lumbered along the shore towards them.

"I told you it was a bear," said Jay.

"What do we do?" said Anthony. His voice high pitched with panic.

"Jump," yelled Jay.

The boys leaped from the cliff. When they came up the bear was nowhere to be seen.

"I think it's gone," said Jackson.

"No, there it is," pointed Anthony.

"Where?" said Jackson.

"In the water; right there. It's swimming this way," said Jay breathless. "Get in the boat."

They grabbed the canoe and tried to all scramble in at once. The canoe fought back and threatened to roll over and play dead.

"Stop! One at a time," said Jay. "Jackson, hurry up, get in."

Jay and Anthony steadied the boat. Then Anthony got in and pulled Jay up and over the side. They grabbed the oars and started to paddle with all their strength. The canoe didn't budge.

Jay looked behind him. "Crap, it's tied up!"

Jay dropped his paddle and worked the knot.

"Who tied this thing anyway?" muttered Jay. The knot, now wet from Jay's hands refused to give up.

"He's coming closer," said Jackson.

Jay broke the branch and pushed off. The rope, knot and branch towed behind in the wake as they rowed furiously. Without a paddle Anthony hung over the side and used both hands to scoop the water. The canoe picked up speed. Being left handed allowed Jay to paddle on the left side and Jackson on the right. They matched stroke for stroke and headed to the beach.

"Here he comes. He's getting closer," said Jackson. The pitch of his voice rose higher and higher.

"Shut up and paddle, Jackson," said Anthony.

"Go away, go away," whispered Jay as the bear caught up to the canoe.

Jay raised his paddle ready to defend himself and his crew.

The bear turned its black snout and round ears towards Jay and the world slowed down. The bear swam easily. Its wide, front paws pulled the water, keeping the wet, black spiky fur above the surface. Breath, like a steam engine, pumped out of the flared nostrils along with the occasional snort of water and snot.

Brown eyes met in agreement. *I won't bother you if you don't bother me.*

The bear swam past the canoe, pulled itself onto the shore and shook off the heavy coat of water. He crashed into the dense black forest and was gone.

The boys pulled their paddles up and drifted onto the beach. The canoe scraped bottom and came to an abrupt stop.

After a moment Jackson spoke, "If I didn't believe it I wouldn't have seen it."

Anthony and Jay cracked up.

"What?" said Jackson unaware of his mix-up.

"I had no idea bears could swim," said Jay.

"And swim good," said Jackson.

The boys climbed out of the canoe. They stood on the shore staring at the forest where the bear had exited.

"I'm in the middle on the way back," said Anthony.

"Why should you get the middle?" said Jackson.

"In case the bear comes back. If my parents pick me up and I only have one leg, they'll never let me come back," said Anthony.

"Who said we want you back?" said Jay.

"Yeah," said Jackson.

"Fine, carry it back yourselves," said Anthony.

"Just kidding. How about rock, paper, scissors for the middle?" said Jay.

Jackson won the draw and the three boys began the task of removing the small boat from the water. The canoe wobbled, half submerged, knowing it's legless body would no longer be the smooth swift vessel carrying the boys to safety but a burden to be carried.

"Jackson, you should get the middle 'cause, man were you scared. I thought you were going to pee your pants," teased Anthony.

Jackson didn't say anything.

"You did pee your pants!" said Anthony.

"Well, I couldn't exactly stop and find a nice tree somewhere," said Jackson.

"I'm glad you didn't," said Jay.

"Yeah, me too," said Anthony. "Hey, too bad we can't ride the canoe down the trail."

"Too bad," said Jay. He and Jackson snickered.

On the way back, to bring the noise level up, they sang any song they could think of to keep the bears away. The songs started out cool like AC/DC's "Highway to Hell" but soon deteriorated to childhood favorites like "Teddy Bear's Picnic" and "Under the Sea" from "The Little Mermaid".

That night, the three boys camped outside in Jay's backyard and counted shooting stars. Jay pointed out Scout, the first star of the night, and said its other name was Fomalhaut.

Anthony said "Foam-a-lot? I don't think so. You guys are just messing with me. It's sounds like some kind of latte my mom would drink."

"Yeah, and it's sponsored by Starbucks, get it "Star"bucks," said Jay.

"Yeah, I get it. Hilarious. What's the streaky cloud in the middle of the sky?" said Anthony. When Jackson told him it was the Milky Way Anthony punched him in the arm and called him a liar.

"It is," said Jay. "See how milky it looks. It's not clouds; it's stars."

"This is better than the planetarium," said Anthony.

Chapter 35

In the morning the boys awoke to the sound of Tatla's excited voice. They had moved inside to the living room when the sun rose and shone directly on them making it impossible to sleep in.

"It's here, it's here," she called.

The boys watched as a white cube van pulled up. Tatla rushed out to greet the driver.

"What's here?" asked Jay. Jay thought the moving van was delivering more lost boxes from the move.

"Wait until you see," said Tatla.

Two men in dirty white t-shirts climbed out of the truck and rolled up the back door. They reached in and slid out a cardboard box almost the size of a billboard.

"Where do you want it?" inquired the tall, unshaven driver.

"Hey, don't I know you?" said Jay.

"Is that you, kid?" said Painter.

"What are you doing here? I thought you were in jail," said Jay.

Grampa, who was sitting on the porch having coffee with Chief George watched with interest.

"I had a good lawyer. He got me work release. It's not bad. I get to drive around instead of being cooped up in jail," said Painter. "How are you doing?"

"Pretty good," said Jay. Tatla quickly interrupted when she realized how Jay knew the driver.

"Put it against the garage over there, please," directed Tatla. She signed the form on the clipboard given to her.

"Sweet mural, did you do this, kid?" asked Painter, bending back his head to get a good look at the raven painted on the garage.

"Yup," replied Jay.

"You would have made an awesome apprentice," said Painter.

The boys, Grampa and Chief George followed Tatla to the side of the garage. The movers balanced the package against an outside wall and turned to go. Tatla handed them a tip, hoping to get rid of them in a hurry.

"See you later, kid," said Painter.

"No you won't," said Tatla under her breath.

"Jay, give me a hand with this, please," said Tatla.

They grabbed the edges of the box and pulled out the large brass staples holding it shut. Once one side was open, Tatla and Jay slid out the frame, being careful not to drag it on the dirt.

Chief George and Grampa's eyes were wide. "Tatla, it's the picture of the potlatch," said Grampa.

"I had one of my suppliers blow it up," said Tatla.

The poster was bronze in color and the cracks from the old photo were now more pronounced. The faces of Jay's ancestors were speckled and pixilated when he looked at it up close but from the other side of the yard it was the same picture he had found during those first days in the village.

"Where are you going to put it?" asked Jay.

"In the longhouse. If it's OK with the elders," said Tatla, smiling.

Jay, Jackson and Anthony shuffled their feet while the adults stared at the poster.

"What are you boys doing hanging out here? Didn't you spend enough time here this summer? Why don't you go to the rope swing?" said Grampa.

"Yeah, let's get out of here," said Anthony.

They grabbed some Pop-Tarts and headed down the path, past the totem poles and the longhouse. Jackson stopped in to the longhouse to tell his mom he was going to the rope swing.

The elders were happy to see a new face. They showed Anthony all the crafts and artwork they had been working on for the last couple of months.

"This stuff is amazing," said Anthony. "My folks would pay big money for this."

Mary grabbed a drum and put it in Anthony's lap.

"Here, paint," she said.

"Paint? I don't know how to paint. What should I paint?" Anthony looked at Jay for direction.

"Paint what you know. What you love. What guides you," said Mary.

Anthony gave it some thought and went with his baseball team crest.

The boys spent the day hiking in the mountains and exploring the many caves. They were so absorbed in what they were doing they lost track of time and almost missed the pole raising.

They ran the whole way back and quickly got ready. Right before sundown the boys gathered with Grampa, Tatla, the entire village and more, outside the garage.

The healthy able adults along with Jay lined up on either side of the totem pole, picked up the ropes laid out underneath and hoisted it up off the sawhorses. Slowly they moved together carrying the totem pole out of the garage. Miles and the gang

256

banged their drums in step and the elders chanted a low melody for the debut of the totem pole to the sun, the air, the trees, and the sky.

Chief George led the way to the longhouse to bless the totem pole.

"To honor our past, our present and our future and to show how strong, proud and resilient our people are, let the totem pole rise," said Chief George.

Jay grabbed one of the many ropes attached to the totem pole and together he, his grandfather, and all the people of the village, pulled until the totem pole stood upright. It proudly took its place next to the other totem poles.

Chief George continued the blessing. He started at the top and spoke of each symbol.

"We are grateful to Moon who watches over us, to Raven who has brought light back to the eyes of our people. We are blessed to see the spirit of Frog who has brought riches to our families by renewing our ancient crafts. We are proud to have these gifts shouldered by Wolf, the spirit of leadership and family to keep the fabric of our village tightly knit."

Jay and Grampa smiled at each other, knowing the totem pole was just as the other had imagined.

Fred and Billy came up next. They placed two ladders under Thunderbird. Together they carried the newly carved wing to the top of the ladder and placed in the slot where the other wing once flew.

Mary spoke. "Today we have mended what was wounded in the past. Let the healing continue."

The people of the village held their hands with the palms upward to the sky.

"Are they checking for rain?" asked Anthony.

"No, they are giving thanks to the Great Spirit," said Jay.

The front of the longhouse was a freshly painted grizzly bear. Its huge mouth swallowed up the tribe members one by one as they entered.

Inside, the longhouse came alive with activity. The fire in the center of the room made shadows across the story totem poles at each side of the doors; Bear, Beaver and Salmon. Their eyes moved with each flicker and their teeth bared, ready to join the feast.

The tribe used carved wooden boxes and beaded bags to decorate the longhouse. The multi-colored blankets were hung on the walls and baskets were placed on the plank floor. The potlatch picture hung from the ceiling at the far end of the longhouse.

"You did a great job on the garage and the totem pole," said Grampa as they entered the longhouse.

"I didn't think I had it in me, but it does look pretty good," said Jay.

"I think you are capable of many great things. I have a present for you," said Grampa. He handed Jay a package wrapped in brown paper.

"What is it?" asked Jay. He forgot about the gift giving tradition of the potlatch. The belief was the more you gave the more you received in return.

"Open it and find out," urged Anthony.

Jay tore the paper from the box. It was a cedar box about the size of a shoe box meticulously painted with the symbol of the mythical double-eyed monster.

"Thanks Grampa. It's nice," said Jay flatly.

"Look inside," urged Grampa.

Jay lifted the lid of the box. "An iPod. Really? Thanks, Grampa."

"I guess the Asking Rock worked," said Anthony.

"This isn't what I asked for," said Jay.

"What did you ask for, a bag of tobacco? Come on let's potlatch 'til we puke," said Anthony.

Jay, Anthony and Jackson worked their way over to the feast set out on the buffet table; deer stew, poached salmon, butter clam chowder and salty, crispy, melt-in-your mouth seaweed. Jay decided it wasn't completely horrible but not something he'd give up spaghetti for.

Not only was the food incredible but also the dishes they were served in. A bowl shaped like a wolf head; the serving spoon held in its mouth. An orca whale whose dorsal fin was the handle used to remove the lid. Wooden clam shells in various sizes held sugar and other condiments. Miniature canoes were filled with more contemporary party snacks like potato chips and cheese puffs. The women kept the bowls topped up with piping hot food all night long.

"Have you tried the seaweed yet?" Mary asked the boys from the other side of the buffet table.

She and May-Belle both wore floor length blankets made of black felt with a huge circle of red felt in the middle. Within the circle was an outline of Thunderbird, sewn in white pearl buttons on May-Belle's blanket and the four winds sewn on Mary's blanket.

"Yes, Grandmother, it's really salty but not as gross as I thought it would be," said Jay.

Mary and May-Belle laughed.

"How come you called her Grandmother?" asked Anthony.

"I didn't know I had," said Jay. He thought about it for a second then replied. "It is a sign of respect to the elders."

"Oh, OK. Which one is Miles?" asked Anthony.

"The big one in the corner," said Jay. He picked up a steamed mussel in a black half shell and slid it into his mouth. Fishy water dripped down his chin. He dragged his right forearm across his face to wipe it off.

Miles sat cross legged in a circle with the other boys and one girl, their drums placed before them creating an inner circle. Paper plates piled with food rested on their laps. They ate with their hands and licked their fingers. No apples in sight.

"He's big but I could take him," said Anthony. Miles turned and stared in their direction.

"Nobody is taking nobody," said Jay. He returned to his food. The deer stew was fantastic.

"What is this?" asked Anthony.

"Deer," said Jay.

"Sorry. What is this, *Dear*?" said Anthony.

Jay, Jackson and Anthony laughed a little too loudly and caused heads to turn.

Courtney snuck up behind Jay and slipped a necklace made of leather, black and silver beads and a bear claw over his head. He turned to thank her but she disappeared into a crowd of her friends.

"Hey, she's cute," said Anthony.

Jay's face felt as hot as the sun. He pulled the bear claw away from his chest and put his chin down to get a closer look.

Fred saw Jays' embarrassment and leaned in to rescue him. He fingered the claw. It was flat and crescent shaped with a sharp tip. The edges were shiny black and the flat part was light grey.

"Looks like a black bear. Rear paw," said Fred.

Anthony's eyebrows went up. "Very cool," he said.

Fred continued on, making his rounds through the longhouse talking to everyone. The children followed him as

260

pennies, symbolic of the copper gifts given during past potlatches, fell from his cedar robes. He pretended not to notice. The children giggled as they scrambled to collect each coin, thinking they were pulling one over on Fred.

Jay watched as everyone mingled. People came up to congratulate him on carving the totem pole, including a local politician he didn't know. He saw Principal Williams, Mr. Dunbar, Mrs. Scott. It was strange to see them outside of school. Mrs. Scott had beaded earrings on and feathers in her hair. A lot of tribe members who had moved away to find work returned for the celebration. Even the Martins came back. Tatla introduced them to Jay. He felt awkward knowing he was living in their old house.

Ronald the rancher sat with Dr. Two-Feathers pointing and laughing at the kids chasing the dogs, almost over turning the food tables. The 3Ds sat with their mom and grandmother eating the bracelets they had made using Cheerios and Fruit Loops as beads. Everyone was happy, admiring each others regalia and exchanging presents.

The kids from the pool charged over to Jay. Breathless and excited they showed Jay the gifts they received.

"See what we got," said Angela, the tallest and oldest of the four. They held up the gifts; miniature dug out canoes each with a different ornamental bow and stern; a beaver, a salmon, a whale and an otter. All faced forward like they were swimming the crawl except the otter which was face up floating on his back.

"Who made these? They are awesome," said Jay.

"We don't know. We found them sitting on those mats with our names on them and a note that said they really floated and we could play with them in our pool," said Angela.

"That's really strange," said Jay. He looked around the longhouse to see if he could figure out who the anonymous gift giver was. His eyes stopped when he noticed Grampa and Tatla speaking to a lady. He didn't know who it was until he looked at her chubby ankles. Tatla waved him over. "Jay, look who came," said Tatla.

"Hi, Mrs. Thornton," said Jay. "How are you?" he asked.

"I am amazed at the wonderful things everyone has made. The food, the music, the costumes," said Mrs. Thornton.

"Regalia," said Jay.

"Pardon?" said Mrs. Thornton.

"The celebration clothes are called regalia not costumes," said Jay. Mrs. Thornton looked sheepish.

"I'm sorry," she said.

"That's OK, I made the same mistake," said Jay.

"Thanks for letting me know. This has been a marvelous experience. I've learned so much about your culture. Maybe I'll suggest all my charges be sent here," said Mrs. Thornton.

"Oh, uh, well." Grampa struggled for the words.

"I'm just kidding," said Mrs. Thornton, letting him off the hook.

"And make sure you ask the dancers before you take their picture," said Grampa.

"Why would I do that?" asked Mrs. Thornton.

"Many believed the camera was stealing their spirit. Now it is mostly a sign of respect," said Grampa.

Mrs. Thornton raised her camera toward Tatla. Tatla nodded her approval and Mrs. Thornton snapped the picture.

The Chief did one more blessing of Skye's baby then a slow steady beat of a single drum indicated the start of the dancing.

Mary, May-Belle and the other elders took their seats of honor in the front row and watched the dancing and singing. They clapped and cheered and raised their palms in thanks.

A beautiful lady in thick black braids with a turquoise blue beaded headband made her way across the floor. Dipping her head, twirling her hands, lightly stepping her bare feet up, out and down. Jay was hypnotized by the fluid motion and the delicate sound of bells around her ankles.

"Who's that lady?" Anthony asked Jay.

"I don't know. It must be one of the guests," said Jay.

The lady continued her dance around the fire, bowing and turning, praying to the earth then to the sky. She made her way toward Jay and winked.

"That's no lady, that's my mom," exclaimed Jay.

"She's beautiful," said Jackson. "Like a princess."

"Stop it, she is not," protested Jay, embarrassed but proud at the same time.

"She's pretty good, eh?" said a voice on the other side of Jay.

He turned to see Grampa, wearing an ankle length yellow cedar tunic made from strips of softened bark that looked like suede and a traditional ring hat.

"Nice lampshade, Grampa," said Jay.

"Hey, watch it. I still have the receipt for your iPod. Teresa just gave these to me. She made them herself from the cedar strips we took from the tree. What do you think of your mother?" asked Grampa.

"I didn't know it was her," said Jay.

"Are you going to try one of the dances?" asked Grampa.

Tatla tried to teach Jay the dances she learned as a child. After having her toes stepped on and tripped up a few times they decided it wasn't safe to have Jay dance, especially near an open flame at a potlatch.

263

"No, it's better for everyone if I just watch. I think my Indian name should be "Dances with two left feet," joked Jay. Anthony agreed.

"Why don't you dance, Mr. Roberts," suggested Anthony.

"No, no, I'm leaving that to the youngsters. I'm going to tell a story later," said Grampa.

Jackson's dad, Stone, brought out more Indian candy in a variety of flavors like teriyaki, garlic, and honey. Jackson motioned for his dad to come and join them. Stone came over carrying a long skinny package wrapped in newspaper.

Jackson took the package and handed it to Jay. A card taped to the package read: To Jay – From Jackson.

"I didn't get you anything," said Jay.

"Whatever, just open it," said Jackson. He shifted his weight from left to right.

Jay peeled the newsprint off the package. "A paddle? You got me a paddle? Gee, I wonder why? It's really nice." The paddle was made from a single piece of yellow cedar and came up to Jay's chin.

"Where did you get it?" asked Jay.

"I made it," said Jackson. He took the paddle from Jay's hands and turned the handle upside down to show Jay the paddle side. "See, this side is Frog." He rotated the paddle. Painted in green the frog image sprang; webbed feet splayed, grin on its face, legs stretched. "And this side is Salmon." The First Nation symbol of renewal painted in red and black showed Salmon's hook nose and bulging eye. The size and shape of Salmon fit perfectly on the paddle end.

"I used Frog and Salmon because I know they like water," said Jackson. "I made one for myself, too."

264

Chief George looked on with pride and remarked that the only thing missing was their masks.

"And Gordon," said Grampa. Jay had seen Johnny Walker at the pole raising. He stood apart from the village and left as soon as the pole was raised.

"Where are the masks?" asked Jay. He looked up at the potlatch picture that showed men wearing masks as big as themselves, carved and decorated to look like eagles and wolves.

"The masks and other treasures were burned or stolen when the Europeans abolished potlatches in the late 1800s. Even up until 1921 people were still being arrested for having potlatches. Some tribes continued to have potlatches but had to do so in secret."

"See in the picture at the feet of the chief? Those were copper gifts to be given to the visiting chief but no one knows where they are now," said the chief.

"Some say they are hidden in the mountains somewhere," said Grampa.

"Buried treasure; we'll have to find it," said Jay.

"Let's go look for it tomorrow," said Jackson and Anthony.

The dancing, singing and story telling lasted until dawn.

The next day the chief dropped by Grampa's house to see how he was feeling. Jay, Jackson and Anthony also stopped by before heading up to the lake for one last swim.

Anthony's parents were picking him up later.

"That was some potlatch wasn't it?" said Chief George, squinting into the sunshine.

"It sure was. Our wives would have enjoyed it," said Grampa. He rubbed Dillon's belly with his foot. Jody lay panting between Jay and Anthony.

Jay touched his necklace and wondered what Courtney was doing right now.

"It's a shame it was probably our last one," said Chief George.

"Why is that?" asked Anthony, scratching the back of Jody's neck.

"More people are leaving than staying. The kids move to the city and never come back. No one can afford to stay here," said the chief.

"My dad said you don't have to pay taxes so why would anyone leave?" said Anthony. "My dad hates paying taxes."

"You need an income to pay taxes. Is it better to pay taxes, rent and childcare in the city or is it better to stay here, not pay the same taxes but possibly live in poverty?" said Chief George. "But enough of that, did you have a good time last night?"

"It was great, Chief. This is the best summer I ever had," said Jay. "Last year my mom sent me to this boring summer camp. It cost her over five hundred dollars and we didn't do anything fun. Don't tell her, Grampa, but it was lame. Right, Anthony?" said Jay.

"Yeah, it was really pathetic," said Anthony.

The three boys headed up to the lake, but left the canoe behind this time in case they ran into the bear again and needed a speedy get away. Jay decided his new paddle was too good to use and hung it up on the wall in his bedroom.

"Take Dillon and Jody with you, in case that bear's around," said Grampa.

"She won't harm them as long as they don't surprise her," said Chief George. "Her cub was hit by a truck so she's not as dangerous. Poor girl."

Jay touched his necklace again. This time he wondered where Courtney got the bear claw.

Was it hunted or did it die in an accident?

"I know what you're thinking, Jay," said Chief George. "The bear claw around your neck once belonged to a bear. The bear is our brother. We have lived together in the forest since time was tracked only by the return of the salmon."

"If he's our brother then why do we hunt them?" said Jay.

"Because they taste good," said Jackson. He laughed at his own joke until Jay scowled at him. "That pepperoni you had last night; bear."

Jay's face dropped. It looked, smelled and tasted like regular pepperoni. He wasn't sure he would have eaten it if he'd known.

"Besides that, we are keeping a balance. Only a few are hunted each year and we use all the parts of the bear. Nothing is wasted. It is a way of conserving the population. If there are too many bears and not enough food the stronger males will kill the weaker youths. The black bear numbers have been steady over the years and nothing to worry about," said the Chief. "Hunting Grizzly is another issue."

"Are there Grizzlies around here?" asked Anthony. He snapped open his pocket knife.

"Sometimes, but very rarely," said Grampa. "Go on, now. Enjoy the day."

"Dillon, Jody, let's go," said Jay. They rose from their sleeping positions. Dillon stretched and Jody copied. Legitimate stretches this time for their health and not for biscuits.

The dogs chased each other through giant ferns, bounding over the granite rocks. Jay thought he'd lost them a few times and then they would pop up, out of the bush thirty feet ahead.

Anthony cursed at them for scaring him. "I thought it was that bear again."

267

A raven called from high in the tree tops answered by another raven on the other side of the forest. The boys listened as the birds exchanged information.

"They sound like a couple of whining old ladies," said Anthony.

"It sounds exactly like my mom does when my dad comes up behind her and puts an ice cube down her back," said Jackson. "He calls it the poor man's taser gun."

The boys stepped out of the dark forest and into the bright sunlight, blinded momentarily by the brilliance of the lake.

They scoured the lake shore for signs of the bear but saw none. Either, the whooping of the kids leaping into the water or the dogs barking at squirrels would be warning enough for any bear. Anthony threw a stick into the lake for the dogs. Jody made a valiant attempt but could never out swim Dillon. Jay wondered who would tire first; Anthony or Dillon. Anthony's arm was strong from baseball but Dillon's stick obsession could not be underestimated.

"Watch this," said Anthony. He picked up a walnut-sized rock. Dillon and Jody, knee deep in water, kept their eyes riveted on Anthony's hand. He leaned back, twisted to his right, pulled his arm back and whipped the rock. It flew high across the lake getting lost in the sunlight. Three seconds later it splashed in the lake, spouting water.

Dillon and Jody dove into the water and dog paddled toward the ripples. After 100 feet Jody made a slow u-turn and huffed and puffed back to shore. Dillon was not deterred.

"That dog is crazy. He's going to swim out there and realize the rock is gone. Then what? Start diving for it," said Jackson. "He'll drown."

Jay saw the determination in Dillon. He knew Jackson was right. It was too far for any of them to swim and no canoe to

268

paddle out with either. Dillon had slowed down to half speed. His nose sprayed a fine mist with each breath. The only thing to do was give Dillon an out.

"Dillon, come on boy. Here Dillon," said Jay. "Here, boy." Jay looked at Anthony and Jackson. They joined in. "Come Dillon. Good dog," said Jackson.

"I've got a stick. Come and get the stick," called Anthony, waving a stick above his head.

Dillon eyed them from the corner of his eye and turned to swim back. He was halfway to shore when his head starting slipping under; his black nose barely breaking the surface. Jay dove into the water. Jody joined him. They reached Dillon as his head went under. Jay pulled Dillon up by the loose skin on the back of his neck.

Swimming with one hand on Dillon and one hand pulling the water side arm, they made their way back. Jackson and Anthony stood waiting waste deep, cheering Jay on. Together they dragged Dillon on to the beach. He and Jay lay panting. Jody hovered over Dillon and licked his mouth.

After a few minutes Dillon got to his feet to have a full body shake. Starting with his head he flapped his ears like a sputtering propeller then he shimmied his shoulders spraying water over everyone and ending with a final flick from the tip of his tail. He trotted over to the forest edge and relieved himself on a sapling, then returned to Anthony, dropping a stick at his feet.

The boys groaned. "That dog has serious brain damage," said Jackson.

"I save his life and he wants you to throw the stick. Thanks a lot Dillon," said Jay.

"What can I say? The dog has excellent taste," said Anthony. "We better get going. My mom and dad will be here soon."

They made a detour to Sadie's for orange pop and ketchup potato chips. Dillon got most of the chips. After stopping by the longhouse to get Anthony's drum they headed back to Jay's to wait for Anthony's parents.

"Mom, have Anthony's parents called?" asked Jay.

"Yes, they called from their cell phone. They're checking out some waterfront property nearby and will be here soon. At least I think that's what they said. The signal was terrible," said Tatla.

"That sounds like my dad; always checking out the real estate. 'Buy waterfront. They're not making more,'" said Anthony, mimicking his dad.

Chapter 36

Eventually they heard the Mercedes SUV pull in. A cloud of dust followed and then overtook the luxury vehicle. Dillon, Jody and four other dogs rounded Grampa's house barking and circling the SUV. Jay cringed when Dillon jumped up on the driver's door.

Mr. Gardener banged on the window. Grampa came out and shooed them away. "Sorry, it's our local welcome wagon," said Grampa.

"More like welcome waggin'", said Jay.

When she was sure it was safe, Anthony's mom opened the door and placed her high-gloss, high-heel shoe on the uneven ground twisting her ankle slightly.

"Mom, we saw a bear," said Anthony.

"How nice dear," she said as she checked her shoe for damage.

After dusting off the toe it finally registered. "A what? You saw a what?" she screeched.

"You saw a what?" repeated Tatla, coming down the stairs to greet her guests.

"We saw a bear. It was totally awesome. We watched it swim across the lake," said Anthony.

"John, did you hear what Anthony said?" said Mrs. Gardener.

"Yes, sounds like quite an adventure," said Mr. Gardener, examining the paint for dog scratches.

"And, look at the drum I made. Chief George even blessed it," said Anthony. He held up the drum and banged out a beat.

271

"That is lovely, dear," said Anthony's mom. "I didn't know you were such a good painter. Maybe I'll have you do something for my next exhibit."

"Pretty cool, huh, dad. I can entertain us on the way home," said Anthony. Bang, bang, bang.

Mr. Gardener rolled his eyes. "For three hours? I don't think so, maybe a few miles." He took the drum from Anthony and examined its structure.

Anthony opened the bag of chips they bought at Sadie's. He'd been saving it for the ride home but couldn't wait any longer. Dillon bowed at the sound of the crinkling paper.

Anthony ignored him. Dillon bowed again. Anthony threw him a chip. Dillon chewed once and swallowed it almost whole. Then he bowed, again.

"That dog worships you," said Anthony's mom.

"He's an awesome dog. Can we get one?" said Anthony.

"He's way too big for an apartment. It wouldn't be fair to the dog," said Mr. Gardener.

"Why don't you get a small one? Dr. Two-Feathers was telling me she just picked up a litter of Chihuahua-crosses before the potlatch," said Tatla. Mrs. Gardener gave her a look.

"Sorry, Pamela," said Tatla, but it was too late. The seed had been planted.

"Can we? Come on, Mom. Please, Dad," begged Anthony.

"Well, we can go have a look but I'm not making any promises," said Mr. Gardener.

"Thanks for having Anthony over, Tatla. I hope he wasn't any trouble," said Mrs. Gardener.

"No, I hardly saw them," said Tatla.

"Come and check out the garage Jay painted," said Anthony. He dragged his parents to the side of the house and told them to wait. The doors of the garage opened and the Raven's wings expanded. The Gardeners were speechless for a minute.

"That is amazing," Mr. Gardener said.

"Incredible. You've really captured the expression of the raven," said Mrs. Gardener. She viewed it with the critical eye of someone who buys, sells and appreciates art.

"That reminds me. Jay, who was the man at the end of the street? When we stopped to ask for directions I thought he looked like an artist I once knew," said Mrs. Gardener.

"He's nobody, just Johnny Walker," said Jay.

"That's what he said. I gave him my card anyway," said Mrs. Gardener.

"Well Pamela, should we get going?" said Mr. Gardener checking his Rolex.

"Yes. Which way to Dr. Two-Feathers?" asked Mrs. Gardener.

"Anthony, take your parents past the totem poles first," said Grampa.

"OK and thanks for the drum," said Anthony to Jay's Grampa. They shook hands.

"See you later, Anthony," said Jay and Jackson.

"See you guys. Thanks for an awesome time," said Anthony.

"Send me an e-mail," said Jay as Anthony walked to the car with his parents.

"How was your visit?" asked Mrs. Gardener.

Jay smiled when he overheard his friend say, "It's really cool being First Nations."

Chapter 37

Jay and Jackson grabbed a couple of colas from the fridge and sat at the kitchen table. They watched the house flies perform perfect squares overhead. The boys were too hot and tired to do anything less mindless. Even turning on the TV seemed like a monumental task.

"Are you excited to go back to school, Jackson?" asked Jay's mom as she put away the breakfast dishes.

"Mom, why do adults always ask that? Of course he's not happy to go back to school," said Jay.

"Well, maybe he is. Maybe he is bored of summer. Maybe he is looking forward to not being the low man on the totem pole this year. Right, Jackson?"

"Hey, remember it's good to be the low man on the totem pole," said Jay.

"I won't be going to Nelson High next year. My dad can't find a job and the fishing this year wasn't good enough to hold us over the winter. My mom's cousin got her a job at the museum, in the anthro-apology department," said Jackson.

"Anthropology department," corrected Tatla.

"That's what I said. She's going to show the tourists how to make baskets and mats," said Jackson.

"Oh, so reduced to a museum attraction? Like cavemen or something?" asked Jay.

"Well it pays pretty well and she can keep the money she collects selling the baskets and mats. We're moving to the city to live with my cousin until we find a place," said Jackson.

"Can I go, too?" asked Jay.

"No, you know you can't," said Tatla.

"Why don't you stay with us until your parents find a place?" said Jay.

"I already asked. My grandmother had a fit. She said they aren't going to split us up again," said Jackson.

"That sucks," yelled Jay. He stormed up the stairs and slammed his bedroom door. The plates on the kitchen wall shook. Jay kicked his desk chair over before diving onto his bed, face first, and punched his pillow.

He knew his mom was right. Grampa was not well. The doctors told him not to drive until he had his blood pressure under control. He had doctor's appointments almost every day. Tatla drove him when she could but without Fred or Billy or Sadie pitching in he would have missed half his appointments.

"Jay, Jackson wants to talk to you," Tatla called through the door.

"I don't care. Tell him to go away," said Jay.

A second knock came a few minutes later. Jay ignored it.

"Jay, it's Grampa. Open the door, please," said Grampa.

Jay unlocked the door but didn't open it.

Grampa turned the handle and found Jay righting his desk chair. He sat down, picked up a pencil and doodled at his desk, keeping his back to Grampa. Jackson leaned against the door jamb.

"Why don't you come out of your room and go do something with Jackson? You've only got two days left before school starts," said Grampa. He sat down on the bed, winded from climbing the stairs.

"What's the point? He's leaving anyway," said Jay and continued to doodle.

"The point is to spend as much time with the people you care about while they are around," said Grampa.

"I don't care about him," said Jay.

"You know back in the old days, boys your age were sent away on quests to prove their manhood. They would hike alone in the woods and survive on nothing but their instincts. There are places near the pictographs where they carved holes in the stones for days to show their endurance," said Grampa.

"What does that have to do with anything?" said Jay.

"They were probably just as scared as you are. No one wants to feel alone, but you carry on and do something about it," said Grampa.

"I saw those holes," said Jay. He put the pencil down and looked out the window. The cedar trees swayed back and forth painting the sky blue with long brush strokes.

"Yeah, me too," said Jackson from the doorway.

"By the stupid Asking Rock," they said in unison.

"Why do you call it a stupid Asking Rock?" said Grampa. "It did protect you from the bear."

"Because I asked for something and it never came true," said Jay, putting down his pencil.

"Me, too," said Jackson. "I asked for my dad to find a job so we wouldn't have to move."

"When did you ask?" asked Grampa. He leaned forward; his elbows on his knees.

"When we went to the lake," said Jay.

"That was only a few days ago," said Grampa. "You can't expect it to answer right away. It's not a vending machine where you put your money…"

"Tobacco," interrupted Jay.

276

"…pardon me, your tobacco in, and expect the answer to fall into your hands," said Grampa. "Be patient, it will come. Now, go on outside."

Reluctantly, Jay obeyed. He and Jackson walked around the village with no particular destination in mind. Everyone who saw them waved or said "Hi". They walked past Courtney's house a few times. Jackson kept his mouth shut when Jay's pace slowed down.

The air was cooling down faster in the afternoons and Jay felt a foreboding sense that summer was over. The coastal rain forest was ready to live up to its name once again. The clouds kept a civilized distance from each other. No tailgating yet. The nimbus grid lock was yet to come.

"So what's there to do in the city?" Jackson asked Jay.

"Lots of stuff. There's a huge mall where you can go skating even in the summer," said Jay.

"Did you ever do that?" asked Jackson.

"No, but you can," replied Jay.

"What else?" asked Jackson. He put his hands in his pockets and walked with his head down.

"A movie complex with twenty theatres that's open all day," said Jay.

"You could watch movies for almost two days without leaving," said Jackson.

"Yeah, you'll like the city," said Jay.

"I hope so. I'm not looking forward to a new school," said Jackson.

"You'll have no problem finding friends," said Jay, even if he didn't totally believe it. He knew the city could be a cold, rough place, where you are just one in a million other people.

277

"Maybe I'll go to the skate park and see where you started your painting career," said Jackson.

"You want my skateboard? I don't use it anymore," said Jay.

"Sure," said Jackson.

Jay knew Jackson's family didn't have money for extras. Maybe Jackson could make some friends at the skate park.

"Why don't you wait until you find a place?" asked Jay.

"No. They don't want me to change schools in the middle of term. I'm stuck with my cousins for the first while," said Jackson. "And if they think I'm sharing a room with Emily they can forget it. I'd rather live under an overpass."

"So you'll have Emily to hang out with and Anthony," said Jay, trying to find a silver lining. Emily was Jackson's second cousin. She was two years older than Jackson and they never really got along but at least he would know someone.

"It sucks that you have to move and I have to stay," said Jay.

"No kidding," said Jackson.

The next morning, Jay helped Jackson and his family load their belongings into the car. Fred, Billy and the 3Ds came to say goodbye. The girls cried as Crystal and Anna hugged them and told them to keep up the beading and jewelry making. When the car drove away Fred broke down.

"It's too much like when the government and the church took us away to the residential schools." He swiped his finger under his nose and put the heels of his hands up to his eyes. Jay didn't know what to do so he put his hands in his pockets and looked away until Fred collected himself. The 3Ds looked scared. Billy put his arm around his dad. "It's OK, Dad. I'll bet they'll be back sooner than you think."

278

"I don't see how," said Fred, sniffling.

Chapter 38

That night Jay tossed and turned for hours. Even listening to his iPod didn't help. Thoughts raced through his brain with no way to turn them off. *Jackson has gone to the city - my city. How unfair is that?* The words of the chief also haunted him. *Could the village disappear? Would everyone leave and there be nothing left? Who'd take care of the totem poles? Who'd look after the longhouse? We should move back to the city in case Grampa has another emergency. No, he'd hate it there, too noisy, too fast, and too busy. He'd definitely have another heart attack.*

He knocked on Tatla's door.

"Mom, are you up?" asked Jay.

"I am doing some research. Come in. Why are you still up?" she asked.

He entered her bedroom. Tatla sat cross legged in pink sweats and typed on her laptop computer. Her hair hung down in front of her face and coiled at her toes. Her bedroom was decorated completely in white; white lace curtains, white dresser, white end tables and a white sheep skin rug she'd laid out to cover the stains on the carpet. Way too girly for Jay's taste but he did like the way it smelled. It smelled like his mom, like vanilla, as if she was making a batch of Rice Krispie squares.

"I can't sleep," said Jay and flopped down face first on the bed. "It's not fair that Jackson has to leave. His family has lived here for hundreds of years."

"Don't worry, you'll make new friends. Maybe even find a girlfriend," said Tatla. She wiggled her eyebrows.

"No thanks, too demanding, and besides, I don't want to make new friends. Why can't we move back to the city? Then I can hang out with Anthony and Jackson," said Jay.

"For the last time, Jay, you know we can't with your Grampa's health. I thought you liked it here now," said Tatla.

"If it is so great here how come you left in the first place?" asked Jay.

"I moved to the city to get a fresh start and leave everything behind. I thought I was too good for this place. I wanted to go to college and then I met your dad and got pregnant. When your dad left I was too humiliated to return. Your grandfather was very angry at me for not finishing college, said I was wasting my life. I was too proud to talk to him after that even though he apologized and told me to come home. It was stupid of me," said Tatla.

"How come you never told me any of Grampa's old stories?" asked Jay. He lied on his back, tossed one of many throw pillows in the air and caught it with his bare feet.

"I should have told you the stories of our people but I wanted to forget the past and live in the present," said Tatla.

"Can you tell me a story now?" said Jay.

"Really?" said Tatla, surprised at her now fourteen year old son.

Jay nodded and scooted up to the pillows.

Tatla removed her reading glasses and set her laptop and notes to the side.

"Ok, well, I can remember one your Gramma used to tell me when I was a little girl. I remember it because I begged her to tell me over and over again. It is more of a girl's story. I am sure she was sick of it but she didn't say anything. She always told it to me like it was the first time. It's called 'The Prince and the Wolf'.

281

A long time ago, in a village nearby, a chief summoned his son to kill a wolf seen near the camp. The chief was worried the children were in danger of being eaten. The prince was very happy to be the one chosen to kill the wolf and left right away in his canoe. The chief needed to test his son. If his son was smart enough and brave enough to catch the wolf then one day he could lead the tribe. The young maidens waved to the young prince as he left but he was not interested in them. He only wanted to hunt and fish. He traveled for many days tracking the wolf along the river. He slept in the canoe which he placed in a tree branch away from animals. The prince was so determined to catch the wolf, he forgot to eat. This made him weak. That night he crawled into the canoe, pulled a blanket over his head and went right to sleep."

Jay's mom stopped for a minute, her chin pushed her bottom lip up. Jay thought she was going to cry.

"Then your Gramma would tuck my quilt in tight around me. It was the best part and probably why I always asked her to tell it," said Tatla hugging a pillow. "Sorry, I'll try to keep it together."

"It's OK, mom. You don't have to finish." Jay had seen enough crying for today.

"No, I'll be alright," she said as she blew her nose into a tissue and continued.

"As the prince slept, a mother wolf and her beautiful cub caught a whiff of him. Before the mother could stop her, the cub climbed up the branch and looked at the prince.

'He smells good,' she said.

Then the cub grabbed the blanket in her teeth and pulled back. When she saw his peaceful face and his thick, dark eyelashes she immediately fell in love.

'Let's eat him,' said the wolf mother.

'No, let's take him home where we won't have to share with the others', said the cub.

282

The wolves carried him in the blanket to their cave. The mother was exhausted when they got home and laid down to rest. 'Good,' thought the beautiful young cub, 'now I can gather 'sleepy leaves' to give to my mother and the boy. They will sleep until I get back.'

The cub set out to speak with her guardian spirit, Elk.

'Elk, I have found the love of my life, but he is a boy. I need you to turn me into a girl so I can be his wife,' said the cub.

'I understand,' said Elk. 'Here is what you must do. Go to the house of the blind witch. Ask her for a maiden's dress. Take the dress and hang it near Still Pond. You will see the dress in the pond's reflection. Dive into the water, emerge through the reflection and put the dress on. You will then be a girl in a dress fit for a princess. It will only happen if you promise to be a good wife otherwise you will come out of the water as blind as the old witch.'

The cub did as Elk told her. She found the dress at the witch's house and swam through the reflection. She climbed out of the water and put the supple buckskin dress on. When she looked at herself in the pond this is what she saw..."

Again Tatla paused.

"Your Gramma would hold up her silver hand mirror to my face and say … she saw a beautiful young girl." She continued with the story.

"When the boy awakened from his sleep he looked around the cave very frightened. Bones were lying everywhere. As he hurried out of the cave he bumped into someone. It was the most beautiful maiden he had ever seen and he fell in love with her instantly.

'Don't go in the cave, it's very dangerous. You must come home with me and be my wife,' the prince said.

'This cave is my home. It is not safe here for you. I will guide you back to your village and be your wife,' said the maiden.

283

The prince watched in amazement as the beautiful girl kissed her sleeping wolf mother goodbye. In a few days they were happily married and she was always a good wife," finished Tatla.

"He married a dog. Ooww ooow oooow!" howled Jay.

"Stop it," said Tatla, slapping his knee. "See I told you it's a girl's story. I knew you would make jokes."

"Sorry, Mom, it's a good story," said Jay. He noticed for the first time that Tatla had put her dolls from the box in the garage up on a shelf.

"Well your Gramma told it better. Can you sleep now?" asked Tatla.

"I'll try but I can't stop thinking about what the chief said. He said if the land treaties aren't settled, people will either get poorer or else they'll have move to other towns to find work," said Jay.

"Well, the chief is right. We need something to keep the village going. Some of the other bands are prospering now because they have logging rights to sell timber or water rights for building dams to generate electricity. Our little village won't have anything like that until we settle our land claims. Don't worry too much about it. My event planning business is doing well so we'll be fine. Except I can't find a place for this mining company to have its annual corporate retreat. They said they wanted something different, not another Las Vegas weekend," said Tatla. She picked up her laptop and started typing.

"Mom, I'm not worried about us, I'm worried about Grampa and the elders and the chief. What will happen to them? I don't think Grampa would do so well in the city," said Jay.

"It would probably kill him. I wish I had the answer. Try to get some sleep. Maybe the person clever enough to come up with rat day can come up with something," said Tatla. She kissed Jay on his forehead and ruffled his hair.

Jay went back to his room and sat at his desk. *Jackson has moved and Grampa's sick. What's the point of staying here anyway? Just because their ancestors lived here for thousands of years doesn't mean I have to. Even Mom left as soon as she could. But now she seems really happy to be back.*

Jay picked up a pencil and started sketching the village. He drew the totem poles, the longhouse, the forest, the lake, the river, the little houses and the small abandoned farms in the outlying areas. As he sketched he thought of the amazing things he did that summer; the stories, painting the garage, canoeing to the pictographs, hiking through the forests, the potlatch, and carving the totem pole.

He picked up Jackson's canoe paddle and examined the craftsmanship that went into shaping it and the skill that went into painting it. *Maybe Jackson can get a job at the museum, too.*

Jay lay in bed and stared at his drawing. The moon was full and filled the room with silver light.

This really was the best summer I ever had. It was like one big summer camp. I can't believe it might all disappear, thought Jay as he drifted off.

Chapter 39

CAW, CAW, CAW.

Jay jumped out of bed. "Thanks for waking me up," said Jay, happy to hear the raven. He reached into a box of croutons he always had for the birds and tossed a few out the window. The raven cried loudly, swooped down and pecked at the crusty bread.

Jay ran downstairs and grabbed his mom by the arm. She dropped her spoon in the bowl of cereal she was eating. When milked splashed over the woven place mat she scowled.

"Come on. I need a meeting with the elders," said Jay.

"What is going on? What elders?" said Tatla, confused, as she blotted the spilled milk with a dish cloth.

"I'm talking about you and Grampa. Let's go. It's important," Jay picked up the first pair of shoes he saw and handed them to her; red high-heels.

"I'm not wearing those," protested Tatla.

"Whatever. Get something on your feet and hurry up." Jay rushed her along.

"OK, OK, I'm hurrying," she said and slipped on a pair of flip-flops.

They let themselves in the back door of Grampa's house, entering through the kitchen, past the fridge. Jay noticed for the first time that clinging to the fridge door with a magnet was his sketch from that awful first ride to the village: a passenger bus going off a cliff and bursting into flames while hawks circled overhead with body parts in their claws.

Jay smiled.

How long has that been there? Jay wondered.

Grampa hovered over the newspaper with a cup of coffee steaming on the table.

"I hope that's decaf. You know what the doctor said," warned Tatla.

"Hmmpf," groaned Grampa.

"Morning, Grampa. Close your newspaper, please. I need to talk to you and Mom about an idea I have," said Jay.

Grampa folded his newspaper, then his hands and gave Jay his undivided attention.

"Mom, remember last year when you sent me to summer camp?" Tatla nodded her head. "Well, it was lame. Sorry but it was. And you paid $500 to send me there, right?"

"Yes, that's right," she said. "I had to save like mad. I even gave up my morning Starbucks. You begged me to go, if I remember correctly."

"Anyway, I told Anthony this was like the best summer camp ever and he agreed. And the chief said we need something to sustain our village and to bridge the gap between the people outside the village and the people inside the village. He said we must pull together if things are going to change," said Jay looking to Grampa for confirmation.

"True," said Grampa. He squinted his eyes and leaned forward. "So what is your idea?"

Jay unrolled the piece of paper clutched in his hand. "I give you, CAMP POTLATCH: a summer camp where city kids have fun and learn about the culture and traditions from real tribes-people."

The paper was a map of the village but it also included some changes. The abandoned farm now showed buildings on it.

287

"The campers would stay in cabins that look like longhouses, have campfires at night and listen to Grampa tell the old stories, if you're up to it. In the daytime there'd be canoeing, archery, hiking to the pictographs and on rainy days make masks, drums, and learn the dances. At the end of the week when the parents pick them up we could have a small potlatch, as a way for them to learn about coastal First Nations. They will see that people just have different ways of being the same. What do you think?" asked Jay, taking in a huge breath.

"Jay, it sounds lovely, honey, but who is going to pay for it?" said Tatla.

"Never mind about the money for now. Don't think of ways it won't work, think of ways it will work. Let's go talk to the chief," said Grampa.

Jay went over the proposal with Chief George.

"It is a very ambitious project you have there," said the chief.

Jay hung his head and waited for another patronizing comment like his mom's.

"I like the idea. I'll call a meeting with the elders. We'll crunch some numbers. Then the qualifying tribe members will take a vote. It may not fly but it's worth a shot. I'm running out of ideas and ready to try anything. The potlatch proved how well we work together and the many skills we have to offer," said Chief George.

Jay was too young to cast a ballot but worked tirelessly that fall going door to door. He explained what 'Camp Potlatch' was and how it would bring work, tourists and revenue to the village. It also kept his mind off Jackson's leaving. When Jackson's family left the whole village seemed to go into a depression. Fred did not come out of his house for a week and May-Belle no longer stood at the window to wave.

"Everyone will get shares in the camp and we will all benefit from the success. When 'Camp Potlatch' turns a profit the money will be split among the tribe," explained Jay over and over. "You can also invest in the camp and buy more shares."

"Buy more shares? I can hardly buy milk some days," said May-Belle.

Jay figured she blew her milk budget on her cats but didn't say anything.

He got the same reaction at school. Not from everyone though. Courtney, Levi and Skye thought it was a good idea but none of them were willing to back it up by going door to door. Skye was back in school on a part-time basis while Teresa looked after Dove.

If only Jackson was here, thought Jay. *He'd come with me.*

The rains followed Jay around the village. He passed Johnny Walker's house. The carport's charred remains stood bleak and depressing. The blackened timber barely held up the frame. One good kick to the support beam and the whole thing would cave in. Jay wondered why he was working so hard to save this crummy village.

I should just give up and go home. I'm cold and wet and nothing is going to change.

Johnny came out the front door and called Jay over. Jay was still mad at him and had no intention of including Johnny in the plan. He wasn't a tribe member and had no voting rights. He couldn't even be bothered to show up for the potlatch.

"Hey, Jay, having a rough time? You look like a wet dog. Why don't you come inside and dry off," said Johnny. "I'll get you something hot to drink." Johnny held up a chipped coffee mug and took a sip.

"No, I'm fine," said Jay.

"Even after the totem pole and the potlatch they're still treating you like an outsider, eh," said Johnny. "Change is hard."

"Yea, no kidding," said Jay. He carried on. Some people didn't even answer their doors.

After a few blocks he came to Mile's place; a two story house similar to Jay's and Grampa's. The same algae spread on the gutters and drain spouts. Moss covered the lawn and the vinyl roof of a two door Monte Carlo. A lacrosse net with a huge hole was set up in the driveway. Jay stood at the front door for a few minutes before mustering up the courage to knock.

Miles' dad, R.J, answered. "You're dreamin', Apple," said R.J. "Why should we listen to some kid who's only been here for a couple months?" Miles snickered from the top of the stairs.

Jay didn't have an answer to this. He passed the mail-box condos and stopped to unload on Chief George and Grampa who were collecting their mail.

"I didn't think it would be this hard," said Jay.

"I remember you thought the same thing before jumping off the rocks into the lake," said Grampa. He sorted through his mail. Jay was silent. Jackson's words came back to him. 'Looking up you see only the height of the cliff. Looking down you see the height of the cliff plus the depth of the lake.'

"We just have to get them to take that leap," said Grampa. He stuffed the envelopes; some manila, some white, into his inside breast pocket to keep them dry.

"It may be difficult for our people to accept this new idea. They are used to the way things are. Even though their situation may not be good, change is still scary," said the chief.

"We have to let them know this will bring prosperity to the village. To allow our elders to stay in their homes and give our young people a future," said Grampa.

"I've told them that again and again. I feel like I'm canoeing with one paddle; going in circles," said Jay.

"You can still row in a straight line with only one paddle. You just have to switch sides every once in while," said Grampa.

Jay looked frustrated and deflated.

"I think what Jay is trying to say is that he needs someone else to help paddle," said Chief George.

"I'll call the village to a meeting. I'll explain the benefits of 'Camp Potlatch' and what we need to do to succeed. We can apply for an economic opportunity grant to get 'Camp Potlatch' up and running but we can't welcome visitors to the village in the state it's in. The old cars and appliances have to be cleaned up. People won't want to send their kids to junkyard camp," said the chief.

"Maybe we could have a spring clean up. I saw on the news how much money you can get for scrap metal. Guys are stealing phone booths for the aluminum. If we sold the cars to the wreckers then people would have money for shares," said Jay.

"You have the spirit of a wise elder inside you," said Chief George.

Grampa beamed with so much pride that Jay thought he might have to give the old guy an extra heart pill.

Tatla said she'd try to communicate the benefits at the women's circle she'd joined a few weeks ago. The ladies met weekly to talk about issues and connect on a spiritual level. A gap had been left by Crystal and Anna's departure. Using her selling and marketing skills Tatla did her best to overcome the women's objections. This week the meeting was held at Tatla's house. Jay couldn't help but listen in.

So far Mary was Tatla's only advocate.

"I think it's worth trying and really what is there to lose that isn't disappearing already," said Mary.

"I don't want to get my hopes up and then have them thrown back in my face," said Theresa.

"I had a job in the city. I made decent money but someone else controlled my hours, my pay, and my security. The decision to start my own business was scary but I did it. Now I am rewarded for the work I do. It is up to me how much money I make by how hard I work and how well I treat my customers. The word is out now and my customers are sending me more customers," said Tatla.

"Last time we let strangers in they ruined our totem pole," said Billy's wife Sheila.

"Fred and Billy fixed it and now it's better that ever. I'm not saying this will be easy but I'm saying it can be done and if we all work together maybe it will be amazing," said Tatla.

Gradually May-Belle came on board and soon Theresa and Billy's wife Sheila followed.

The group held hands and said a prayer and the ladies left smiling and chatting about the possibilities.

When Chief George addressed the men things were not as polite. They gathered in the longhouse, sitting in a circle around the fire pit on fold out chairs.

"It's a damn waste of money. Shouldn't we concentrate on fixing the potholes or getting rid of the mold in our homes or buying school computers?" said Fred. He had just picked up his mail; another batch of rejected resumes.

"The grant is for economic stimulus. To qualify we need a business plan. The government is not going to hand out money to fix potholes," said Chief George.

"We can use the camp profits to fix the potholes and the mold and get computers for the school," said Grampa. He had to watch his blood pressure. Tatla didn't even want him to attend the meeting because she knew how heated they could get.

"What about all them strangers coming through our land?" said R.J.

"We need to keep our children safe. I don't want any molesters hanging about here," said Billy.

"I understand your concerns. We'll do this right. The only people who'll want to come here are parents with children. The land we need to get is on the other side of Dr. Two-Feathers. It won't be on the reservation. You and I both know the bank won't approve the loan without the security of property. Since this isn't our property yet, we have to go outside the reservation," said Chief George.

"We also have to get a bank loan?" groaned Fred. "What is the point? They won't give us one."

"Yes they will if we can get the government grant," said Grampa.

"If we get the grant? That's a big if," said R.J.

"I guess we'll just keep things the way they are then. The government won't change, the banks won't change so we won't change either. Thanks for coming out and listening," said Chief George. He stood and folded the chair he'd been sitting on, prepared to place it in the corner with the other extra chairs.

The men grumbled amongst themselves.

"Hold on Chief," said Fred. "We hear what you're saying but we're not sure. On the other hand, no one is knocking down my door to give me a job." He threw his rejected resumes into the fire. "Can we have a few days to think about it? See what our wives think?"

"Absolutely," said Chief George.

"That's all we ask," said Grampa.

Chapter 40

The next week all the qualifying tribe members gathered together for the vote.

Jay was asked to explain the camp's location, the buildings required, the jobs created, the number of campers, the camp fees, etc. He answered all of them with a little prompting from Tatla.

Since he was not eligible to vote Jay paced outside the longhouse waiting to hear the outcome. He looked at his fingers and realized that sometime over the summer he had quit biting his nails.

To pass the time Jay watched the maple trees sway; their branches circling in front like arms drawing in the wind, bending backwards, inhaling as much air as possible before thrusting forward, blowing out and coughing up dozens of spinning red and yellow leaves. Courtney, Levi and Skye with baby Dove in a snuggly joined him. At last the door swung open and Chief George came out. He put his arm around Jay.

"Well Jay, we tried our best. The vote was really close. I know how bad you wanted this," said Chief George.

Jay felt his heart pound while his stomach did flip flops. *We didn't get it.*

"That's why I wanted to be the first to congratulate you." Chief George smiled and reached out to shake Jay's hand. "You've got your Camp Potlatch."

Jay heaved a sigh of relief, letting out about twenty pounds of air. Courtney, Skye and Levi whooped and hollered. Dove let out a wail.

"Way to go, Jay," said May-Belle. "I'll bring you an extra special batch of bannock tomorrow."

"Thank you, Grandmother," said Jay.

"Jay, because of you, I can stay in my home," said Mary. She reached up and patted him on the head.

Fred picked Jay up and swung him around. "This is a great day for our band," he said, dabbing his eyes.

The 3Ds broke away from their mom and leached onto their dad. When he shook them off they grabbed his hands and made him dance in a circle with them, ring-around-the-rosy style.

Jay's cheeks hurt from smiling.

"Now the real work begins," said Grampa.

For the next month the entire village pulled together. Fences were mended, windows replaced and the garbage was picked up. It wasn't perfect but it was a good start. Once the grant money came through they could start on the camp compound itself.

"Hey Jay, good news." It was Jackson on MSN messenger from the public library in the city. "We are moving back. Dad will be the head carpenter and care-taker for Camp Potlatch. I'll be back after Christmas. BTW - saw your work at the sk8 park. You're way better now," wrote Jackson, with a smiley face emoticon.

Jay was about to reply when he heard his mom calling him.

"Jay, can you come downstairs, please?" asked Tatla.

"Sure," said Jay. He signed off from Jackson, closed the laptop and went to the living room.

Tatla, Grampa and Chief George were there. No one smiled. They looked like someone had died.

"What's up?" asked Jay.

"I just received a fax from the government grant office. They said they can only give us about half of what we need to get the camp going," said the chief.

"What does that mean?" said Jay. He searched their faces for signs this was some kind of prank.

"We'll have to come up with the rest or there'll be no camp," said Tatla.

"What about the bank?" asked Jay. He knew this was no prank.

"Without the grant money we don't have enough for a down payment," said Grampa.

Tatla got up from the couch to give Jay a hug.

"No," said Jay. He backed away from her, confused. "They can't do that. They promised."

"I know, Jay, it's disappointing. This is what we've been going through for years. The government says one thing and then does another or tangles it in red tape until we're hog tied," said the chief.

"So that's it? We just give up?" asked Jay.

"Unless we come up with something else," said Grampa. He ran his fingers through his hair as if the answer lay hidden inside.

"Let's get the village together," said Chief George.

"I'm not looking forward to this meeting," said Tatla.

When the village had gathered again in the longhouse the mood was very different from the potlatch. The kids sat at their parents' feet. Some of the women and Fred were wiping their eyes. The men were split between being angry and disgusted.

"That's typical," said Miles' dad after Chief George had delivered the bad news.

296

"I knew it wouldn't happen. It was a dumb idea anyway," said Miles.

"No, it was a good idea. It's still a good idea. Let's not give up yet. We need $50,000 and that sounds like a lot but if we keep selling the baskets, mats and blankets maybe in a couple of years we can have the money we need," said Grampa.

"If the grant money isn't used within a year then we lose it," said the Chief.

"The village will be gone by then," said Miles' dad. "We're moving to the oil fields as soon as we can."

"Don't leave yet. We'll think of something," said Grampa. Jay looked up and saw Johnny Walker slip out the door.

The rest of the village followed suit. They left the longhouse to go back to their houses and decide what to do with their future. Some of them gave Jay dirty looks as if it was his fault for getting their hopes up.

"I really wanted Dove to grow up here," said Skye as she walked past Jay.

Jay was stunned. "How can they just give up?" he said to Grampa.

"They don't know what else to do," said Grampa.

"Sometimes when it's over, it's over," said Chief George.

Jay ran out the door pushing past the slow moving crowd. He ran past the totem poles through the trees and down the trail. He couldn't face them anymore. *How was he going to tell Jackson?*

When he reached Grampa's garage he looked down the street and saw Johnny Walker standing on the road staring back at him. The sun was setting and Johnny slowly turned into a black silhouette. The silhouette raised its arm to finish whatever was left in the can it had been holding.

Jay thought about all the junk Johnny Walker had in his yard and how he sold it for beer money. Jay stopped the people of the village as they headed home. He asked them to bring all their scrap metal over to Grampa's.

"No, way, forget it kid. We are sick of your harebrained ideas," said the adults as they disappeared into their homes.

The kids congregated on the street and speculated about what would happen to them now. "I don't want to leave," said Donna. "I'm afraid to go to a new school," said Deanna. "I thought the camp was a great idea," said Courtney.

Jay appealed to the kids.

"Go and bring all the metal you can find lying around the village and in the ravine. Put it in front of Grampa's garage. It's worth money and who knows maybe it will be enough to keep going," said Jay. When no one moved Jay figured his idea would be shot down.

Then they ran off in all directions and a few minutes later Jay heard the clang and groan of metal being dragged down the streets. Clothes dryers were hauled on wagons; a chrome bumper was dragged with the effort of two small girls in matching dresses, boxes of small appliances were dumped into the pile.

Sadie chased down her daughter and grabbed the toaster from her hand claiming they still used it. Kelly drove up in his 442 and popped the trunk filled with sheets of aluminum and bent porch railings. The pile reached as high as Grampa's garage.

The adults came over to see what the commotion was. "Good work kids," said the chief. "I'll get Stan the Scrapman over here tomorrow to see what he can give us for it."

"Jay," said Grampa when everyone had gone home. "This would have been your chance to go back to the city. Without Camp Potlatch the whole village including me would probably have to leave. Why did you do it?"

298

"Because of the moon," said Jay.

Chapter 41

Jay had a hard time sleeping. He wanted Stan to come over right now and give them an estimate. In his mind he could see Stan holding up one of those giant lottery checks with $10,000 or $20,000 written on the amount line. Jay was snapped out his daydream.

He looked out his bedroom window and saw a shadow moving across the fence. He went into his mom's office to see who was out there. Jay pushed aside the curtains and peeked out, trying not to attract attention. Picking through the scrap metal pile was Johnny Walker. Jay felt the blood boil in his veins.

"What a jerk. He's stealing our scrap metal for beer money. I'll kill him," said Jay under his breath.

Scrambling back to his room he bashed his knee on the corner bed post, just to add to his foul mood. Jay pulled on a sweat shirt and sweat pants and slid bare feet into running shoes. He ran downstairs and out the front door not stopping to close it. He leaped from the verandah, losing a shoe, and hobbled across the yard to the pile of metal in time to see Johnny Walker disappearing into his yard.

Jay found his shoe and scuffled his way down the road to confront Johnny. A blue light glowed in the kitchen window. It flickered and pulsed reminding Jay of the night in the alley when he stumbled across the chop shop. The voice inside Jay's head told him to turn around, go home and forget about Johnny Walker. One or two pieces of metal aren't going to make a difference, but Jay was still angry at Johnny for not helping Grampa.

The loss of the grant money and the disappointed looks on the faces of people like Mary and May-Belle was too much.

Johnny Walker wasn't just stealing from Jay he was stealing from Grampa, Chief George and everyone who voted for Camp Potlatch. Jay wanted to explode.

He flung the door open and stormed into Johnny's kitchen. "I saw you take the metal. Give it back. We need it to save the camp. Wait until Grampa hears what you did. It'll kill him, you know. He is the only one who ever helped you and this is how you repay him? You are just a selfish drunk that thinks of no one but himself," shouted Jay.

Johnny stood in the kitchen with a blow torch in his hand. He let Jay vent.

"The scrap metal will get you maybe a thousand bucks. It's not enough to save Camp Potlatch," said Johnny as he turned off the blow torch. The bottom tray of a barbeque lay on the Formica kitchen table.

"But it's enough to get you a case of beer," said Jay.

"I haven't had a drink since the night you took your grampa to the hospital," said Johnny.

"What's that?" said Jay, pointing to a can of Pepsi on the table.

"It's Pepsi," said Johnny.

Jay grabbed the can of Pepsi and pulled at the label. When he couldn't unwrap it he put the opening to his nose and sniffed; Pepsi.

"Why did you take the metal?" asked Jay, putting the can on the table.

"I'm sorry. I'll bring it back tomorrow. You should go home. It's late," said Johnny Walker. He ushered Jay out the door.

Jay took his time walking home. Something was off. Johnny Walker looked different. His clothes were clean, his house was clean and Jay didn't have to step over anything in the yard.

After a sleepless night Jay heard Stan-the-Scrapman pull up. The morning was cool and overcast. All the kids and a few of the adults gathered around the huge heap of metal to see what the tally would be.

Stan jumped down from his beat up flat bed truck. He had installed a four inch lift kit and large knobby tires. No matter what type of road he drove on, asphalt or dirt, the ride was always loud and bumpy. Stan was also a little beat up, a little loud and a little bumpy.

He had on a plaid shirt with the sleeves cut off and his muscled arms were covered in tattoos. His forehead protruded farther than his cheek bones giving him a Neanderthal look. His hands and fingernails were stained black from grease and oil. A couple of his knuckles had chunks out of them.

"That's a whole lotta metal," said Stan. "Where did you get it?"

"From yards, garages, basements, ditches wherever we could," said Chief George. "We need the money to keep Camp Potlatch alive."

"The price of metal has gone down quite a bit; everyone's suffering from the lousy economy. I can give you seven hundred dollars," said Stan.

"Is that all?" said the chief.

"'Fraid so," said Stan as he walked around the perimeter of the pile.

"Johnny Walker said it was worth at least a thousand dollars," said Jay.

"That drunk? He doesn't know what he's talking about," said Stan.

"Whatever he is, he does know his scrap metal," said Grampa.

302

"Well Stan, what do you say? Can you do better than seven hundred?" asked the chief.

"I'll give you nine hundred but you have to help me load it up," said Stan.

"You've got a deal," said the chief.

"Nine hundred? That's it?" said Jay. "It's not enough, is it Chief?" asked Jay.

"No, it's not enough. But it's a start," said Chief George.

But Jay didn't hear him. He ran to the pile, pulled out a bumper and threw it, almost hitting the 3Ds who stood watching. They jumped back and screamed. Next Jay picked up a toaster and smashed it to the ground. He was about to grab an iron when Grampa grabbed his arm.

"Jay! Jay!" shouted Grampa. "Stop it, stop it. That's enough. It's over."

Jay collapsed to the ground. "We gave it a shot. Jay, we know you tried hard but some things just aren't meant to be," said Chief George.

Jay wanted to cry but held back. He swallowed the lump in his throat and looked up at the sky to stop gravity from dragging the tears from his eyes. He didn't want his Grampa or the rest of the village to see how upset he was, but no one was looking at Jay. Their attention had turned to the sound of a shopping buggy rolling down the street.

"It's Johnny Walker," said Stan.

"He's just bringing back the metal he stole from the pile last night," said Jay as he stood up and dusted off his pants.

"You can keep the metal, in fact you can take the whole stupid pile, if you want," Jay called out to Johnny.

"Chief George, Grandfather, Jay," said Johnny. "I want to give this to you. Maybe it will help you like you helped me."

303

The metal in the shopping cart was barely recognizable as the metal borrowed from the night before. It had been shaped and welded to look like the Indian masks found in the old potlatch photo.

"It's one of your sculptures," said Tatla. "It's amazing. Is it for the longhouse?"

"No, it's for you to sell. Raise money for Camp Potlatch," said Johnny Walker. "I can make more. Maybe it will be enough if people still want to buy them."

"You don't have to do that. Why don't you keep the money for yourself?" said Grampa.

"Because of the moon," said Johnny. Grampa clapped him on the shoulder.

"That's nice work," said Grampa.

Jay's eyes were fixed on the sculpture and the man behind the shopping cart. Both man and metal were transformed.

The crowd around them was growing. The entire village was there now; kids skidded up on bikes, Skye moved in with Dove on her hip, Mary and May-Belle linked arms and shuffled in closer.

"Hey, look what Johnny Walker made," someone said.

"His name is Gordon," said Jay.

Chapter 42

Jay sent a picture of the sculpture to Anthony to show his mother.

Mrs. Gardener was thrilled and said she could easily sell anything Gordon made.

Jay told Gordon the news. "Mrs. Gardener wants to have a show for you. Isn't that great," said Jay.

"I can't do it, Jay," said Gordon.

"What do you mean? You have to do it. Don't you want to sell your stuff?" said Jay.

"I can't go to the city. I can't be near all those people again. I just stopped drinking. It's too much for me," said Gordon. He ran his hands through his hair and paced around the kitchen.

"I thought you didn't want to turn your back on the village anymore," said Jay.

"I don't. I'm not. Everyone has been so supportive of me. Not just because of the sculpture but because I stopped drinking and cleaned myself up. May-Belle even brings me bannock every day which might not be such a good thing. But at least I don't feel like an in-law. You go to the show for me," said Gordon. He lit a cigarette with shaky hands.

Jay didn't want to force Gordon to do anything that would set him back. He seemed fragile and uncomfortable around too many people.

Mrs. Gardener was good to her word. Realizing time was short she pulled together a guest list and made catering arrangements within three weeks.

Jay was eating a bowl of cereal for dinner; he was lucky there was even that in the house. Tatla was run off her feet with the gala and running her business and shuttling Grampa to his doctor's appointments.

"It's all set," said Tatla. "Mrs. Gardener wasn't sure she'd get enough people to commit on such short notice so I called all my customers and most of them said they could make it. I even got the head of a major hotel chain to come." She grinned from ear to ear.

"Just the head? Why not the rest of him?" joked Jay.

Jay, Tatla, and Grampa honored Gordon's request and took his place at the show.

The masks were set up at Mrs. Gardener's gallery. Jackson and his family and Anthony came out for the gala opening. The three boys did their best to answer questions about the artist and the artwork. The guests were disappointed they did not get to meet Gordon. Jay thought they were secretly intrigued by the mystery of the introverted artist.

"What can you tell me about this piece?" asked a lady. She was dressed head to toe in a black velvet body suit. A thick braided silver chain hung loose around her neck plunging to her waist. Her jaw-length platinum blond hair was cut so perfectly straight it looked like her hair dresser had used the school paper slicer, aka the guillotine, instead of scissors. She held a glass of red wine in her manicured fingers. The nail polish color matched the wine exactly. It took Jay a moment to realize she was speaking to him.

"This piece?" asked Jay. He pointed to one Gordon had made as a gift for the potlatch but then chickened out. It was in the shape of a salmon. The same size as Jackson's Tyee and made from empty soup cans. Layer upon layer of curved, rippled aluminum created the shiny scales like a suit of armor, bottle caps for the eyes, a red pop can with a silver wave placed in the middle was molded into the dorsal fin.

He had listened to Mrs. Gardener talk about art pieces. It didn't matter what she said. She was an expert and the customers ate up every word and every appetizer she served them.

Jay put his hand on his chin in contemplation. "Well, this one is an interesting piece. The artist was going through great turmoil at the time. Not sure whether to swim upstream or downstream," said Jay. He looked at the lady from the corner of his eye.

She hung on his every word, never taking her gaze from the salmon. "Yes, go on," she said, swirling the wine in the glass. "What's the message?" Jay scrambled for something to say.

"I believe the artist was saying to make lemonade out of lemons," said Jay. He looked around the room hoping Mrs. Gardener was nearby to bail him out.

"Yes, of course, I love lemons on my salmon," she exclaimed, throwing her hands up in the air nearly splashing red wine on Jay.

Did she really just say that? thought Jay.

"What is it called? I must have it," she said taking a sip of her red wine, leaving an imprint of her bottom lip on the rim.

Jay had no idea what it was called. "I'm not sure it has a name," said Jay.

"Well, it must be called something!" she said. "How will I tell people what I bought?" Her alabaster cheeks were turning pink. Annoyed she turned to examine the next piece.

I'm losing her, thought Jay. She took two steps. Jay stared at the salmon made from aluminum cans.

"Uh, uh, it's called 'Canned Salmon'," Jay almost shouted at her.

She spun 180 degrees on her four inch heels made from the same material as a golf shaft. "See that wasn't so hard, was it?" she said and ran her fingernail along Jay's jaw line. "I'll take it."

Anthony and Jackson witnessed the whole thing. When the lady was a safe distance away they grabbed Jay and pulled him into the back office. They shut the door to muffle the sounds of their laughter.

"'Canned Salmon', are you serious? Where did you come up with that?" asked Anthony.

"Yeah," said Jackson, running his finger along Jay's jaw. Jay swatted it away and told him to get lost.

Red dot after red dot was placed on each mask and sculpture until every item was sold.

"I am delighted with the show. When the final tally comes in I'll bet it will be one of my best shows ever. When can Gordon make more?" asked Mrs. Gardener.

"He did these for us and for the village. He may not want to make any more," said Jay. "It takes a lot out of him."

"Well, maybe he'll change his mind when he sees how much money he brought in," said Mrs. Gardener.

They drove home immediately after the show and straight to Gordon's place. It was 3 a.m. A light was on and they figured Gordon was still awake.

"I can't believe it, over sixty thousand dollars. You did it," said Jay. There was no giant check to present but it didn't matter.

"Way to go, Gordon. This is the most exciting thing that's happened to our village since that moose gave birth in Sadie's front yard," said Grampa.

"If it wasn't for you, Grandfather, helping me out when my house blew up and Jay not taking any of my crap, I'd either be dead or too drunk to know I was alive," said Gordon.

"Is it enough for the camp?" asked Gordon.

"It is more than enough," said Tatla. "I met someone at the show. They were looking for you. When I told them you didn't make the trip she asked me to give you this." Tatla handed Gordon a piece of white folded paper.

"What is it," asked Gordon.

"It's your wife's phone number," said Tatla. Gordon smiled and hugged her.

Chapter 43

For the next nine months the entire village pulled together, planning the camp and getting the permits. When the ground thawed it was time to start on the camp compound itself.

Washrooms, showers, a modern cafeteria and a fully stocked store were constructed. Jay insisted spaghetti for dinner and peanut butter and jam sandwiches for lunch were on the menu at least once. Canoes and an archery range were purchased. A fire pit was built in the centre of the compound where the campers could sing songs and listen to the old stories.

Under the direction of Jackson's dad, five small longhouses for the kids cabins were built, each with ten bunk beds and adorned with authentic Indian mats made by Crystal and Anna. Jackson and Jay painted huge, First Nations symbols on the façade of each longhouse; Raven, Eagle, Grizzly Bear, Frog and Wolf.

"Are you and Jackson interested in the jobs for camp counselors?" asked the chief.

"Sure, what do we have to do?" asked Jay, putting down his paint brush.

"You make sure the kids are taken care of. Get them to bed on time, supervise during swimming, archery, canoeing, etc. Just be sure they have a good time and they are safe," said the chief.

"Sounds kinda fun," said Jackson. He wiped his nose and made a long red paint smear down his face. The chief and Jay chuckled.

"What's so funny?" asked Jackson.

"Nothing. What about the girls?" asked Jay.

"Courtney and Emily will take care of the girls," said Chief George. The twinkle in his eye made Jay feel like his thoughts were being read.

"You will have to take a first aid course and get swimming medallions before the end of June," said Chief George.

"No problem," said Jay and Jackson, proud to be asked to do such an important job.

"We can be their elders," said Jackson.

"You already are elders in training," said Chief George.

Tatla and Teresa ran over as they were talking.

"We are officially booked to capacity for the first two weeks," she announced. The ladies from the women's circle took turns manning the phones and taking reservations.

"We're taking reservations for the reservation," said Teresa. She giggled behind her hands.

Tatla had taken on the task of marketing Camp Potlatch. Ads were placed in the newspaper. A TV news crew came out and did a story on the latest summer camp.

"Check out the web site," said Jackson. He had worked on it for weeks getting as many people to pitch in as possible. Miles and his gang recorded the sound of the drums for the background music. Teresa took photos of the longhouse, the totem poles, and the lake which Jackson posted. A store had been set up so people could order crafts, medicine bags, or even Gordon's art online. To enter the web site the visitor had to click on the raven's wings painted on a longhouse. The doors opened into the mythical magical world of the coastal First Nations people.

The day had arrived. Even the weather co-operated. The week long forecast called for sun and high temperatures. Jay pulled on his Camp Potlatch t-shirt and ball cap, headed to the school bus drop off point and waited for the first group of campers.

311

The excited travelers bounded off the busses to claim their backpacks, pillows and sleeping bags.

"Come on over here," said Jay waving the crowd in closer. "Quiet, please. Settle down."

"I need the boys on the left and the girls on the right," said Jay.

Backpacks and pillows careened into one big tangle. Jay and Jackson watched in fascination. After a few minutes the mob divided like an amoeba into two cells; girls on one side; boys on the other.

Once the jostling stopped Jay continued. "Girls age 9-10 you are in Frog house, girls 11-12 you are in Raven house, girls 13-14 are in Eagle house. Boys age 9-11 are in Grizzly Bear house and boys 12-14 are in Wolf house. Grab your stuff and put it on a bed of your choosing. Once you're done meet me in the longhouse. That's the big one over by the fire pit. You have two minutes. Last one there peels potatoes for dinner."

The kids grabbed their stuff and hurried to their houses to get the best bunk beds.

As the crowd dispersed Jay noticed a little girl in a pink hoodie and jeans, clutching a stuffed bear close to her as she sobbed into its plush fur.

Jay looked at her, not knowing what to do and more than a little scared to approach her. *I'd take Miles' bullying over a little girl crying any day,* he thought to himself.

He gathered up the courage to ask, "Hey, what's wrong? I was only kidding about the potatoes," said Jay.

Courtney came over to see what was going on.

"Are you homesick, Sweetie?" asked Courtney.

"I don't know which one is the frog," she said as her lip quivered.

312

"Oh, OK," said Jay. "What's your name?"

"Olivia," she said.

"Here Olivia, I'll take you. It's this one right here," said Courtney. Jay picked up the little girl's sleeping bag and Dora the Explorer backpack and led her to Frog house.

Olivia took Courtney's hand and looked up at her, "It doesn't look like a frog, you know."

"I didn't think so either the first time I saw it," said Jay.

"It is a First Nations frog. You'll learn about it this week. They bring good fortune to people. You are lucky to be in Frog house," said Courtney.

She seemed pleased to hear this and was Courtney's shadow for the entire week.

Once everyone was inside the longhouse the chief entered and spoke. He wore his cedar shawl over jeans and moccasins.

"Hello, everyone. Welcome to Camp Potlatch. I am Chief George and for the next seven days you will be honorary band members."

"Where's your head dress?" heckled one of the older boys.

"It's at the dry cleaners," quipped Chief George, and the kids giggled.

Jay and Jackson stood shoulder to shoulder, arms crossed in front. "Looks like we have a 'Miles' in the crowd," said Jackson to Jay.

"Where is Miles? I haven't seen him around," said Jackson.

"He's working in the bush for the logging company this summer," said Jay.

"These fine young ladies and gentlemen standing behind me are your elders this week," continued the chief, motioning behind him to Jay, Jackson, Courtney, Emily and six other kids

313

from the village. "You must do as they say for they have much wisdom," continued Chief George.

"Like what kind of wisdom?" piped up the same boy.

"Like where the washrooms are and what time dinner is served," said Chief George, to more giggles.

The boy rolled his eyes. He nudged the kid beside him and said, "This is lame."

Jay stepped forward. "Also what to do if you see a bear," said Jay. He wanted to put Miles Junior in his place before he ruined the week for everyone else.

Everyone in the room gasped.

Oh, crap. I've scared them all, thought Jay.

"Don't worry. Singing and laughing will keep the bears away. We have lots of fun things for you to do and learn. I hope you have a wonderful time and we are very happy to have you in our village as honorary tribe members at Camp Potlatch," said Chief George.

The "elders" sang the "Journey Song" for the journey the children were about to take into the land of the First Nations people. It took Jay weeks to learn and Mary had almost given up on him ever remembering it.

Each child received a white Camp Potlatch t-shirt with a traditional Indian symbol in red and black designed by Jay and Grampa. Encircling the symbol were the words 'Camp Potlatch – Different ways of being the same'.

Gordon crossed the campsite to Jay. A boy about nine years old and a girl about eleven years old followed behind carrying something in their hands. She had on a sunny yellow beach hat and sunglasses, the boy had on a white tee shirt with an urban design. Gordon placed a hand on each of their heads and said, "Jay, I want you to meet my children. This is Vincent and Monet."

"Hi, nice to meet you. Are you going to Camp Potlatch?" asked Jay.

They looked down and shook their heads no. Jay had a close look at what they carried. It was the same canoes as the pool kids had at the potlatch. Jay smiled to himself.

"Maybe next year. This summer I want to spend as much time as I can with them," said Gordon.

"Your kids can come here anytime they like," said Jay.

"I know. I get the family discount," said Gordon.

Chapter 44

During the week the honorary tribe members were taught how to maneuver a canoe, how to shoot bows and arrows, how to tell what the age of a tree is and what kinds of plants, birds and animals live in the old growth forest. Dr. Two-Feathers made arrangements with some of the ranchers for horse-back riding in exchange for veterinary services. They rotated a few of the horses every two weeks. The ranchers were happy the horses were being taken care of and getting lots of exercise.

Courtney was in charge of the horses. On his way from the archery range to the mess hall Jay saw her sitting on a bale of hay in the barn. It was dark inside. Her head was down and her hands wiped her eyes. A speckled grey mare and a sorrel wandered outside near the entrance. They nibbled at the grass while their reins dragged behind them.

"Courtney? Are you alright?" asked Jay. He stepped into the shadow covering Courtney. Her face was wet with tears. "How come the horses still have their saddles on?"

"I can't do it. It's too much," said Courtney. "I have to look after all these horses and keep the kids entertained. It's impossible." She wiped her eyes with the sleeve of her t-shirt.

Jay sat beside her on the hay bale.

"They need to be brushed, fed, watered, their hooves scraped, their saddles put on then taken off," said Courtney. She sucked in her bottom lip to keep from crying.

"Who? The kids?" asked Jay.

She frowned and looked up at Jay. "No, the horses." When she realized he was teasing her, she punched him on the knee and laughed.

It was cooler in the barn. Jay had a hand in the upgrade. A green metal roof, a coat of tan paint, galvanized steel latches for the stalls and a new floor for the storage loft. A mixture of hay and manure created a sweet and tangy aroma. Jay could have sat there all day but he knew the horses had to be groomed. If the ranchers thought the animals weren't being looked after, the camp would lose its privileges.

"Seriously, though. I can't do it all," said Courtney. She sniffled a bit.

"I'll help you," said Jay.

"You can't help me and supervise the archery lessons," said Courtney.

Jay stared outside. A couple of girls from Raven house were petting the horses and feeding them strands of loose hay.

"What is it about girls and horses? They just can't leave them alone," said Jay.

"Are you jealous?" said Courtney as she bumped Jay with her shoulder. Jay smelled strawberries again.

"No," said Jay. "Well, maybe a little bit."

Courtney laughed and then froze. Her eyes were wide open.

"What is it?" said Jay. *If she starts crying again I'm leaving.*

"That's it! You did it! Thank you," she said. She grabbed Jay's face and kissed him on the mouth. Then she jumped up and ran out of the barn toward the girls.

"What did I do?" Jay said out loud. "Tell me so I can do it again," he shouted.

317

Courtney was out of earshot by this time. Jay watched as she spoke to the kids. The girls smiled and nodded. A couple of them jumped up and down and clapped their hands, spooking the horses.

What the heck are they so excited about? thought Jay.

It didn't take long to find out. The whole gang of girls stormed the barn. They surrounded Jay.

What are they going to do to me? Jay leaned back on the hay and lifted his feet up to keep the girls away. His adrenaline was still pumping from Courtney's kiss.

"You have to move," said Amelia. At least Jay thought that was her name. He had come to think of her as 'Licorice'; no matter what time of day it was she always had a piece of red licorice in her mouth. She was shorter than the other girls and her belly drooped over her black yoga pants. Despite her small stature she seemed to be the leader of the gang.

"No I don't," said Jay.

"Yesh, you do," she said, stepping forward. Jay backed away to avoid a chunk of licorice being spat on him while she spoke.

"Yes, you do," said Courtney who had walked in behind them.

"Why?" said Jay.

"So we can feed the horses, duh," said Amelia. She pulled on the licorice and Jay wondered if a tooth might come out.

"Yes, the girls have agreed to brush, feed and water the horses every day," said Courtney. Her face was beaming.

"That's a great idea. You know we are not allowed to treat the kids like slaves though," said Jay.

"It's not like I'm making them muck the stalls," said Courtney.

318

"What's that?" asked one of the girls.

"Shovel the shit," said Amelia.

"Hey, watch it," said Courtney.

"Sorry," said Amelia.

"I don't know. Maybe I should ask the chief," said Jay.

"Please, please we want to do it. We love horses and we never get to see them in the city," shouted the girls.

"Plus, we get a piece of licorice every day that we help," said Amelia, pulling a fresh piece out of her pocket and winding it around her finger.

Jay looked at Courtney for confirmation.

"What can I say, she drives a hard bargain. Besides it was sort of your idea. You said girls and horses can't leave each other alone," said Courtney. Jay saw the smug look on her face when he walked past in surrender.

Chapter 45

During rainy days the campers were shown how to make traditional First Nation masks using Papier-Mache, drums from frames made by Billy and Fred and woven mats using cedar strips.

The first night after the drums were made was a disaster. Drums echoed through out the camp. At first it was just random drumming. Then Grizzly bear house would drum out a beat and Wolf house would repeat. The sequences got longer and more complicated.

Jackson and Jay shared a small cabin between Wolf and Grizzly Bear house. "Do you hear that?" said Jackson.

"Yes, even the elders can probably hear that," said Jay. He was exhausted and just wanted to sleep.

"What do we do?" asked Jackson. He reached in between the beds and turned on the shared lamp.

"I'm sure they are just wired from being here. They will tire out soon," said Jay. But they didn't.

Jay and Jackson got up several times to tell them to stop but this seemed to energize the kids more. Jay put a pillow over his head and Jackson slept with his fingers in his ears. The next morning no one wanted to get out of bed. Jay knew how his mom felt now.

"Come on. Rise and shine. It's a beautiful rainy day," said Jackson, flicking on the light in Grizzly house.

The children groaned and snuggled further into their sleeping bags.

"How come you guys are so tired? Didn't sleep much?" said Jay. Jay eyed a drum lying on the floor under a bunk bed. He nodded to Jackson.

They each picked up a drum and began banging loudly and chanting. The children cried and moaned. "We'll stop as soon as you get up," said Jay.

After five minutes all the kids were up except one boy named Evan. Jay and Jackson stood over his bed beating the drum until Evan finally relented and kicked his sleeping bag off, looking grumpy and disheveled.

Jay and Jackson kept the drums in their cabin at night.

A few of the younger girls were away from home for the first time. The beating drums had scared them so Tatla suggested they make 'Dream Catchers' to hang on their bunk beds to stop any bad dreams. Crystal and Anna showed the children what to do.

"Twist two lengths of red willow into a wreath then loop string every inch or so around the red willow leaving a gap between each knot. Next tie the string in the middle of each loop and repeat until the string reaches the centre completing the web where the bad dreams are captured. Then the beaded strings with colored feathers are attached. See how they dangle from the edges and the middle," said Crystal.

One afternoon the girls in Frog house had a surprise for Jay and Courtney.

"You gotta come see what we made," said Olivia.

They entered Frog house. Jay and Courtney suppressed their laughter. The girls had built their very own totem pole by stacking up their stuffed animals one on top of the other against a middle support pole.

"It's fantastic," said Courtney.

321

"Yes, I've never seen anything quite like it; the first totem pole to have a hippopotamus, a kangaroo and a 'Groovy Girl'," said Jay. Jackson took a picture to post on Facebook for the parents to get a glimpse of how the kids were doing. Cell phones were not allowed as there was not much service in the deep valley of the coastal mountains. The thirteen year old girls looked like they had been told the family pet had died, but Courtney kept them busy and after a while they didn't miss their phones at all.

Jay and Jackson made up some silly races for the first ever Camp Potlatch Games, like the 'build a human tee-pee' contest, the three legged snow-shoe race and Jay's favorite, a relay race where the campers balanced a beach ball on the end of a lacrosse stick, ran down the field, turned around, ran back and passed off the ball to the next person; chaos on a windy day.

For the adventurous campers a variation of 'Capture the Flag' was played. Each person selected a piece of paper from a ring hat telling them what team they were on. Once divided, each person then selected another piece of paper from the team ring hat telling them if they were a spy. A treasure was given to each team, usually a small wood carving. Each team would have five minutes to hide the treasure and then meet back at the hats. The goal was to get the other teams' treasure and bring it back. They painted their faces to look like tribal warriors.

"It's kinda scary," whispered Jackson to Jay, as the kids yipped and hooted, pumping their fists in the air.

"A bit too realistic," agreed Jay.

Jackson headed up the first game. The whistle blew and Jay stood as Jackson and his whole team set out into the forest, to hide the treasure, howling at the tops of their lungs. When they were out of sight Jay selected two players to hide their treasure.

Jackson and his team returned a few minutes later.

"How come you aren't out hiding your treasure?" said Jackson.

"I sent out two players to hide it. With a spy amongst us you don't think I'd let everyone know where the treasure is, do you?" said Jay with a grin.

Jackson knew he was beat but the kids still had fun. More important; the campers were exhausted and slept well that night.

May-Belle and Mary taught the kids how to make bannock. They gathered around the long tables set up in the mess hall. Bowls, spoons, measuring cups and the ingredients were already set out.

"Now, before we get started you must all take the oath," said May-Belle, she held her right hand up like a stop sign. The kids did the same. "Repeat after me – I solemnly swear." A girl around eight years old with huge blue eyes and teeth too big for her face frantically waved at May-Belle. "Yes?" said May-Belle.

"I'm not allowed to swear," she said.

"Oh, of course not, sorry. Let's try again," said May-Belle she held up her hand again. "I promise."

The girls repeated. "I promise."

"To never tell anyone the secret recipe."

"To never tell anyone the secret recipe."

"For May-Belle's bannock."

"For May-Belle's bannock."

"Ok, let's get started then," said May-Belle.

"Ok, let's get started then," said the girls. May-Belle and Mary and the girls all laughed.

The older group did everything from scratch; combining the flour, baking powder, salt, sugar, butter, eggs and water but the younger kids mostly rolled the dough and added whatever extra ingredients they wanted like raisins, cinnamon, or chocolate chips. Olivia saved a piece for Jay to try. He bit into it. "Mmmm,

323

delicious," he coughed. Olivia had not mixed the flour completely into the dough and Jay's mouth filled with dry flour. He blew it out like smoke. Olivia laughed a wicked little giggle. Jay washed the rest of it down with water and made a promise to himself to take smaller bites next time.

The kids also enjoyed exploring the ancient rain forest. Mary gave them a list of plants and insects to look for. After the first group of campers brought her back jars full of bugs and baggies full of fungus she learned her lesson and instead told them they weren't to touch the items only check them off the list. The first one to complete the list won a prize.

Fred and Billy took turns demonstrating carving techniques and by the end of the first season had finished a replica of the logo and the Camp Potlatch tag line – Different Ways of being the Same. The Chief insisted they hang it up at the entrance to the camp to welcome the visitors. The children copied the carving techniques practicing with soap, clay or wood depending on their age.

At night around the campfire Grandpa repeated the old stories.

"This is the story of Ghost Lake. Many, many, moons ago two young women were picking berries to feed their people. They found an abundant patch near the edge of a lake with no name. It was a favorite lake of the tribe for drinking water, fishing and swimming. The baskets were getting very heavy and the two women decided it was time to return to the village. When they turned to leave, a grizzly bear jumped out and said, 'Why are you stealing my berries?'

The women replied, 'We didn't know they were your berries.'

'Well, you do now,' he said as he struck them down with his 6 inch claws.

When the women did not show up for dinner their families were very worried. A search party soon came across the bloody bodies. The scratches showed it was a grizzly bear. The chief was very angry and sent his two best hunters to seek revenge. After two days the hunters were still not back. Another search party went to look for them.

They couldn't believe it. There in the same spot as the women were the hunters, struck down by the grizzly bear. The chief and the elders decided this was no regular grizzly bear but an evil spirit disguised as a grizzly bear. They told the tribe to stay away from the lake. No one was to visit the lake for any reason.

For a few years no more deaths occurred until another tribe moved in nearby. The chief warned them of the danger but they did not listen. Two of their tribe members were found dead in the same spot as the women and the hunters. The second tribe realized the chief was telling the truth about the evil spirit and kept away from the lake.

The evil spirit protected his lake by allowing many grizzly bears to feed and live in the area. The lake had so many bears even the European hunters with guns and traps kept their distance. Still today only the grizzly bears are brave enough to visit the shores of Ghost Lake."

The kids listened, mesmerized, just like the kids a hundred years ago did. Olivia fell asleep in Courtney's lap on more than one occasion.

If the night was clear the campers were allowed to stay up past curfew and watch the Northern Lights cast ghostly rainbows across the sky.

When the week was over the parents were invited into the longhouse for a potlatch. The children came out wearing their handmade masks and banged the drums they made while the little ones performed the 'Canoe Dance'. At the end of the potlatch the 'elders' sang the 'Return' song, sending the campers back to the arms of their parents with gifts of beaded neck-laces and dream-catchers.

Chapter 46

Jay, Tatla, Grampa, Jackson, Courtney and Chief George waved as the last bus drove away from the village.

"That's the last one. The first season of Camp Potlatch is over," said Jay. "How did we do, Chief?"

"This year we employed twenty full time people, forty part time people and we'll have enough revenue to get the school new computers, and start a scholarship fund for students who want to go on to college," said Chief George.

"And with the money from the weekend corporate retreats we can pay some dividends to the band members," said Tatla.

"First we rebuild Gordon's carport," said Chief George.

"I am so glad his wife is giving him a second chance," said Tatla.

"I guess the Asking Rock really works," said Jay.

"Why do you say that?" asked Grampa.

"I asked for something I thought would never happen. I asked for the village to stay together so you wouldn't have to move," said Jay.

"You really are the Raven. Transformed from a delinquent graffiti artist to the bringer of light to my life," said Grampa.

"And to the people of the village," said Chief George.

"My people," said Jay.

***

Coming soon, *"The Copper Raven"*.

Jay searches for the missing masks, hidden during the Potlatch abolition but will he find them before the eagle poachers do?

Acknowledgments

Thank you for reading 'Because of the Moon'. If you wish to contact the author please email ccutayne@gmail.com.

Like this book on Facebook.

Thank you to my husband Bruce for his unwavering support. To Danielle Ackerman, who painstakingly edited this book, my unending appreciation. Gratitude also goes to my family whose quirkiness is scattered within these pages.

Thanks also to Leslie Picton, an amazing First Nations dancer, and Nicole Lalonde, my beautiful sister-in-law.

This book would not be possible without the First Nations people of the Pacific Northwest. Their stories, culture and spirit inspired me to learn more about the people whose land I live on.

The characters and places in this book are all fictitious except for the Asking Rock which is found outside the town of Lytton, BC.

The legends are found in museums such as the Museum of Anthropology in Vancouver and the Royal BC museum. *The Cannibal Ogress, the Prince and the Wolf,* and *Ghost Lake* courtesy of Hancock House, www.hancockhouse.com.

Pepsi is a registered trademark.

Manufactured by Amazon.ca
Bolton, ON

26755529R00181